GOING DEAF FOR A LIVING

GOING DEAF FOR A LIVING

Steve Lamacq

To Zoe
Love
Steve Lamacq

BBC

Published by BBC Worldwide Ltd,
Woodlands, 80 Wood Lane, London W12 0TT

First published 2000
Copyright © Steve Lamacq 2000
The moral right of the author has been asserted.

ISBN 0 563 53749 3

Commissioning Editor: Jessica Gibson
Project Editor: Erica Jeal
Art Director: Pene Parker
Designers: John Calvert and Isobel Gillan
Cover design by Microdot
Picture Researcher: Miriam Hyman

Text set in Minion, News Gothic and Compacta MT Bold
by Keystroke, Jacaranda Lodge, Wolverhampton
Printed and bound in Great Britain by Butler & Tanner Ltd, Frome and London
Colour separations by Radstock Reproductions Ltd, Midsomer Norton
Colour sections printed by Lawrence-Allen Ltd, Weston-super-Mare
Cover printed by Belmont Press Ltd, Northampton

PICTURE CREDITS:
First section 1t LFI/Paul Canty, 1b Redferns/GAB, 2t LFI/Simon Fowler,
4t Retna/Ed Sirrs, 4b Retna/Steve Double, 5bl Retna/Ed Sirrs, 6b Retna/Ed Sirrs,
7 Retna/Ed Sirrs, 8t Retna/Ed Sirrs, 8b Martyn Goodacre
Second section 1t LFI/Kevin Cummins, 1b LFI/Andrew Catlin, 2b Retna/Colin Bell,
3t Martyn Goodacre, 3b BBC, 4t Retna/Steve Double, 4b Paul Slattery, 5 courtesy Hut
Recordings, 6t Redferns/Sheryl Stevoff, 6r Redferns/Sheryl Stevoff, 6b Retna/Tim
Auger, 7t BBC, 8 BBC
All other material courtesy of Steve Lamacq

Postcard reproduced by kind permission of Mega City 4.
Lyrics from *Song From Under The Floorboards* © Mute Song Ltd, reproduced by kind
permission of Howard Devoto.
Every effort has been made to contact the copyright holders of the material included
in this book. If any copyright has been overlooked, holders are invited to contact the
publishers.

CONTENTS

All You Good Good People

Neil Pengelly, Steve Harvey, Jeff Smith, Mark, Julie, Nicole and everyone at Wise Buddah, Juliet Sensicle, Alan Lewis, Mick Mercer, Mark Henwood, Liam Fitzgerald, Graham Bell, Alan James, Tony Smith.

Also thanks to:
John Peel, Jo Whiley, Matthew Bannister, Andy Parfitt, Chris Lycett and everyone I've worked with at Radio 1.

The people who helped in the making and research of this book, including Phil Lawton, Monica Wolff, Claire Pattenden, Andy Rogers, Sam Cunningham, Stephanie McWhinnie and Bethan Davies. Also to all the photographers who contributed.

The BBC publishing team including Jessica Gibson and Erica Jeal.

The Pubs: The Ship, New Cavendish Street and The Old Red Lion, Kennington Park Road (including Pat and Jack, my Sunday lunchtime saviours).

The Family: especially Mum and Dad for putting up with that racket upstairs.

And of course, Fischer Z for the title ...

Special respect: Simon Williams

Steve Lamacq, Kennington, May 2000

Up the U's.

INTRO & HEALTH WARNING

If a cat has got nine lives, then I've come to the conclusion that your average pop music obsessive probably has nine second childhoods. By my reckoning I'm just up to number five. And this book is the product of the first four.

It is about 20-odd years of alternative music, 10 years of Radio 1's *Evening Session*, and the search for the Holy Grail. Well, all right, forget the bit about the Holy Grail (unless your vision of the Holy Grail is a copy of *Scooter* by The Mice). What you have here is a collection of pub theories and anecdotes; explanations and excuses; and quite a few mentions of The Lurkers.

It's not, I should add, a definitive history of the music itself. There is some history in it, but it's the history of my pop world, because as we all know, everybody's pop world is different. Everyone has their own version of events. What was important, what was inconsequential ... and, depending on the reliability of your memory, what happened next. So, this is a random selection of important stuff to me – including some of the bands who've entered my orbit over the last few years.

But *Going Deaf For A Living* isn't just about the groups themselves. In a way it's my attempt to explain the relationship between us and them. The sometimes turbulent, often distant rapport we try to keep up with the people on the stage who have a disturbing capacity to cheer us up and let us down.

Oh, and there's another thing.

It's only after reading this book as a whole for the first time that I've realized how many metaphors I've accumulated for pop music over the years (if you have a metaphor allergy, I'd put this volume back on the shelf and walk away). I could give you a couple of reasons for this.

One is that metaphors are a good journalistic crutch that we lean on when our stories don't have legs. The second is that these metaphors are there to give the impression that we exist on the same planet as everybody else. I use everyday images, I think, to claim a relationship with the Real World, when the truth is I can go for days without relating to the Real World at all. Oh, I go outside and talk to people and read newspapers and do radio programmes. But everything, bar the records and CDs I play and the tunes that swim between my ears, passes by in a haze. I forget to make phone calls, or pay bills, I studiously overlook Real World chores like shopping and sending birthday cards. And I exist in my own little world with its suitably chaotic soundtrack.

This is probably not the healthiest state of mind for a person to go through life with. For a start, you can become completely socially inept. At parties or in pubs the conversation drifts all around you as you sit there thinking about the latest record you've bought or the next gig you're going to see. And where there should be well-reasoned opinions of the Blair administration, there are song lyrics and trivia about the original drummer from Pavement (Gary. The crazy one who used to do back flips on stage).

I've learnt to disguise this a little now. I mean, it's not as if I couldn't tell you who's running the country, or what's wrong with the NHS, it's just, well … you know … have you heard the one about Mark E Smith locking the rest of The Fall in a dressing room in Sheffield and then losing the key?

If you recognize any of this, then, listen, your secret's safe with me. This might sound like an erratic, insular, odd sort of lifestyle … but I like it.

• 1
AIN'T GOT A CLUE

It's just gone five o'clock and there are two of us standing outside the backstage door at the Ipswich Gaumont. The one with glasses and a parka is me, the other one with glasses and carrying a variety of record sleeves is Graham Diss, who I sit next to in double history at school.

Inside the building, and we know they're there because we can hear them soundchecking, are The Undertones. The real, in-the-flesh, live Undertones. The same Undertones whose logo appears on our history roughbooks and who we've seen on *Top of the Pops* doing *My Perfect Cousin*. Graham Diss even has one of their hits, *Jimmy Jimmy*, on green vinyl, which makes me obscenely jealous.

Some minutes later the noise of soundchecking stops and the stage door opens to reveal two fellas looking a little flustered. HELP! One of them is Feargal Sharkey, the band's singer. The other one, we deduce, is the tour manager. Just as we're about to pounce on them they disappear back inside and we return disconsolately to our game of kicking stones around the car park.

Another five minutes pass and the TM is back. 'Do either of you two know where Radio Orwell is?'

'Yeah, I do. It's about five minutes' walk.' I've got one up on Graham Diss at this point because I spend every other Saturday hanging around record shops in Ipswich and he doesn't know the area so well.

'Can you tell us where it is, only we're supposed to be doing an interview there,' the TM adds, only in retrospect it sounds more like: 'Well bloody give us the directions, you little brat, because we're late.'

'Well, if you want,' I say, trying to sound cool, but stuttering slightly. 'I'll take you up there.'

And that is how I came to save The Undertones' tour.

Of the many features we've ever run on the *Evening Session* the most successful is still Do You Remember The First Time? It was a simple enough idea. Just write in and tell us about the night you lost your gig virginity. Which band did you see? Did the earth move? The mailbag was full for weeks.

There were tales of lost tickets and broken limbs, the vagaries of public transport, there were family disputes (usually with elder brothers or sisters), and then explosive accounts of the headlining band walking on, and playing an immaculate set which included every song the listener had wanted to hear ... and more.

The question is, were any of these accounts actually true? They were true in the minds of the letter writers, but you exaggerate your first gig, don't you? If not at the time, then at least in later years. Or maybe exaggerate is the wrong word. What I've found is that we personalize them and make them revolve more around ourselves. This is why everyone's first gig story will have different highlights – even if they happen to have broken their duck on the same night watching the same band.

Your first gig is also a subject that's guaranteed to crop up when you're sizing up new friends or acquaintances, like your first single or the first band you pinned a picture of on your wall. It's a good barometer of age, taste and attitude. It's like fingerprinting for pop fans. Although it is one of the most widely shared experiences we have, everyone's tale is unique.

But there are parts of the story that we will allow ourselves to share. Parts of the excitement and the trauma. Which is why I have honed my 'first gig' story into a shape I'm happy with. It was a band called The Lurkers – a second-wave punk group whose third single *Ain't Got A Clue* had, unbelievably, been made Record of the Week on Kid Jensen's Radio 1 drivetime programme. They were without doubt my favourite band of the era (I'd been too young for the first wave of punk and was scrabbling around for the best of the rest when I found them on the radio). I didn't have the album yet, but I did have permission from Mum and Dad to go and see them at the Chancellor Hall in Chelmsford, a venue better known for its amateur dramatics and wrestling nights.

Now, blow by blow, minute by minute, I couldn't tell you exactly what happened when the gig finally arrived. But this is how I tell the story. Stop me if you recognize any of these symptoms:

I spent two hours before leaving deciding what to wear.

Mum and Dad gave me a lift and dropped me off – not outside the venue, because that would have been too embarrassing, but at the end of the street.

They both raised their eyebrows as they surveyed the motley collection of people who made up the queue outside. At least, I think they raised their eyebrows. I don't think I actually saw them do it – after all, I was in the back seat of the car and unless I was scouring the driver's mirror for a reaction, I wouldn't have been able to see them. But they definitely shifted in their seats a little, which is a sure sign of eyebrow action.

I had a ticket and no-one else seemed to. I was quite chuffed when it had turned up in the post. Ticket number 0012. I thought this made me one of the elite (surely the lower the ticket number, the cooler you are?). Little did I realize that advance ticket sales for The Lurkers were probably in the region of 30. And that when a bouncer shouted, 'Anyone with tickets can come straight through,' I would be the *only* person to shuffle from the queue and walk in, past the scornful looks of a hundred or so punks.

At the end of the night, there was a piercing ringing sound in my ears. I actually thought they were broken, that I'd done some irreparable damage to them. I was so scared that my parents might ban me from further gigs if they found out, that I kept schtum. It took two and a half days for the noise to stop.

The actual details of the gig aren't that important. But, being older and wiser now, I wince at the vision of the unhip me who got to the gig too early, stood right at the front, got spat on by the singer of the support band (a local Essex group called The Sods) and was then crushed against the front of the stage as The Lurkers arrived and everyone tumbled onto the floor from the bar.

I scrambled out halfway through the set and watched the rest of the gig from beside the PA, but it was too late to save myself. I was infected with something more virulent than whatever might have been lurking in the singer's saliva. I had contracted some kind of live music disease. I know, it sounds embarrassing doesn't it? (And it's worse if you say it out loud.) But honestly, I think that The Lurkers at the Chancellor Hall was the most exciting moment of my life up to that point. I mean, there wasn't much to compare it to (winning a school art competition and getting a Christmas card from Linda Audsley were good, but they weren't a patch on The Lurkers). And from the moment I left the gig, all I wanted to do was go to another one. And another one.

And that's where my problems began. Living in a small Essex village 10 miles from Colchester didn't give you much opportunity to join the live circuit. No-one seemed to play in Colchester or Chelmsford, or even further up the A12, in Ipswich. On reflection there must have been gigs going on, but either I didn't spot them or there were reasons (school, lack of transport, poor finances) that must have prevented me from going. The worst disappointment of all was that The Undertones were due to play the Chancellor Hall a month after The Lurkers … and having kept quiet about the business with the faulty ears, my parents had once again agreed to give me a lift there. Then, with just days to go before Gig 2, the show was cancelled. I cursed and sulked and sat back on my bed and waited impatiently to see when they would tour next.

In the end it was three years before The Undertones finally played near enough for me to see them on a non-school night. And by that point the entire musical landscape had changed.

Punk had been and gone and what remained of the new wave was an overexcitable and underachieving mess. The onset of the 80s signalled a tawdry Top 40 which, apart from the odd 2-Tone or Jam single, was full of charlatans and chancers as far as I could see. A bunch of FAKES. And, being a teenager whose only take on pop music came through the radio and the pages of a paper called *Record Mirror*, I didn't understand what was going on. Who was responsible for this? Why had all the bands I liked started to go out of fashion? What was I going to do now?

But the worst moment of all – the point when I knew that punk and new wave were really, finally all over – was when the Big Boys stopped going to the youth club. Every Essex village has two Big Boys. They're compulsory. They're there as a reference point for your parents, so they can say things like 'You don't want to end up like them'.

But at 13 you do want to end up like them, and I wanted to end up like one of them in particular, because he had a leather jacket and an amazing record collection. Each week the Big Boys would idly slouch into the youth club, flick a couple of small children to the floor and then march up and commandeer the record player.

Before I discovered John Peel they were responsible for much of my musical education (even if was just Sham 69 and the Smirks and 999). Also, to break up the monotony of village life, the youth club would hold discos every month or so and the Big Boys would pogo and I'd stand in the corner and gawp at them. Then one week they stopped going. And the next week it was wall-to-wall Bee Gees records and that was that. The mighty punk revolution, which had promised so much, had fallen at the first hurdle. It had lost the battle for the Colne Engaine Youth Club record player.

And I think I could have handled this if I hadn't invested so heavily in music in the previous couple of years. But after the Lurkers gig I'd started to use pop music as a cover for my lack of real identity. I wasn't particularly gregarious, I wasn't terrifically good at sport, and I wasn't even that good at being the sort of rebellious swot who never seems to try, but gets great marks. I was the classic OK pupil in the top stream of an OK Essex comprehensive who wanted to be something one day, but didn't know what it was he wanted to be.

The nearest I got to being enigmatic was when our frightening English teacher set our group an end-of-term crossword competition. 'And 14 down,' she hollered, 'is for you, Lamacq.' The clue was 'Murderous group (10 letters)'. It wasn't much of a deification, but it was enough to give me a certain amount of notoriety for a time.

But something was definitely missing. And if I had to pinpoint it, I think it was the lack of interaction between me and pop music. I bought records and taped songs off the radio and stuck pictures on my wall, but that's just being an armchair supporter (or, in reality, a lying-on-the-bed sort of supporter). No, I needed to work on this relationship between pop and me because it was too one-way.

Then sometime in 1981 The Undertones came to Ipswich on their 'Positive Touch' tour and I met Feargal Sharkey. During the walk to Radio Orwell I was barely able to speak for fear of saying something stupid or soppy. This is a situation, I can happily report, that has not changed to this day. Only now it's not just Feargal Sharkey who makes me tongue-tied. It's Dave Grohl from the Foo Fighters, Bob Mould, Jarvis Cocker, a hundred other people in bands and the entire Colchester United first team squad.

I can talk to them when there's a microphone around, but say they were standing at my local bus stop ... I'd have to cross the road to avoid them. The problem with these chance meetings with pop stars is that you know you've only got a limited amount of time with them (in

Feargal's case, a five-minute walk). So where do you start? Everyone has chat-up lines for the opposite sex but, 50 years after inventing rock'n'roll, no-one's come up with an infallible chat-up line for singers in bands. One that will leave said singer thinking (a) nice chap rather than (b) saddo.

What did I want to say to Feargal anyway? Still haven't forgiven you for cancelling Chelmsford? Any new songs in the set tonight? By the way, what are the publishing deductions like in your EMI contract?

No, I think all I wanted to say was thanks for making good records. Thanks for still being there when so many of my other favourite groups had already given up the ghost. 'Cheers, Feargal, you're a real brick.' No, bugger, maybe not. I think I managed a strangled enquiry about how the tour was going and then fell silent again. Within minutes Feargal was inside Radio Orwell, and Graham and I were on the pavement outside, looking in.

But despite the lack of any real exchange, we were jubilant. Come the gig, we could stand in Row F and look up and say, 'That's our mate Feargal. We were chatting to him this afternoon.' My lust for interaction had been cured.

As a postscript to this, when we invited listeners to send in stories about meeting their favourite or most influential pop heroes, I got an e-mail from an Oasis fan who lived near Aberdeen. The teenager in question had been on his way back to school after his lunchtime break when he ran across the road and was nearly mown down by an impressive – not to say, incongruous – looking limo.

As he gathered himself up from the road where he'd fallen, he saw the passenger window wind down, and a head poke out of the window. It was a concerned Noel Gallagher. 'Watch yourself, man,' Noel said, 'you could get killed doing that.'

Now honestly, what wouldn't you give to be nearly run over by your guitar hero?

b side

I started buying records when I was nine years old. I started plastering my bedroom walls with ripped-out pictures of bands when I was ten. And I started having to answer for my actions when I was thirteen. It's a very early age to be put in the dock, isn't it? The question is, how long does it take us to realize that it's pointless 'discussing' pop music with our parents? A week? A month? An entire adolescence? Don't we ever learn?

I had a debate once with my dad about The Police's *Message In A Bottle*. It went roughly like this.

Me: 'It's on green vinyl, so it's a collector's item. It's worth £5 at least.'
Dad: 'It's only worth £5 if someone's willing to pay £5 for it.'

Like many of the final words that my dad has uttered, there was no answer to this. I probably said, 'Well, loads of people would.' But the harsh truth was that I didn't know *anybody* who would shell out a fiver for the Police single – and if I'd known then how Sting's music would turn out in the future, I would have probably given the thing away anyway.

But the exchange is typical of the ones that happen daily between parents and their budding pop kids. My mum and dad were extraordinarily lenient in some ways. They didn't shout when I woke them up returning home late from gigs and, before I had a decent bank account, they didn't mind when Dad had to write out cheques for mail-order companies that specialized in difficult-to-get indie singles.

So, I've a lot to thank them for. But at the same time I didn't get off that lightly. Mum and Dad asked all the rhetorical questions that all parents specialize in. Here's a few, with the translations in brackets. You can add your own as well.

- Do you need all these CDs? (You DON'T need all these CDs.)
- You can't still play all these. (So why not get rid of some of them?)

- What happens when they go out of fashion? (What a waste of money!)
- I thought you had that one already on the album. (What a waste of money! Remix.)

Possibly the best one is the exasperated 'Just how many records do you need?' How many? Hundreds. Thousands. Every single great record ever released and probably some of the bad ones too so I've got something to compare the good ones against. Then there are ones for compilation tapes, ones for tacky parties, ones to impress your mates … how many's that so far?

Part of the objection parents have to your CD and record collection is the clutter. So what on earth will parents have to sigh about when MP3s take over the world and pop music is filed away on a hard drive without hindrance to a passing duster or hoover?

There are more serious aspects to the relationship between pop and the nation's parents though. During Britpop my mum used to send me cuttings from the local paper about Blur and Elastica and they started quite liking the music. This was unheard of. They'd always winced or backed out of my bedroom, shaking their heads, when I played them records as a teenager. I don't remember them actually saying it, but at some point they must have come out with the famous 'It hasn't got a tune,' or its cousin 'They all sound the same to me.'

And this was happening all over the country. *Top of the Pops* – one of the programmes that you could usually rely on to emphasize the generation gap in your house – began turning into an all-ages show. It was very confusing. How can you call pop music your own and use it as a statement of your youth if your mum is humming along to Oasis?

No wonder there was room for a rock revival at the end of the 90s and the start of the noughties. Mum, Dad, this is Slipknot.

It happened in dance culture too. The neater and tidier mainstream house music became – the more it turned into the sort of music that drunk uncles could shake a leg to on the dancefloor – the more you needed an extreme alternative. And thankfully, so far, I haven't been to a single wedding that's played Goldie or Ram Trilogy, or the latest trance or speed garage dubplate.

I think my parents could see that something was going wrong in my teens. They tried occasionally to lever me out of my bedroom and away from the radio or the record collection. But in the end they must have conceded that this shy son of theirs wasn't going anywhere unless it involved a gig or a record shop. Even when we went on holiday to Germany once, I came back with two import 12-inch singles and a couple of German pop magazines.

And anyway, underneath it all, my dad's just as bad. He goes to jazz gigs all the time, and when I went home last Christmas I found his CD collection had outgrown the sideboard and his storage cabinets. Not only that, but he has 18 Chris Barber CDs. EIGHTEEN! I mean, he's never going to play all those.

• 2
BUBBLEGUM

Have you ever wanted a haircut like someone in a band? And if you have, did you end up going to the hairdresser with a picture of the pop star in question and saying: 'I WANT TO LOOK LIKE THIS'?

Then I hate to tell you, but you're in trouble. You're on the slippery slope. Your relationship with pop music and fashion has gone past the stage of just holding hands. The next thing you know it'll want to meet your parents, and eventually it'll want to move in with you and rearrange your furniture.

I should know, because I've been there. At 13 I decided I wanted a haircut like the bass player from The Skids (*the bass player!*). I took the sleeve of their *Into The Valley* single to the hairdresser in town and pointed at it. He looked at my head and gave out a curious sound that I later discovered was exactly the same as the one an electrician makes when he gives you an estimate on rewiring your house. Fair play, he made a go of it, and I'm sure he wasn't lacking in barbershop skills, but when he'd finished and I looked in the mirror, I still wasn't the bass player from The Skids.

I gave up on trying to look like people in bands after that. But other aspects of my appearance – and my whole outlook on life, to be honest – were changing. When I was 10 I wanted to be a DJ (and you can blame the Radio 1 roadshows and me being a reclusive only child during the summer holidays for that). Then I wanted to draw *Marvel* comics. I used to spend hours sitting in my room, inventing new superheroes and copying pictures of Daredevil. Then as I tripped over the tail-end of punk, via my bedside radio, my only ambition was to live in London. Preferably near a tube station.

There is an interesting passage in *A Beat Concerto*, The Jam's official biography by Paolo Hewitt, describing Paul Weller's early life in Woking. Interesting to me anyway, because although Colne Engaine wasn't suburbia and I didn't want to be a guitarist, there were definite similarities between Weller and Lamacq in their early teens. Hewitt describes how Weller would make trips up to town with an old-school radio cassette recorder and when people asked him what he was doing, Weller used to say, 'I'm going to *record* London.'

And it wasn't just this obsession with London – where, in our young repressed minds, everything was happening – that connected us. Hewitt also reveals how Weller's circle of friends began to change, the more obsessed he became with music and then his band. Back in Essex, the same thing was happening to me. As I wandered through my teens, I found I knew more about The Vapors than I did about who was top of the Football League. I stopped going to watch matches with my dad and used to spend the long Saturday afternoons in record shops instead.

It was obvious that as my own interests began to move on, then my circle of friends would too. It set a pattern for the rest of my life, if I'm honest about it. But that's the deal with being a pop fan. You start to choose your friends through music – or in some cases, music chooses them for you.

And this is what happened with Maggot. Maggot was a couple of years older than me and, as I later found out, worked in the old DHSS office in Colchester. His nickname had attached itself to him at school – when his hobby was fishing – but he'd kept it anyway, probably because it sounded quite punk.

We first met at the 100 Club, after striking up a conversation because we were both standing on our own and were bored between bands. It transpired that we lived quite close to each other in villages on opposite sides of Colchester and shared a similar taste in music (we liked the Newtown Neurotics, and disliked Crass). But there was other good bonding material between us. Maggot had already done a hundred glamorous things that a gig-novice like myself had only dreamed of: he'd missed the last train back to Colchester and slept in the toilets at Liverpool Street Station; he'd met one of Peter & The Test Tube Babies.

Maggot's favourite story was of a punk gig in Norwich where, to quell the threat of violence, the promoters had forced everyone entering the venue to take the laces out of their boots. The only problem was that they threw all the laces in a cardboard box which meant no-one knew whose were whose. At the end of the night they put the box at the exit … and there was a full-scale fight over the last remaining set of red DM ones.

This was the downside to gigs in the early to mid 80s that sometimes gets forgotten; the smell of trouble that hung in the air at many post-punk gigs. We were used to occasional grief in Colchester – mostly at the hands of squaddies from the local barracks – but in London the second wave punk shows were dark and scary affairs. Travelling in twos helped allay fears that you would leave for home with the imprint of a skinhead's fist down the side of your cheek.

So Maggot and I became Essex County's most well-travelled gig-goers. I had old school and college friends – some good mates – but Maggot was my link with the world outside of education and family. He started writing for my fanzine, *A Pack Of Lies*, which was my first venture into print. We even followed bands on tour, sleeping in my car to save money (I always lost the toss and got the front seat, where the handbrake would bite into my ribs). One night, parked in a lay-by near Sunderland, we were woken by two bullish military police officers who thought we were two squaddies on the run. One flash of the torch at the creature lying under a donkey jacket across the back seat was enough to convince them that we weren't. That was Maggot. We lost touch when I started work, and the music scene began to evolve, but I'm sure if we met now, we'd talk about the same nonsense.

And that's the point. You can meet people by chance who you were at school with for years and shared some of your most traumatic times with, and not have more than three questions to ask them. The conversation is stilted and uncomfortable and set in the past. But meet somebody who you know through music, and there's always some common ground.

I keep in touch with a couple of my college friends – noticeably the ones who were most into records – but the mid 80s for me are marked out by people whom I met while I was writing or selling my fanzine. I can – and have – gone for years without seeing them, but sooner or later they pop up again and you just carry on where you left off (can you imagine that happening with old next-door neighbours or workmates?).

A good example of this is Lawrence Bell. When I started *A Pack of Lies* I filched many of the ideas from an Ipswich-based fanzine called *Harsh Reality*, which had folded just before my first issue had come back from the printers. Then, one afternoon in Parrot Records, I was trying to persuade the assistant behind the counter to stock my latest issue when a young chap picked up a copy and began flicking through it.

'What's this then?' he asked, with a nice mix of enthusiasm and nonchalance.

'It's my fanzine. It's like a Colchester version of *Harsh Reality*. Look, see that bit, I nicked that from *Harsh Reality* ...'

Smiling, he nodded his head. I felt the full sales pitch building up, so I forged on: 'Do you remember *Harsh Reality* at all?'

'Remember it?' He grinned. 'I wrote it.'

'YOU'RE LAWRENCE!'

And that was it. We chatted for a while, I off-loaded 10 copies of issue two on the shop's assistant manager and I didn't see Lawrence again for years. Then one night I went to see a band called The Adicts at the 100 Club in London. And, to my amazement, who should be the singer in the support band Perfect Daze? It was Lawrence. This time we kept in touch for a while and when I joined the *NME* (*New Musical Express*) I wrote a couple of favourable reviews of the Daze, who went on to gig with several fashionable Ipswich skate-punk bands and released a handful of energetic pop-punk singles.

Then inevitably we lost touch again. I don't know why. A couple of unreturned calls, then you lose a phone number and your life fills up with other people. One night I was out with Dave Bedford from Fire Records who told me about their plans to start a new guitar offshoot label. It was going to be run by some chap they'd found who knew all there was to know about the American scene and had a good ear for a tune. 'Can't tell you who it is at the moment, it's a secret,' added Bedford conspiratorially, 'but he really knows his stuff.'

'His name's not Lawrence, is it?'

'How did you know that?!'

Just a guess. And so Lawrence started the great Roughneck Records. He lived in London and used to drop round the *NME* with his latest releases by Leatherface or The Lemonheads, and it was nice to have him around again – and have someone to stand with at gigs. I think there was another six months when the phone calls dried up (later explained by his departure from Fire to start his own label, Domino Records, home to people like Pavement and Sebadoh), but apart from that we've done quite well.

But Lawrence – and a few others – make up some sort of loose gang of friends who are also fans. People who knew me before I was at Radio 1 and are therefore well qualified to tell me when I'm turning into a pain in the arse. There's my gig guru Simon Williams and Graham Bell (Tall Graham), whom I met when I was living in Harlow and who introduced me to not just the local music scene, but also to the local greyhound racing track. And there's Neil Pengelly, who was a singles buyer at Virgin when I first knew him and now books the bands for the Reading Festival. All these people, hopefully, forgive me for being useless at returning calls and understand that our shared lunacy when it comes to music is enough to cement our friendship for years to come. I haven't checked, but at least two of them definitely did that thing with the picture and the hairdresser.

Back at Halstead's Ramsey School it wasn't hard picking friends into music. You just had to know where to sit in class.

The Ramsey School obeyed the universal laws of seating arrangements-to-musical taste, i.e. boy-band-supporting pop kids at the front, obscurist indie fans and metalheads at the back. You can't place the dance fans, because they keep moving about all the time. And I know some schools flout these laws, but it's not a bad rule of thumb. We all had to sit somewhere near the back because the logos of the bands we liked were more complicated to draw than everyone else's. Hidden away behind 20 other heads we could spend an entire geography lesson on them. Then there's the business with making lists (Top 10 current favourite singles, Top 10 all-time best bands, and the Top 10 records I would like to buy if I could get a decent Saturday job to pay for them). It's no wonder I didn't get around to filling in those entry forms for university. I was too busy working out which was the all-time greatest Blondie single.

The fact that I wasn't going to uni, though, made me something of a pariah in the eyes of my school. Out of all the pupils in the Upper Sixth, I was the only one who didn't get the traditional end-of-school interview with the Headmaster. At least I think it was because of this. It could also have been because a month before the end of term I strode out to bat in the Sixth Form vs The Teachers cricket match, dressed not in the regulation whites, but in black DMs, black jeans and a T-shirt which bore the legend 'Chronic Generation'. I hit a four off my English tutor and was out for six.

Instead of university, I'd passed the entrance exam for a course in journalism run from Harlow College. And, of course, within a week of arriving, I'd hand-picked most of my best friends-to-be based on either (a) geographical location (a couple of them came from around Colchester) and (b) musical taste. It's important to add that in some cases it doesn't matter WHICH bands people like, as long they like them with the same, insane, obsessive approach that I have. My new best mate was Greg Fountain, son of an important PR man at Vauxhall Motors in Luton, who lived and breathed Bob Dylan. I knew I had made a good choice in Greg when, within a couple of months of the course starting, we had to bunk off college one day and drive to Luton to buy the new Dylan LP *Infidels* on the day of release. A day late wouldn't have been any good.

And I couldn't abide Bob Dylan. But then again, Greg wasn't a big Partisans or Pistols fan either, so the arrangement worked quite well. The most important aspect of living in Harlow, however, was that I was finally within striking distance of gigs in London. Once, maybe twice a week, I'd walk a mile through the town park to the train station and head for the Smoke. Financially this would have been a struggle, but I soon discovered that there was never a ticket inspector at Harlow station to greet the last train home. So all you needed was a single to town and you were sorted.

It was a rule that only failed once. One night, ticketless and penniless, I began walking toward the exit, before spotting the orange bib of an inspector who was still on duty. Panicking slightly, I was forced to turn back on to the platform and make good my escape (this involved leaping over two sets of live rails, scaling the wall into the Post Office car park and then sprinting to safety).

I wasn't the only one who occasionally diddled the ticket inspectors. On my third Harlow–London expedition I met ranting poet and writer Attila the Stockbroker on Liverpool Street Station. I introduced myself as a local fanzine writer and asked if he'd like a hand carrying his bags and mandolin. 'No thanks, I'll be needing these,' he said, as he set off like an overburdened mum with too much shopping. The guards simply looked at him sympathetically as he made a failed attempt to find a ticket, and waved him on his way.

We chatted on the train home, and I got his phone number. And through him I found the Newtown Neurotics, the only band I'd heard of from Harlow. I didn't quite realize quite the impact that meeting them would have, but then I hadn't taken stock of where my interest in music was really going. Mostly it was based on bands I read about in the press. But via the Neurotics I became involved with the local music scene and Tall Graham's fledgling record label, Davy Lamp, which had just released a benefit EP for the striking miners and went on to put out a compilation album for the anti-Apartheid campaign. Not only that, but, following the Neurotics around to gigs, I met new groups like Action Pact, the Redskins, and The Men They Couldn't Hang. I went to exciting and sometimes scummy new venues, met fanzine writers and ranting poets, and got nicknamed Hovis by the Red Action skinheads because of the flat cap I used to wear. The hat had started as a tribute to the old fellas on the terraces at Colchester United, but it finally found fame of its own when Phill Jupitus (then performing under the name of Porky The Poet) wore it on stage one night supporting Billy Bragg. All a little surreal, but that's how I spent the early 80s. The Neurotics unlocked a new underground world for me – at the same time as the rest of the UK student population was busy 'saving' the overground one.

We used to listen to the first Smiths album all the time during my year at college. Well, not ALL the time, but there were days when you suspected that the entire student population of Britain had decamped to college carrying nothing more than an optimistic packet of three, a couple of hip T-shirts and the first Smiths LP.

During the first few months I went round visiting some of my old school friends at their various universities and they all had the Smiths album as well, except, ironically, my mate Steve Cooke, who studied on The Smiths' home turf in Manchester. Instead, Steve had found somebody called Indians In Moscow and Martin Stephenson & The Daintees who had both played at his local SU in the first term.

Bands do brilliantly on the college circuit in the autumn because everywhere they go there's a cheap beer promotion.

Elsewhere, though, it was The Smiths and New Order. When I visited Sheffield a mate told me that New Order's 'Blue Monday' was the in tune to get laid to and you could tell when someone was having sex because it would start blaring through the corridors of his hall of residence. That's when all the big alternative bands of the time started to make sense. New Order (getting laid). The Smiths (not getting laid). Then came Billy Bragg (politics) and, a year later, The Pogues (drinking) and that was your University of Life soundtrack pretty much sorted. Everyone was allowed their own maverick variations, but no college jukebox could survive without the Big Four.

And so some of the ground that had been lost in the charts after the demise of punk and 2-Tone started to be reclaimed. I'm sure it wasn't just students who were buying the alternative music of the time – like me, most of them were probably taping it off the radio or other friends – but the student dollar is still an important factor in pop's make-up.

You can tell an incredible amount about who's in and who's out of fashion by inspecting the posters that adorn the walls of halls of residence around the country. It stands to reason. First year freshers, faced with four blank walls, either bring or buy a selection of posters to wallpaper their rooms with at the start of term (have you ever been to a university that doesn't have a man come round once a week selling huge posters in the sports hall?).

Each influx brings the hippest groups of the moment. I mean, suppose you do manage to pull a second year and get him or her back to your lair, you don't want it papered with someone who a has credibility rating of zero. You want a collection of artful, trendy, romantic, sexy and intellectual types. You don't even have to like them that much, but it's important to look like you're buying into the culture of the future.

In 1992 it was Nirvana; in 1993 it was Rage Against The Machine and Cypress Hill; in 1994 and 1995 Britpop; in 1996 it was Trainspotting; and in 1998 and 1999 it was the Chemical Brothers and Fatboy Slim. I've often pondered whether there is a relationship between the three-year student cycle and the rise and fall of various alternative groups. Because if you take a look at some of the most student-friendly bands, they appear in the first year, reach their peak in the second and then after three years they start to fade. Musical scenes have been known to go through the same fate.

Take Britpop for instance. If your average fresher arrived in the autumn of 1994 with their Oasis posters, and championed the Britpop bands through their three year course … then by the spring of 1997 they're returning home and it's all over. No more cheap beer or bands. It's off to work, more responsibility and a huge loan to pay off. The gang of mates you used to go to gigs with has been broken up, and there might not be the money around to indulge in so many CDs.

The bigger bands survive, but the rest – the ones who'd failed to make it past being another cult college group – seem to wither and disappear. It's just a thought.

I didn't have a three-year cycle. I was only at college for a year, but my musical taste was going haywire. I'd been through a stage of championing some good and not-so-good punk and indie bands because there didn't seem much else to do.

Then everything started to change. I moved on from New Order, Orange Juice and the Psychedelic Furs and ended up somewhere else. In a world outside the charts. That's when I rediscovered John Peel.

• 3
GETTING NOWHERE FAST

Unbelievably it was my dad who introduced me to John Peel. Not literally of course, because apart from them both watching Ipswich Town on a regular basis, there's very little chance of them ever bumping into each other. But one night, before going to bed, Dad was fiddling with the radio, flicking through the dial, when he chanced upon some extraordinary piece of folk music.

As his ears pricked up, he pushed the record button on his cassette player and caught the final three minutes of the song. At the end of it, the voice of Peel back-announced the track – don't ask me what it was – and then went into a song from his session guests Generation X. Dad switched off.

A couple of nights later, under the cover of darkness in my bedroom, I found this John Peel character again. It was like discovering life exists on a different planet. It took me a couple of months, sizing up possible career options, but eventually I decided I wanted to be John Peel. Well, not him, but I wanted to be Somebody Like Him: playing records he liked and then talking about them. And not just any records. Records that were *weird*.

The punk and new wave era had boasted three very good radio shows: Peel, Mike Read, who was given the 8–10pm slot on Radio 1 to cater for the music spilling over from John's show, and Stuart Henry's *Streetheat* on Radio Luxembourg on a Saturday evening.

Of these, Read's slot was the most obvious forerunner of the *Evening Session*. Not just because of the time slot, but also because Read played a slightly more accessible range of tunes than Peelie, which complemented John's two-hour magical mystery tour. After Read moved on to daytime, the *Evening Show* (no-one had managed to find a name for it in those days) continued to exist, although it did have its ups and downs. Kid, now David, Jensen took over from Read, as the new wave began to fall apart. And then Richard Skinner arrived, slightly burdened by the lack of great alternative music at the time (which was probably why he played the American band Green On Red on every show). Skinner was there when I rediscovered Radio 1 at college, but he was later followed by Janice Long, whose enthusiastic delivery became a big influence on the *Sesh* in the days of myself and Jo Whiley. Long was bubbly and effervescent and sounded like one of your mates. She was ageless and infectious and played Blyth Power and the Loft. I liked her.

But as my college exams drew ever closer, it was the return of Peel to my daily routine that made the most impact. When I first listened to him I did what countless young fans of the time did. I listened at home, on school nights, with my headphones on and the bedroom light switched off so that my parents didn't know I was still awake. In return for this surreptitious set-up he'd introduced me to all sorts of bands – groups whose records I still treasure, even now: The Blue Orchids, The Fire Engines, Gang Of Four, Girls At Our Best, Silicon Teens. Even the early Adam & The Ants singles like *Zerox* and *Cartrouble*. You can still hear the influence of these early 80s independent bands today if you listen closely enough (check Elastica, Pulp, Tindersticks and numerous others). What Peel had managed to do was to gather up the shrapnel from punk and make sense of it.

When I do radio shows now, I present them in the hope that some-where along the line, one or more records I play each night will have a similar impact on a listener that Peel's playlist had on me in my teens. Mind you, listening to Peel caused untold misery as well. What's the single most frustrating thing that can happen to an overexcitable, young and foolhardy pop fan? It's hearing a record on the radio, saving up your money and then going to the shops on Saturday only to be told they haven't got it. Not only have they not got it, but THEY'VE NEVER EVEN HEARD OF IT!

All that expectation, the thrill of the chase – and then at the end of it, nothing. As a last-ditch solution I used to send off for records from mail-order companies – in the same way that the internet is now taking up the slack left by poor shop distribution – but it wasn't the same. I always forgave Peel though. After all, it wasn't his fault that Parrot Records didn't have *Hold On* by Terminal (a record I'm still looking for if anyone happens to have a copy). Anyway, who else were we going to turn to for advice on music? Peel was our personal tutor.

For many kids, me included, my bedroom was both my sanctuary and my own private world. And during homework hours Radio 1 became the soundtrack to it. The only people I would let in my bedroom – if they weren't looking for dirty clothes or bringing me cups of tea – were Mike Read and John Peel. Metaphorically speaking, Peelie has been in more bedrooms than any other person in Britain over the years.

It's also partly his fault that I launched myself into that other bastion of bedroom culture – the fanzine. I used to have this Peel Show ritual where I'd write three-line reviews of some of the records he played (rather scarily, I also had a marking system, which I later found out is exactly the same system that Peel has used for years to denote his favourite tracks). From these three-line reviews, I got into writing for other fanzines, and then I launched my own.

A Pack Of Lies Number One carried 22 pages, had a print run of 300 copies and came out while I was in the Lower Sixth at school. I sold it by post and at local gigs by groups like Colchester's Special Duties (whose singer Steve Green I still stand next to on the terraces at Colchester United). By the time I got to college I was on to issue four and a print run of 400. I did the Neurotics, plus a Welsh band called the Partisans, and filled the rest with reviews and waffle. At college the National Council for the Training of Journalists had put all its students into digs – which meant I lived with a landlady on one of the estates near the swimming pool. She didn't mind my increasingly nocturnal lifestyle, but she did mind the rattle of the front room ceiling as I stapled 100 copies of Lies in a single night in my bedroom upstairs. Once again, Peel was the noise in the background.

I got through college, but only just. I revised for my law exam on the tube going to Hammersmith to see a band called Twisted Nerve. When it came to the all-important shorthand exams, I failed three times before finally passing the required 100-words-a-minute barrier on the last day of term. I thought I'd never see Harlow again after that, but I was wrong.

After college I returned to Colne Engaine with its one shop, one pub and one village green, and mooched around the house, plotting the future of my fanzine. I applied for a few jobs – partly to keep my parents happy – and, scarily, was offered an interview with a paper in Shrewsbury. But

Shrewsbury was nowhere near London and London was where all the gigs were, so I blew the interview by saying that I might be unsettled living so far from home and went back to daytime TV and photocopying.

Then, out of the blue, Andy Griffin, a classmate from college, tipped me off about a job on the *Walthamstow Guardian* and within two weeks I was behind a desk sharpening my shorthand pencil. Not in Walthamstow – I'd missed that one – but on one of its sister papers, the *West Essex Gazette* in Loughton, a quietly anonymous suburb attached to the capital by nothing more than the Central line. As a junior reporter I got the Golden Weddings, the primary school picture captions and the High Street vox pops (the weekly feature where you stop people in the street and ask them their views on proposals for a new bus stop by the fire station).

It's fair to say that I didn't settle in straight away. In fact, it's truer to say that as my three-month probation period came to an end, the Editor expressed doubts about my ability and promptly gave me a fortnight in the central office to prove myself. In the end they relented and I went back to Loughton to write such memorable stories as Mum Gives Birth To Baby In Front Seat Of Mini and the tale of disgraced Spurs goalkeeper Tony Parks. It's the latter which shows what an ingenious coward I used to be when it came to hard news.

Parks had appeared in court on a drink driving charge at a time when magistrates were making examples of fallen footballers and handing out custodial sentences instead of fines. Parks escaped the rumoured prison term, but he couldn't escape the determined hacks of the local press.

Having written up the court case, the Editor threw the story back in my face claiming that – quite rightly – the tabloids would beat us to it. 'What I want you to do, Steve, is phone him up and ask him about his marriage and whether he's got a drink problem.'

On balance I didn't much fancy the idea of tackling a six-foot goalkeeper with claims that his personal life had driven him to ruin, but given my precarious position on the paper I had to show some willing. I found his number and made the call. I let the phone ring twice, put the receiver down with lightning speed, and then announced, 'He's not in.' This was on Friday. Our deadline day was Wednesday. I repeated this process on Monday and Tuesday and then it came to press day.

'Give him one last go,' the chief reporter sighed.

By now I was so confident that he'd gone abroad, or was staying with friends until the fuss had died down, that I let the phone ring four times. And then he answered it.

'Erm, it's Steve Lamacq from the *West Essex Gazette*, I wonder if you could spare me five minutes ...'

Parks said this was fine. And I set off looking for a way of avoiding all talk of marriage and booze. If I could just get him to say something like 'I am not the bad boy of soccer,' that would be OK. The phone call seemed to go on for hours, but after what was probably 15 minutes of unadulterated pussyfooting, I gave it one last shot at goal. 'Well, thanks, Tony, and I just wondered ... a lot of local kids look up to you as their hero ... so do you have any message for them now?'

'Um, yes,' Parks considered. 'I'd just like to say I'm not the bad boy of soccer.'

THANKSVERYMUCHGOODBYE.

Sensing that maybe hard news wasn't my forte I was moved again, this time to the Sports Desk at the *Harlow Gazette*. This suited me fine. I was living back at my old landlady's, and covering local soccer matches on a Saturday, so I got Fridays off to go record shopping (by now I'd discovered a terrific little shop in Walthamstow called Ugly Child Records. What a brilliant name for a record shop. 'Oi, spotty kid with a carrier bag, do you know Ugly Child?'). I'd even managed to find a girlfriend who didn't mind too much that I'd disappear for nights on end to staple fanzines or write incomprehensible reviews of bands I'd seen at the Hammersmith Clarendon. In fact, quite the contrary. Helen was the music writer on the *Gazette*'s rival paper, the *Harlow Star*, so we were always going to gigs together and if we argued about anything, it was usually over the relative merits of Half Man Half Biscuit vs Pop Will Eat Itself.

The *Gazette*, meanwhile, was staffed by a good bunch of reporters – many of whom have since moved on to bigger and better things (Mark Hill, whom I used to sit next to, is currently producing Steve Wright's Radio 2 show and has won a couple of Sony Awards, while Garry Thompson has risen through the ranks of various national newspapers). I moved out of my landlady's and bought a flat. And, despite my relative inexperience, I was made Father of the Chapel of the local branch of the National Union of Journalists. Morale was low after a six-week strike prompted by a case of unfair dismissal. We'd lost, and had gone back to work with our tails between our legs. But it was important to try to rally a positive mood for the next battle (the onset of computer technology and direct input. The same factors that on a bigger scale had prompted disputes all over Fleet Street and then Wapping).

In the meantime I received the odd verbal warning from the über-bosses at head office about 'burning the candle at both ends' and turning up half asleep after being at a gig the night before, but otherwise life had become almost settled. I think I nearly knocked my music biz aspirations on the head around this time … but then I got sucked back in.

After a year the *Gazette* promoted me to Sports Editor and gave me our pop music page to play with as well (even if it did, in keeping with local newspaper law, have a cringeworthy title, namely … Our Generation). Anyway, you might not think that there is much pop music to cover in Harlow but, let me tell you, Harlow was a hotbed of talent.

Real by Reel, The Sullivans, Some Other Day, The Tender Trap, Austins Shirts, Paul Howard & Joe Clack, The Pharoahs, Blue Summer, the Pressure (later The Internationalists), the Hermit Crabs, the hippy group whose name I can't remember … ring any bells yet? No? Well I suppose that's the point.

There are hundreds of local scenes in towns all over the country. Hundreds of bands from places like Portsmouth or Doncaster or Peterborough, the sort of places that in rock'n'roll terms are forever overlooked and always out of fashion. The problem is, these towns have no pop heritage. They can't boast of previous successes (or if they can they're like Harlow, whose only Top 40 band had been a group called Roman Holiday who were so embarrassingly lightweight that we did everything in our power to wipe them from memory).

The other drawback with these places is that bands are often shockingly uninformed about the way the industry works and about the way you can cheat or shortcut your way to a record deal or a feature in the music press. Unless you happen to have a retired member of a former Top 30 band living on your doorstep, or you've made a couple of good contacts in the industry, you can find yourself banging your head against a wall until finally frustration forces you to give up.

But that didn't stop us banging on about the local groups at the time. I even ended up 'managing' one of them for about three months one summer. Some Other Day were a four-piece whose name unfortunately shortened to SOD. During my time at the helm, I spent £100 on a demo and endless hours inventing new ways of making them famous. 'Listen everyone,' I told them one night, at a specially convened battleplan meeting in the bar of Harlow Town Football Club, 'we're not going to play bog-standard venues, we're going to play cinemas and theatres.'

Apart from the ill-fated theatre tour (one date in Sudbury, which fell through), I tried every idea in the book. Worse still, I thought they were all original. I never once considered the fact that, just possibly, a million other bands had got there first. So we tried sending in the rave reviews from the local press (the ones that start 'Local band The Hit are top of the pops with music fans' or something similar). We tried nice cassette sleeves and fancy biogs. And then, gaining in confidence – i.e. increasingly desperate – we went for the Teaser campaign.

If there are any current or would-be pop managers reading this, whatever you do, don't try the Teaser campaign. I'm so embarrassed by this one, I'm going to leave the room for five minutes.

Somewhere along the line, another local journalist had described Some Other Day as making 'delightful trouser music'. Nobody knew what this meant, but we decided that Trouser Music was the enigmatic, hit-making formula of the future. Before sending out the new demo, we drew up a hitlist of A&R people and journalists and sent them a single photocopied note which claimed, 'Trouser Music is coming'. No mention of the band whatsoever, just the Trouser Music. That would get them thinking.

Next was a second photocopy – this time with the name of the group in bold at the bottom. Then we followed that a week later by sending the lucky few a pair of Action Man trousers. Clever, eh? Finally we unleashed the demo with an invitation to see Trouser Music in the flesh: Some Other Day at the Mean Fiddler in Harlesden.

Nobody turned up. Strike that. A coachload of fans from Harlow turned up, but the rest of the music industry had remained unfathomably un-teased. Still, at least we didn't go as far as the interesting box.

Once a month I arrive in the Radio 1 office to find a massive or oddly shaped box sitting on my chair. As soon as I arrive, a small crowd gathers and the following exchange takes place.

'Go on, open it.'

'I wouldn't get excited, it'll be a demo tape.'

'Don't be silly. In that? Go on, open it.'

First you have to get past the layers of gaffer tape. Then once inside, it's like a bran tub full of the foamy stuff you get with new electrical gear. And then somewhere at the bottom ... there's a demo tape.

'Oh. Is that all? I thought it was going to be exciting.'

Well, it might be. It might be the future of rock'n'roll or the reinvention of rap music or an illicit bootleg of some early Foo Fighters sessions! But it never is. I've had demos that have come in pizza cartons, boxes that once held kettles and toasters – and it's never been exciting. I mean, I live in hope. How great would it be to appear on a programme in years to come, explaining how a band the size of U2 first sent you a tape in a wheelie-bin? And before you get any ideas – don't try it. I once wrote a piece for a musicians' magazine in which I explained that the packaging of a demo has no bearing on whether I'll play it or not. 'For all I know, the best ones will come wrapped in toilet paper,' I concluded. You can probably guess the rest. Didn't need to buy loo roll for a month.

Working on this theory, can I rewrite that last bit? Wouldn't it be great if a band destined to be as big as U2 sent you a demo wrapped in an executive season ticket for Colchester United? I mean, that really would be something.

b side

Working with a band didn't make me rich, but it did give me my first real insight into what bands are like. How they function, and well, to be honest, how they malfunction.

How every small bit of good news is a signal that 'yes, at last, we're on our way' and how every crumb of bad news means it's the end of the road before they've even started. Over the years I've seen it time and time again, and I've thanked my lucky stars that I never wanted to be in a band.

Oh, there was a while when I did I suppose. Aged 10–15, I did the whole air guitar thing in my bedroom and if I got really carried away I'd imagine myself and my band being mobbed by fans. In this imaginary group I was always the bass player. Looking back, I guess this indicates a certain ambivalence or lack of self-belief to start with. Why wasn't I the singer or the lead guitarist, like my mates were in their heads? Why? Because, realistically, I thought the bass would be easier to learn. And it seemed to me, from looking at pictures of bands, that as the bassist you didn't have to be particularly good-looking or articulate to pick up your wage. All you had to do was play the bass as far down by your knees as possible and occasionally supply backing vocals to prove to the audience that you were still breathing.

But then, around 16, it struck me that being in a band wasn't a career I was either (a) capable of or (b) that interested in. It looked like it was actually bloody hard work. And besides … I didn't have a bass guitar and I didn't look like Joy Division's Peter Hook, who I thought was the coolest bass player on the planet. But I really wasn't that fussed, so before anyone trots out the line about journalists being frustrated musicians, think again. For all the writers who have tried and failed in bands before becoming critics, there's an equal amount who never really gave it that much thought.

It's not same for everyone, though. There is that scene in *Withnail & I* when Richard Griffiths as Uncle Monty is recalling his failed acting career. Mournfully and theatrically, he finishes by saying: 'It is the most shattering experience of a young man's life when he wakes one morning and says quite reasonably to himself, "I will never play the Dane". When that moment comes, one's ambition ceases.'

And I imagine some would-be pop stars go through the same trauma. Only it's not playing the Dane, it's playing on *Top of the Pops* or at Wembley Arena or being chased by screaming Californian groupies through the corridor of a five star hotel.

I was lucky. I think it was because I'd studied pop stars (what they looked like and the way they talked) that I knew I wasn't one of them. I wanted an escapist dream, but it wasn't this one. I did finally buy a bass guitar when I was 18 – £35 including the case, through a friend in a band called The Mysterie Boys – but I've never stood on a stage with it. Crazily, two bands have asked if I'd guest with them in the past, but I ran and hid both times. Still, I have taught myself most of The Ramones' back catalogue and *Clean Sheets* by the Descendents, so I'm happy enough. And I do follow the bass-playing rules laid down by Hook and the punk movement.

It's an easy litmus test of how good a group are: the lower the bassist's guitar, the better the band. Level 42, UB40, too high, rubbish. The Ramones, New Order, the Mary Chain, bass by their ankles. Good. I thank you.

So I didn't ever exist in the dreamworld that new bands live in. And I've never had to book a rehearsal room or sack a drummer or wince when the dopey guitarist tries to shoehorn an AC/DC solo into one of my songs. But being a critic you can live a vicarious lifestyle, standing on the edge of all these groups and watching them going through the whole process.

For a start, there's an awful lot to practise. How to stand. How to walk. What to say in interviews. What *not* to let your drummer say in interviews. Then there's the whole problem with your signature. Even I will own up to this one. I spent days once as a teenager practising new signatures, because my regular run-of-the-mill chequebook one looked like the creation of a two-year-old with a blunt crayon. So I invented new ones (dozens of them) before finally deciding on the one I use now.

As musicians grow older and wiser they begin to move the goalposts of what they want to achieve (first it's sex, then it's respect. At the outset it's records sales, later it's credibility). I know I'm generalizing here, but 90 per cent of young guitar bands live in a colourful and romantic Walter Mitty world.

Everything, when a group forms, is a step closer to fame. The first rehearsal, the first two new songs ... then, the first gig. Then you get to make a demo – in a real recording studio (they'll probably throw in an ex-member of a 60s beat group as an engineer into the bargain. And even if he does bore you senseless with stories about the Cavern and makes the guitar sound skinny and useless, who cares, because there're the songs on tape).

Next it's a support slot to someone semi-famous, then the first London gig (embarrassingly, filmed by one of your parents, who are standing proudly on a chair at the back of the gig) and if you're lucky your first radio play or first review. And this is where bands go in separate directions. The lucky ones get record label interest and major deals, and are on their way to the Top 10 and tours of Japan. The unlucky ones, the ones that aren't very good, or don't happen to be in the right place at the right time, suddenly discover that the world is a horrible place.

It could be the umpteenth rejection letter from a record label, or the 400 unsold copies of your first single gathering dust under the guitarist's bed. It might be a bad gig or a scathing review or anything. It could just be the onset of jealousy as you see all these bands who are *quite patently not as good as you* receiving all the acclaim and attention that you, by rights, deserve. But sooner or later, it's time to concede defeat and pack it in.

And I don't know what's worse here. Would you rather have got quite close to fame (a record deal, a couple of tours and a Top 75 hit maybe), or would you rather have called it a day before having the rock'n'roll lifestyle dangled in front of you and then cruelly snatched away again? Whichever. There has to be a day, doesn't there, when you realize it's never going to happen.

This is harder to face for some musicians than for others. On the one hand, that's why there are so many Ex bands in existence (featuring former members of formerly quite good groups who are simply hooked on the lifestyle and obsessed by the dream). On the other, there are bands who've been kicking around for years and have never given up hope that one day their break will come. Demos regularly turn up at Radio 1 from men in their late 20s or early 30s from Hertfordshire or Huddersfield. And it's not the age that's against them, necessarily, it's the look. Most of them resemble an artist's impression of what the Mock Turtles would look like in the year 2010.

I'd like to tell them the bad news. That they've got no hope of being the Next Big Thing, or being besieged on their doorstep by autograph hunters. That their chance has gone.

And before you shoot the messenger, I'm not the one making the judgement here. If you think that music critics are harsh, have you looked at the record-buying public recently? They just don't seem to want to know about bands comprised of four fat, balding men from Bedford or wherever. The press and the fans even turned on Robbie and Gary when they had to add an extra notch to their belts, so what chance does that give an unknown bunch of 20-somethings who haven't even passed go yet?

As with many of pop's unspoken rules, there are exceptions. The more left of centre the music, the less your looks or your age or anything other than the music really matters. Or, better still, you could be American (bands like the excellent Grandaddy have done pretty well, thank you very much and they've got beards for Christ's sake).

Maybe one day the Glasgow Barrowlands or the London Forum will ring with applause as four men from a local Sunday football team walk on stage and open with a rehash of *I Wanna Be Adored* or *Louie Louie*. But I doubt it. It's more likely that the people involved will give up the ghost and form tribute bands, or take up Monday night residencies in the corner of their local wine bar.

And for all the terrific times I would have had, through doing gigs and telling my mum I'd soon be on *Top of the Pops*, I don't think I could've coped with being so near but yet so far.

• 4
WHENEVER I'M GONE

Everyone has a band that they think should have been massive, but never made the Top 40. They could be mates from your local town, or a group signed to a major record label who looked like they were going places. It doesn't matter. They were great – and the rest of the world just didn't see it. Being me, I've acquired about a hundred of these bands (quite a nice collection). But if I had to pick just the one, then it's The Prisoners.

I'd put my fanzine on hold for a year while concentrating on the pop page of the *Harlow Gazette*. But *A Pack Of Lies* returned with three issues in quick succession, starting with number eight, which was a comeback special featuring loads of incomprehensible reviews. But it was good to be back. I'm not sure if it was a particularly good time for fanzines, but through the 80s many of the future music press writers cut their teeth in the underground world of photocopy machines and High Street print shops. By issue number nine the print run was up to 700, and copies came with a free flexi disc (*de rigeur* for 'zines of the mid 80s) featuring a track each from Colchester's sleazy-rocking Mysterie Boys and an Uxbridge-based guitar foursome called The Price.

The peak of the scene for me was when a bunch of us set up a fanzine stall in London's Brockwell Park, where the GLC was staging a free outdoor gig (The Damned played I think, and probably Aswad. It's a bit of a haze because the GLC was always putting on gigs around the time of the miners' strike and the Wapping dispute. I think that's why a certain age group of Londoners has always been so supportive of former GLC leader Ken Livingstone. They associate him with cheap tube fares and being able to see The Smiths and The Redskins for free on the South Bank).

Our stall was on a walkway between the two live music stages and was run by Dave Hurt (*Love & Molotov Cocktails* fanzine), Richard Cool Notes and his mate, me and future *Loaded* Editor James Brown. Brown was always the most entertaining. Midway through the afternoon he stopped two passing policemen and, in a display of salesmanship that was second to none, flogged them not only a copy of his own fanzine *Attack On Bzag*, which was a riotous mix of pop and politics, but one of mine as well.

That was the thing about being a fanzine editor – it made you part of a little community with a spirit all of its own. Sure, there was a certain amount of cliquiness and rivalry around, but between them the fanzines and bedroom indie labels formed a small pocket of resistance to the generally bland mainstream of the time. It's that world outside the chart again. A scene that still exists now, nurtured by the chat rooms and message boards of the internet as well the current breed of home-made A5-sized pop manifestos.

In those pre-net days, we swapped letters and cassettes and phone calls and you didn't rely on the press to tell you what was going on, because each week someone you knew or had just met would introduce you to a new band or great record. Through *A Pack Of Lies* I met Andy Peart, who was behind the excellent *So What* fanzine; and through Andy I met Leigh Heggarty from flexi stars The Price (whose post new wave guitar pop was another sorely overlooked gem). And through Leigh I found The Prisoners.

Andy and Leigh have introduced me to a lot of music over the years, but it's The Prisoners that I really owe them for. They couldn't have suggested a better band if they'd gone through some kind of Dateline selection process matching me to my perfect partner. The Prisoners were, without doubt, the most sullen, angry, embittered and endearing four-piece I'd ever heard. They scowled for Britain. One evening we blagged our way into the soundcheck of their gig at Uxbridge University – I think because The Price were supporting – and waved at them as they arrived. They completely blanked us. Brilliant.

If that sounds masochistic, then doesn't everyone go through a stage of loving someone who behaves appallingly back to them? What was that the Buzzcocks said about falling in love with someone you shouldn't have fallen in love with? Their names were Graham Day, Jamie Taylor, Alan Crockford and Jamie Symons. And they had a song called *Melanie*. A heart-wrenching, gritted-teeth love song that made me fall head over heels for them.

And I wasn't alone in this. Although they received very little press coverage at the time save for some enthusiastic LP reviews, several of today's *NME* writers revered them, as did various bands, including the Charlatans and the Inspiral Carpets, who later namechecked them as a major influence. The two girls from the band Lush were even at some of the same Prisoners gigs that I was at, long before we ever met, or they formed their band.

There are several Prisoners albums to choose from if you want to hear what they were like, though personally I'd go for the third LP *The Last Fourfathers*. It's got some of the saddest and some of the most vitriolic songs I own. And if I felt a bit of a misfit, which I think I did at the time, then The Prisoners understood. They felt the same way. They even had a song called *Here Come The Misunderstood*.

There are probably loads of reasons why their career together never truly got off the ground. Despite emerging from the fleetingly talked-about Medway scene, they weren't the hippest new band around. The music papers were having a mid-80s identity crisis (leading up to the invention of the C86 movement on the one hand and Grebo on the other). And their faces didn't fit. You could even make a case for saying that they were slightly retro-sounding even then.

But they did OK for a time. They were filmed live for Channel 4's *The Tube*, they toured the UK and were Big In Europe. And after *The Last Fourfathers* they finally signed to a bigger label, the quirky Stiff Records, which had grown out of the pub-rock and punk scenes of the late 70s. It would have probably been a good move, had it not been for the fact that Stiff was just about to hit financial trouble. And, according to the band, the A&R staff kept leaning on them to clean up their sound and go for the Big Hit Single. A fourth album *In From The Cold* was preceded by a reworking of *Whenever I'm Gone* (rerecorded from *The Last Fourfathers*) as the potential Top 40 chartbuster. I dashed off to Ugly Child to buy it on the day of release, but it steadfastly refused to chart and the situation between band and label worsened.

Reaching the end of their tether, they arranged two farewell gigs in London. I don't think they were announced as farewell gigs at the time, but as anyone on the fanzine grapevine knows, news travels fast. The first was at the Fulham Greyhound, which I couldn't go to for some reason. But I bought a ticket for the second one at the legendary 100 Club in Oxford Street. They played out of their skins on the night. They always played like the world was ending round their ankles, but at the

100 Club they were on fire. All the anger, all the venom, all the frustration that had built up inside them – it all came out. Perversely, they even played two new songs, including one called *Pop Star Party* which was dedicated to Stiff (there is a rarities compilation which features a demo of this track. Halfway through, it stops and there's a five second gap. In Day's sleevenotes, he explains that's where the master tape snapped as they were trying physically to wrestle the tapes out of the hands of someone from the label).

Whatever other demons they were wrestling with at the 100 Club, they must have been out of their trees as well. By the time they launched into the final number of the encore they were passing round a bottle of Jack Daniels mid-song. Meanwhile, Day, during an elongated instrumental middle section, started announcing their future career plans: 'On drums, Johnny "I'm going back to college" Symons.'

After it was all finally over, Jamie Taylor staggered off stage and, trying hard to focus, walked through the crowd to a corner of the club. Swaying slightly, he arranged four chairs in a row, and lay down on them … and promptly fell asleep. Before leaving, Leigh and I went and just stared at him.

'What a man,' said Leigh.

Scarily, it was like paying your respects to someone who had passed away. I was going to say that he might still be there now for all I know, but Taylor rose again. Within a year he was back with the James Taylor Quartet. Crockford joined him on bass for a while, but soon departed.

There were rumours that they didn't get on very well. But Crockford and Day returned with a new band called The Prime Movers and, in the mid 90s, they finally relented and reformed The Prisoners, releasing a single and playing several dates. We all went along. Despite my fears. (I hate bands reforming. They're a reminder of how much we've all aged. And the energy and the hunger that was part of the group when you first saw them has begun to drip away.) But The Prisoners were as disgruntled and evil-sounding as ever. They were a bit slower maybe (certainly they'd lost more hair, or they'd put on some weight). But fuck me – it was still The Prisoners.

PUMP UP THE VOLUME

Somewhere in the files of the *Melody Maker* there are a couple of issues from 1985 which feature live reviews by a girl called Julie. That's me.

Well, desperate measures for desperate times and all that ... But I came to the daft conclusion that having written a fanzine, the next step in championing new bands was to write for the music press. So, like scores of would-be journalists before and since, I sent in a couple of unsolicited reviews and waited for them to appear in print. They never did.

Years later, I found that the main papers hardly ever run unsolicited work, but at the time I was hopelessly ill-informed and carried on my letter-writing campaign for months. Matters became worse when I read an article about how Garry Bushell, the former *Sounds* journalist turned *Sun* columnist, had got his break. Allegedly he'd been to see 10 gigs in 10 consecutive nights and reviewed all 10, a day at a time. Every morning the Reviews Editor arrived and opened his post – and there was another review from Gaz.

So I tried this. At the end of the 10 days (and nights) I phoned the Live Desk at the *Melody Maker* and weary Section Editor Barry McIlhenny said yes, he'd read them, and yes, if a trial review came along for me to do, he'd phone me. He never did. I actually thought I'd driven him over the edge because, checking in the staff box (the list of the paper's contributors) a month later, his name had vanished.

The upside of this was that there was a new guy in charge who wouldn't recognize my style of writing. He might even like it. But wait. First I found a band that the paper wasn't covering – in this case Action Pact – and then I jazzed up the writing a little and signed it off with a girl's name.

A fortnight later, standing in a newsagent, having bunked off work for half an hour, I opened the *MM* and the review was in. I slowly closed the paper ... then opened it again. It was still there. Fame and fortune at last. I'd arrived. They hadn't even changed much of the copy. I sent them a second review, this time of the Neurotics, and that went in as well. Then a third ... which didn't.

Of course, I should have phoned them – or got a girl to phone on my behalf, to keep up the ruse – but I couldn't face being Julie for the rest of my life. Besides, all I had to do was wait a couple of weeks and write in under my real name and everything would be fine.

But as I went back to Steve Lamacq they went back to ignoring me, and I gave up. Even worse, I arrived home one night to find my landlady writing 'Not known at this address' on the cheque which they'd sent Julie for her efforts. Actually, she might as well have sent it back.

Have you ever tried convincing the Co-op bank that a cheque with a girl's name on it is really for the skinny young man standing in front of them?

There had to be an easier route than this.

It was my girlfriend Helen who got the first break. Having had a few reviews printed in *Smash Hits*, she landed the job of Live Reviews Editor at the *NME*, while I shambled around trying to work out my next move. It's blindingly obvious now. I should have just twisted her arm, or emotionally blackmailed her into giving me some reviews to do. But at the time the thought never crossed my mind. I think I was desperate to prove myself on my own terms (either that or I was simply too proud or too dumb to come up with the idea at the time). So I hung around on the periphery of the press and waited for the next vacancy.

Eventually there were not one but two job ads in the papers in one week. The first was in *Sounds*, the second in the *NME*: 'Sub Editor wanted'. This was it. Unbelievably, having fired off the two CVs, enclosing a recent issue of *A Pack Of Lies*, I was offered interviews by both.

Now, I wouldn't normally have known anything about any music paper editors, but I remembered Alan Lewis's name from the old staff boxes in *Sounds* in the glory days of the early 80s. Lewis was now *NME* Editor, recently installed to help stabilize the paper, whose sales had fallen beneath the magic target figure of 100,000 per week. I remember precisely nothing about the interview, apart from the fact that I wore a suit and wished I hadn't and that Jam biographer and *NME* staff writer Paolo Hewitt passed me by the lift.

Over at *Sounds*, then based in the austere Greater London House near Mornington Crescent tube station, Tony Stewart made more of an impression because he hit me with a barrage of difficult questions about pop music boundaries and defining genres. Even then, though, I had a few half-cock theories which I trolled out, mixed up with a bit of punk rock spite, which seemed to do the trick. It was Stewart's closing question that took me most by surprise: 'Are you going for the *NME* job?' Now, what was I supposed to say to this? 'No, I am 100 per cent *Sounds* through and through and I would not sully the good name of your paper by setting foot behind enemy lines'?

The way it came out was: 'Um, yeah, but I haven't heard anything ...'

A day later, *NME* secretary Karen Walter phoned and invited me for a day-long trial in the subs room. And then everything went haywire. I heard, via my girlfriend, that a senior member of the writing staff had been fired and that the day of my trial coincided with a day of possible strike action over claims of unfair dismissal.

'Well, that's just typical,' I humphed. 'I finally get a break at *NME* and I can't go, because I can't cross a picket line.' Only I think I used more expletives than that, and I may well have had a couple of drinks to soften the blow.

In the end the strike didn't happen. But the threat of it was still hanging in the air as I arrived in the secretary's office for a start time of 10.30 a.m. Lewis looked harrassed and troubled and took me to one side. 'Day's trial, oh yes. Right, erm, well, I've got one or two things to sort out, and erm ...' (at this point he paused and looked distractedly in the direction of the editorial room). Finally, turning back he added, 'So, erm. Well look, do you want the job?'

'Well, yeah.'

'OK, good. See Karen on the way out and let her know how much notice you have to work, and when you can start. Welcome aboard.'

Two minutes later I was back out in New Oxford Street. Slightly stunned.

The first year at the *NME* was like an apprenticeship. There was a lot to learn about the music industry and the media. But then again, the music industry had a lot to learn about itself. Change was in the air.

The first *NME* I ever worked on had Public Enemy on the cover. A month later the front page was headlined: 'HOLD AND STORE:

Coldcut, MARRS And The Art Of Sampling.' Technology was starting to infuse dance music with new ideas and, though the Christmas cover that year still featured old troopers like New Order and U2, you could feel the growing appetite among bands and fans to move on. It would take another year of slow progress before anything much blossomed, but the seeds of the 90s were already being planted.

On a personal note, I had a bumpy first few months at *NME*. What am I saying? I had a bizarre first three days. On day two I stood quivering at the gents' urinals next to Mark E Smith from The Fall. On day three, long-standing skinhead writer Steven Wells stomped into the subs room and slammed a heap of copy down on the desk in front of me, while barking, 'YOU! NEW BOY! Who are you, then?'

Bloody hell. It's Tom Brown's Schooldays. Any second now, this mad ranting poet-turned-music-scribe, this muscley ball of suppressed energy, is going to put my head down the bogs. Strangely enough, in his book *Enough Candy*, former *NME* Reviews Editor Alan Jackson reports a similar incident on his first day. Only neither of us got our heads flushed down the loo and like a lot of the staff, Swells's bark was worse than his bite. Nevertheless, it took time to get to know all the larger-than-life staff and freelances and their individual crusades and foibles.

I'd just started to find my feet when I split up with Helen. We'd been drifting apart for weeks, but then she started going out with a freelance at *NME*, so I'd see them together all the time (and if you want me to up the stakes any, then the split came just a week after Valentine's Day. Trust me, I've never bought a card since). Two days after we had a showdown/split-up conversation in the pub, Alan Lewis called me into his office and, for the second time in consecutive jobs, I had my three-month trial period extended because I wasn't living up to expectations.

Among their duties, as well as writing headlines and captions, sub-editors are responsible for checking the spelling in features and reviews. It hadn't taken Alan that long to tumble that I couldn't spell, and they extended my trial for another month. Quite how I was going to learn to spell in that time I couldn't work out, but I ran around looking extra enthusiastic, and put in all the hours I could, and Alan, to my eternal gratitude, took pity on me.

It was a horror week, though, which ended with me being virtually scraped off the floor by Alan Jackson, who bought me beer and chips and told me not to worry, and that there were plenty more fish in the sea. Even better, he introduced me to a couple of Graham Parker & The Rumour records I didn't have. After that I took a week off and went on tour with the Janice Long-championed Moss Poles, before returning home and throwing myself into work.

One of the highlights of that first year was getting to review singles for the first time. I've done scores of singles pages since, but I remember the first one more vividly than most. There is the initial excitement of opening all the mailers marked 'singles reviews', and then the crushing realization that it's going to take hours to listen to them all – and that most of them are rubbish. Then, like homework, you put off the actual writing until the last moment, and end up finishing at 3 a.m. So, think about this, bands, because if your record has ever had a good kicking in the press, chances are the review's been written at the end of the writer's tether at 2 a.m. (approximately two hours after his supplies of lager and cigarettes have run out).

But the first singles page came in an issue which revealed a lot about alternative pop culture in 1988. Morrissey was on the cover talking about the collapse of The Smiths and the arrival of his solo LP *Suedehead*. Inside there were pieces on The Fall, The Triffids and Ennio Morricone, plus a full-page ad for Sting's new single *Englishman In New York*. The news pages included stories on Billy Bragg, Madness reforming and Mozzer again. It looks stale and lifeless and tied to the past, though at least the paper had dropped its weekly strapline which exclaimed, 'Over 25 albums reviewed inside' (a sign of the times. These days, magazines would be boasting of 250 rather 25).

There were some specks of light though: a feature on Fon studios, a rabid and enthusiastic critique of Dub Sex, and a lead album review for Justified Ancients Of Mu Mu. For my part I weighed in with a mixed bag of mainly dull records (The Sugarcubes: 'Radically remixed, devastatingly soporific'. I bet that had them quaking in their pixie boots, eh?). The one bright spark was the Single of the Week. It arrived just before the deadline, and I knew nothing about it, save for the press release, which was a bunch of made-up old tosh anyway, but the best single of the week was *Beat Dis* by Bomb The Bass. It was a sign of things to come.

For the following year I kept my head down in the subs room, wrote the occasional article or review, interviewed bands that no-one else liked (The Godfathers, Voice Of The Beehive ...) and went to more gigs. Then I got another lucky break. Denis Campbell left his post as Assistant News Editor and I replaced him as second in command to News Editor Terry Staunton. Out of the subs room, and on the News Desk, I was a proper journalist again.

Terry was a terrific tutor in the ways of the press. And he's got a wickedly sharp sense of humour as well. He taught me how to fill in an expenses sheet and deal with PRs. And at the start of my second week, the two Karens from the Beggars Banquet press office took us out to lunch and gave me my first ever free CD – *Greatest Hit* by The Lurkers. For a fortnight I was so happy, I thought my head might fall off.

• 6
SEVERE ATTACK OF THE TRUTH

Simon Williams is as nutty as I am. If not more so. After I'd seen 197 gigs one year, Simon beat that with well over 200.

It's easy to see how we became friends (even though the first time I met him, I wanted to maim him). After work at the *Harlow Gazette* on a Monday, I used to drive down to Dingwalls in Camden. Dingwalls ran a regular Monday nightclub called the Panic Station, which used to showcase some of the best indie and alternative bands around at the time. Not only that, but it was a good place to sell fanzines. If you got there early enough you could off-load up to 30 copies in a night, and have enough money to keep you in cider and chips until the end of the week.

The Dingwalls crowd had a strange quirk though. No matter how much they were into the bands and the music, they'd only ever buy one fanzine a night. So if you arrived late and found another magazine had already done the rounds, well, that was that. You might as well go and impale yourself on a mic stand.

Sure enough, I was late the night I met Simon. My heart sank as I walked into the venue and, *en route* to the bar, passed various floppy-haired indie kids all flicking through a 'zine called *Jump Away*. That was my drink budget up the creek for a week! I bumped into Williams later on and we introduced ourselves to each other and swapped fanzines (he only had two left! I had a carrier bag heaving with copies).

I'm sure we must have seen each other around at gigs after that, but our friendship didn't really start to form until after he'd packed in his job as a shelf-stacker at Sainsburys and begun freelancing for *NME*. Having come from a similar fanzine background we were both charged with the same desire to storm the barricades.

It's a true fact that the *NME* is always split into militant groups: little gangs with their own manifestos, and ways they think the paper should be run. To be honest, that's what makes the paper work – although the real power still lies within the inner circle of the Editor, the Deputy and the Features Ed.

Outside all this, by 1989, Simon and I had formed an unlikely rebel alliance. We used to have a war office in the Stamford Arms pub next to IPC every Tuesday lunchtime, and go to gigs at the Kentish Town Bull & Gate and Camden Falcon every week. Every time we had a review cut or a feature turned down we'd retire to the pub and rant and moan. We were the Blues Brothers of Indie. We were on a mission. Or in Simon's case, he reviewed The Mission.

In 1989 God gave us Madchester and the continuing rise of rave culture. But he gave us quite a lot else too. The indie label scene was beginning to flourish again after an awful two years. And the live circuit suddenly began to fill up with rabid new bands, who could recite the name of every service station between London and Leeds because they'd passed them so often while journeying up and down the country to gigs.

It definitely felt like 1989 was the end of something, but what was it? It wasn't just the end of the decade; it felt like it should be the end for drab old middle-of-the-road alternative music as well. Many of the bands that would shake up the 90s were either just beginning to break through or lying in wait in the shadows.

And in the meantime, what were Simon and I doing? Well, enmeshed in fanzine culture and reeking of beer, we were the self-appointed A&R scouts of the *NME*. In the making of this book we've both checked our diaries for 1989 and we were out all the time. I'm not sure about Simon, but my own selective process couldn't have been that consistent, because there are bands here who I have no recollection of. For instance, who were Kiev Exocet (George Robey, 4 January), or Trashcan Soul (Bull & Gate, 13 January), The Toll (100 Club, 13 March) Kid Glad Glove (Walthamstow Royal Standard, 1 August. The Royal Standard?!), Fat Controllers (Robey, 8 August) or Bad Caesar (Marquee, 9 October)?

There must have been reasons for seeing these horrors. It's not like we just selected bands randomly from the *Gig Guide*, or wandered the streets of London until we heard the noise of rock guitars emanating from inside a pub. There were good gigs of course, as well as the bad ones.

And then there was the most poorly attended gig I've ever been to. This dubious honour falls to a group called Last Party, who had just recorded a John Peel session and released an acerbic and atmospheric single called *Die In A Spy Ring*. The venue for the gig was a bit off the beaten track – the New Pegasus in Stoke Newington – but Simon and I decided to go anyway.

Now, there could be several reasons why this gig was so under-populated: lack of advertising; it was a drab Tuesday night; the Pegasus wasn't exactly well served by public transport. But by the time we arrived, the man on the door looked like he had given up the will to live. The sight of two punters arriving appeared to cheer him up momentarily, but then we were on the guestlist, so he went back to his emotional nosedive.

So we walked in, and that was when it hit us. We were the ONLY people there. No, tell a lie, there was a girl behind the bar. But apart from her, the promoter on the door and us, that was it. About 10 minutes before the band came on another lonely soul (a young indie chap who had heard the band on Peel) arrived, AND PAID. But that was the crowd. A total of three people and two staff.

When the group arrived, Simon, the indie bloke and I arranged three chairs in front of the stage and cheered the Party on. When they finished we applauded and shouted and made them do an encore.

To their credit, the band took it all in good heart. Were they used to playing to three people? Was it in fact a good night for them? Their big-hearted singer, also called Simon, came off stage and bought the entire audience a drink.

It wasn't all bad though. Through 1989 we discovered a series of bands who would go on have a measure of success in the next few years. Simon uncovered Lush, I stumbled across Ride who were supporting a Brighton band called the Pop Guns at The Falcon, then there were the Family Cat, the Inspiral Carpets, Carter The Unstoppable Sex Machine, Senseless Things, Snuff and Mega City 4.

The Megas held a particular place in our hearts, for all sorts of reasons. We liked the music and Wiz's lyrics (there was a time when I thought the first MC4 album, the ace *Tranzophobia*, said more about my life than any other single record). We liked the fact that they'd play any time, any place, anywhere; and that this was an important factor in the revival of small club gigs around the country. And we liked the lack of posturing, pretentiousness and pop star nonsense.

But underlying all this, I think we used the Megas as a metaphor for our position at *NME*. They were outsiders, and unfashionable, and if they wanted to make something happen, they had to get out there and do it for themselves.

I saw the Megas an awful lot in 1989 (I daren't actually add up all the mentions in the diary). But they provided a lifeline at times. I suppose if I'm really honest I used the Megas to haul me clear of the two-day depressions I went through for a couple of months when I thought (a) I'd never get another girlfriend or (b) I'd never get another feature commissioned.

Yet at the same time, the Megas stood for something very positive too. Their gigs were energetic and celebratory (they showcased the rise of the moshpit and stage-diving) but at the same time Wiz's songs were also incredibly well-observed and sometimes deceptively fragile. We used to holler and dance a bit, because their gigs gave us a sense of release – and the further you got out of London, the crazier the scenes and the madder the audiences.

There is one batch of dates, though, that I remember more vividly than any others. I had a week off, so with nothing else to do I drove up to see them play at Norwich Arts Centre. Having nowhere to stay afterwards (money was tight and the Megas had probably cornered the market in kipping on people's floors) I tried sleeping in the car again, in a nearby car park. At about 2 a.m. there was loud tapping on the window. And sure enough, it was the police come to arrest me.

'Are you the owner of this car?'

'Yes. Well, no. It's my dad's. I've borrowed it.'

'Can you prove that?'

What, at 2 a.m.? 'Look, what's up?'

'We've had a lot of trouble with vagrants breaking into cars in this area and sleeping in them and we believe that …'

They think I'm a vagrant. They won't go away. Finally, after I've bored them silly with stories about Mega City 4 and they've checked the vehicle records, they mope off, looking exceedingly disappointed ('thought we had one there …').

The next day, freezing cold and on four hours' sleep, I drove north to Hull to see the Megas again, at the Hull Adelphi (a converted terraced house on the outskirts of the city). And then the next day it was on to

Birmingham, where I had work to do. Even though it was officially my week off I was down to review the Beautiful South on their first UK tour at the Irish Centre. First, though, I had to meet their press officer – and possibly members of the band – at a hotel in the city centre.

I was walking up the steps to the entrance when a man in a top hat stopped me. 'I'm sorry, sir, you can't go in there looking like that.'

'Pardon?'

'You can't go in there looking like that,' he says again, with his arm barring my way and his eyes looking straight over my head.

'I'm a resident. Well, I will be if I get in. I'm meeting people in there. Look, really. I'm not a vagrant!'

'Sorry, sir.'

Any suggestions? Help at this point? The penguin waddled off and then returned two minutes later. 'You may use the tradesmen's entrance. It's round the back. Take the lift to reception.'

Despite all these sorties around the country I think I only went to Manchester twice around this time. But Manchester was where it was all happening at the end of the 80s. By the start of 1989 the Happy Mondays were in the news every week. And in the same way that DJs now spend their summers commuting back and forth to Ibiza, a growing number of industry folk started spending their weekends in the north of England.

At the beginning of the year I don't think many of us knew why they were going (after all, they'd return a couple of days later saying they'd had a great time, but they looked awful). And they'd started talking in that funny way where your intonation goes up at the end of a sentence. What was that all about? I don't think the Manchester bug – or even Manchester's real influence on latter-day pop – made much sense to me at the time. That is, until I went on the road with, of all the unlikely messiahs, My Bloody Valentine.

It was a live page feature for the *NME*, taking in two nights; the first at Nottingham Trent Poly and the second at Manchester University. Both gigs were good but it was the second night, in Manchester, which ended with the most eye-opening of experiences – at the Hacienda. If I hadn't fully seen the foundations of Madchester before then, a lot of pieces suddenly fell into place that night.

But let's get My Bloody Valentine out of the way first. MBV have their own, very definite place in the history of alternative music in this country. Born around the time of the cutesy C86 movement – the hard-to-categorize indie-pop uprising which I'll touch on later – they grew from a floppy-fringed fey pop band into a monstrous sounding rock group. One whose experiments with sound and structure were possibly among the few things we had in Britain that would stand up against the likes of Sonic Youth's serrated-edged rock in the States. That was my angle anyway. My Bloody Valentine guitarist Kevin Shields was more modest and abstract in his view of the group. He was also one of the most softly spoken men I've ever met.

As I interviewed him in one of the Student Union offices at Trent Poly on the first night, Shields was so quiet that he was barely audible over the air-conditioning, let alone the support band soundchecking. The whirr of the cassette recorder was louder than his voice. But he was thoughtful and courteous as well as pensive and reserved. The tour, meanwhile, was among the best they ever did. It was just as they had started including 10, 12 or 14-minute versions of *You Made Me Realize* that shouldered up against tracks from their *Isn't Anything* album. They were astonishingly loud, and lost in their own world on stage. They were mesmerizing, they really were (and the Nottingham gig was in a room that looked like a sports hall. It shouldn't have worked at all, but it did).

The following night they did it all over again at the Manchester Academy. But this time they had the added benefit of being the soundtrack to an increasingly surreal evening. I had travelled across from Nottingham with Jeff Barrett, part-time London promoter and press officer about town who handled the publicity for the bands on Creation Records. It was Barrett, strangely enough, who brought Madchester and the Happy Mondays to London and got them to play at the Black Horse in Camden (he later went on to start Heavenly Records and work with the South's answer to the Mondays, Flowered Up). That night, after checking in, we met in the oddly ornate bar of the hotel where we were staying, just off the Oxford Road. It wasn't the weird décor that was the centre of attention though, it was the people. Sprawled in the corner were various Creation folk, Manchester friends and hangers-on, and in the middle of this motley crew of 24-hour party people was Creation boss Alan McGee.

I'm not sure how many times I'd met Alan at this point – if indeed I'd met him at all – but with his ginger hair, gesticulating hands and wild eyes he was the most passionate man on the planet that night. Every sentence, every proclamation about his label or one of his bands ended with him saying, in his fired-up Glaswegian accent: 'Do you see it, right, Steve … D'ya get it?' It was if he was holding in his hands an idea or a vision of the future, which included both his bands and his label, and which you needed a key to unlock. It was fascinating.

We moved on to the gig and MBV were out of this world again. There really were very few groups who could touch them at the time. (Note: I tried to come up with a list of my favourite 10 gigs of all time for this book, but it was too big a task. By number seven I already had two MBV appearances, though, this one and the night they played in New York supported by Pavement and Superchunk.)

We finished off at the gig and left the indie-noise behind. Then the increasingly large party hit the Hac.

It throbbed. Not just the building, but my head. Still reeling from the onslaught of My Bloody Valentine (and the consequent ringing in my ears caused by Kevin Shields's guitar), we walked into the Hacienda and I swear I just stood there blinking and throbbing.

So this was what all the fuss was about. It was rammed with people. And the speakers were spilling out a tune which had dressed itself in dayglo before going out for the night. If MBV had wiped out the treble in my hearing, then the Hac did for the bass. And I don't think I would remember so much about the night if one of our party hadn't had his first experience with E. Ecstasy was still in its infancy at the time. Or at least it hadn't made the sort of impact it would later in the 90s as it began crossing over from the dance clubs into gigs and pubs and front-page stories in the tabloids.

All I knew was that it was supposed to make you dance all night like you had a Duracell battery stuck up your arse and it made you want to love everybody.

The trouble was that my E-virgin mate had got hold of one of the more powerful strains of E that were doing the rounds. After the initial boredom of waiting for the drug to take effect, he suddenly went very pale. Then he turned around and said, 'Steve? Steve. The floor's turned to rubber.' And then his legs turned to jelly. No Duracell battery at all. I sat him down in a quiet corner and fetched him a glass of water (these were the days before drug awareness campaigns advised people on E to drink as much fluid as possible. But it seemed like the common-sense thing to do). Amazingly, he recovered and bunny-hopped off into the crowd.

Odd night.

As one of the most talked-about clubs in Britain, the Hacienda also played a significant role in one of 1989's biggest stories: the arrival of the Stone Roses. Simon and myself had first come across them through their *Made Of Stone* single, which was one of our favourite records of the spring. Then there were all the stories that started filtering through from Manchester: the graffiti campaign which had seen their name daubed over various public buildings, and how they were gigging all the time because their manager ran two of the city's venues.

A five-track album sampler cassette followed the single. And just before it went ballistic I saw them on tour at Uxbridge Brunel University. The students at Brunel never seemed to take notice of any of the gigs on their own doorstep, so despite the first wave of rave reviews in the press, the place was half-empty. You could walk right to the front, where there were about 20 early hardcore fans dancing in a small group. I took Tall Graham and his girlfriend with me to show them the future of pop music. And though we'd never agreed on any band before, we spent the entire car journey home along the M25 going on and on about them.

It was a good time to see them too, because it was the calm before the storm. Everything was about to come up roses for the Roses. Manchester was cool, club culture was beginning to entwine itself with rock music and there in the middle of it all was this group who walked and talked like a real band. They had a solid masterplan as well. Just as the buzz surrounding them was reaching fever pitch, they staged a jam-packed showcase gig at the Hacienda. Their PR company took a handful of important journalists up to Manchester for the gig. And the Roses were showered with incredible reviews.

I saw them a couple of months later at the ICA in London on the night of a bus and tube strike (so I must have been quite committed) and they were growing in confidence and swagger all the time.

I wrote the review in my head, while trying to get back to Liverpool Street Station in time for the last train back to Harlow. The rest I scribbled on the back of a flyer the next morning on the way to work.

There are three reasons why the Stone Roses are our favourite band of the month and why suddenly, hearteningly, they have their debut album tussling with the lame competition in the Top 30. First though a quick précis of tonight's gig. They go late (nobody cares); they play the oddest ever ICA gig (nobody flinches) and perversely they tart around with the running order of the set and they don't do an encore.

The three reasons cited for their imminent rise to megastardom were: the songs; the fact that they'd got immeasurably better than 'when we saw them at Central London Poly' (sadly a gig I don't even remember); and that 'everyone wants to like the Stone Roses at the moment'. Not be like them. Just like them. To make some connection with them.

Vocalist Ian Brown, the unlikeliest hero of the year, has the crowd falling over themselves to get their attention. He skulks around looking mischievous, a wee bit aloof, while the band shimmy through 35 stylish minutes and into the final 'letting loose' instrumental climax.

They hack down their instruments and amble off leaving the encore shouts to rise and fall, unrequited. They are what favourite bands are all about.

And that was it. They were a group – after a period of uncertainty – that everyone could agree on. A group you didn't want to argue with.

By the end of the year, they were pictured on the *NME* cover standing at the summit of a mountain with the headline 'Top of the World'.

Simon got to write the first feature on the Roses for *NME*, but we didn't always land the articles we wanted. I don't think we ever claimed to be the best writers on the paper in 1989 (for a start we knew it wasn't true). But that left us in a difficult position at the time. We were going out and finding new bands, and often writing the first introductory pieces on them. But when it came to the follow-up feature or the first cover story (articles that involved trips to Holland or America or, gulp, Japan) then we rarely got a look-in.

So come the end of the year, we didn't get the pay-off junket to New York or Amsterdam. We ended up stranded in Wolverhampton.

It was four weeks till Christmas, and we decided to start the festive celebrations early by reviewing Ned's Atomic Dustbin's big Midlands homecoming show at the Wolverhampton Civic Hall. Neds had had a terrific year. They were good fun to watch (no, really). And the bill also featured Mega City 4 and the Senseless Things. Hurrah. Three of the least hip groups in Britain. Journo credibility rating two out of ten. Should be a good night then.

After the gig and post-show drinks we staggered into the street to find it had started to snow. And I don't want to sound cheesy but life seemed very good. Life was not so good the following morning when I woke up with an extraordinary hangover and found that the TV in the hotel room wasn't working. Cursing and bumping into things I made for the bathroom and the light refused to come on. The whole room was broken. Outside in the corridor it wasn't any better. No lights. No lift. No, erm, sound.

I headed down the stairs and into the hotel reception and found myself in a scene from *The Shining*. The place was deserted. There was a single candle burning on the reception desk itself and there was snow up to the window ledges. I was just waiting for a small boy to creep up, muttering 'redrum, redrum'. Then a member of staff ran in through one door and out another. Was she being chased by a man with an axe?

No, she was followed by a man in overalls. We were in Wolverhampton in the middle of a blizzard and the whole town had been plunged into chaos by a power cut. But there was worse news to come. After the power was restored, Simon and I checked the travel situation and found that nothing was moving. No buses, definitely no trains all day … and by the way, the town centre is closing at 3.30 p.m. We were stuck. Not only that, but we were stuck in a hotel which we'd booked into for only one night – and we were skint.

We sat in the lobby by the Christmas tree and weighed up our options. Then we phoned the Neds' press office to explain our predicament. The girl at the other end of the phone seemed to have some difficulty believing us ('It's not snowing in London,' she told us, helpfully), but eventually, after convincing her that our only other option was to huddle together for warmth in a shop doorway, she said she'd sort something out.

It was a rubbish situation. We were due back in London to hand in our review of the Neds gig in 24 hours' time, and we could barely get out of the hotel, let alone Wolverhampton. And on top of that, all we had for musical inspiration was Sir bleedin' Paul McCartney.

As we sat around the tree, the hotel's music centre – powered by the emergency generator – jollied into life, and what did it spark up with? *Simply Having A Wonderful Christmas Time.*

Aaararaarrrggghhhhhhhhhhhhhh HHHHHHH.

All right, it was funny the first time. But it soon became apparent that there were only seven tracks on their Christmas tape. That's one round of *Simply Having* every 23 minutes (punctuated by Greg Lake, Jona Lewie, *Lonely This Christmas* and three other songs I've blocked from memory for fear of going completely doolally).

It was two days before they cleared the tracks and we got a train home.

• 7
YOU LOVE US

Whatever you've read is probably wrong. Apart from the date and venue – and aside from the chapter in Simon Price's book *Everything* – the accounts of the night that Manic Street Preachers guitarist Richey Edwards inscribed the legend '4 REAL' into his arm have become more and more distorted.

For instance, one recent music paper article reported that it was me who called the ambulance for Edwards after our ill-fated conversation. In reality I was standing outside the Norwich Arts Centre, the scene of our showdown, confused, shaken up and drawing rather desperately on a cigarette.

If you're unfamiliar with the incident, these are the bare bones of what you need to know. The Manics were an aspiring, ambitious rock'n'roll four-piece from Wales. I was the journalist from the *NME* sent to review them. After a post-gig interview in which we discussed both their methods and their merits, guitarist Richey Edwards invited me backstage for a final word. Edwards, while still talking, then cut '4 REAL' into his arm with a razorblade.

Those are the raw facts, the bits of information that I trot out when people stop me at gigs and ask what happened. But those aren't the images that really spring to mind. In order, these are the things I remember most vividly about the 4 REAL night:

- The cigarette machine at the venue was broken, and photographer Ed Sirrs and I were down to our last Silk Cut
- Nottingham Forrest were playing and bassist Nicky Wire and singer James Dean Bradfield spent their pre-gig downtime in the hotel bar watching the match on TV
- James was wearing a ludicrously long shiny mac. During the 15-minute drive to the venue, he sat at the back of the bus and refused to be drawn into conversation. I remember thinking, 'Well, this is a good start. He hates me and I don't like his coat'

- Richey's eyes
- The point when the guitarist, in his gorgeous, softly spoken Welsh accent, said, 'We are for real.' That's the point when we were history.

The Manic Street Preachers had first come to the attention of the *NME* through a self-financed double-A-sided single, *Suicide Alley/Tennessee I Get So Low*. I've still got one somewhere. It has a blue and white sleeve featuring a picture of the band on the front, striking a pose straight out of The Clash's picturebook circa 1977.

I'm sure they telephoned and wrote to loads of people around this time (I've got a letter from them and so has Peelie). Mine was scribbled on a yellow piece of A4, a really scrawly, handwritten note that savaged the Shoegazers, the Madchester scene – including the Roses and the Mondays – and rejected the whole 'trip out and tune in' mentality of the time. The final line said: 'PS If we do some London dates, would you come?'

A few weeks later I spoke to the group on the telephone and they were nice people. Eager to further their career, they said they needed a press officer and asked if I had any ideas. The only person of any use that I could suggest was Philip Hall. Hall had been a journalist with the music paper *Record Mirror*, before working for Stiff Records and then starting his own independent PR company, Hall Or Nothing. Philip was a gent. My main dealings with him had been to do with The Sundays and the Stone Roses, whom he represented, but his punk/mod background indicated he might be on a similar wavelength to the Manics.

It transpired that this wasn't a bad call. The Manics approached Hall who went to see them with his brother Martin in rehearsals in Wales and – despite seeing a band unexpectedly stricken by nerves – took on the role, not just of PR, but of their manager as well. In the meantime, another contact-cum-friend had arrived on the scene. Ian Ballard from an independent label called Damaged Goods had offered to release the band's next single. Dam Good had started life as a punk and garage reissue label, but was branching out into new acts who had the contemporary feel of some of the punk predecessors. The Manics were perfect.

Ballard saw the band play at a tiny but now infamous gig in a pub near Great Portland Street in London and did a handshake deal with them to record an EP. When it arrived, *New Art Riot* was an improvement on *Suicide Alley* but still fell short of what the Manics were reaching for. The same went for some of their gigs. The first time I saw them play was at the Kentish Town Bull & Gate, where they appeared in the same – or similar – boiler suit chic that had featured on the debut record sleeve.

In a smaller, sweatier club, with the audience slap bang in their face, they would have probably won me over in a shot (this is why I regret not being at the earlier Great Portland Street gig, which had earned them a rave review in *Melody Maker*). But in a deathly quiet, two-thirds empty Bull & Gate they didn't live up to the early press reports. They sounded spindly and looked like they'd come out of a box marked 'punk rock action figures'.

And there was another problem too, which I'll admit coloured my judgement. I was terrified that we were about to witness a rerun of the rise and fall of Birdland. Remember them? They were one of the biggest hypes of 1990 (even I ended up writing a cover story about them). They were four peroxide blondes from Birmingham and were hailed as the future of rock'n'roll. Birdland played 30-minute, amphetamine-thrash-pop sets, teased and abused their audience, slated all other 'indie' bands for being dull and unambitious and dressed all in white. With the benefit of hindsight the Manics were a superior band (they had an appreciation of hip-hop and rap and more drive and insight). But at the time a cursory glance at their manifesto made them look uncomfortably close to what had gone before. Given that Birdland's star had shone and faded within a year, then, in context, I think a bit of scepticism wasn't uncalled for.

The trouble was, the playful banter began to get out of hand. They released the fantastic *Motown Junk* (their first single for Heavenly, and a record I still play regularly at home) at the start of 1991 and we ran with an On page 'tips for the year' piece on them. But come the time of the follow-up, *You Love Us*, we'd started to fall out in public. They had a dig at some bands I liked; I had a dig back, making some rather unkind comments about them in a review of another band called Bleach. In retort, they dedicated *Starlover* to me at their next gig (which I didn't see, but a gleeful Andy Peart phoned me up and told me). It was all a bit petty, but I guess it must have been serious stuff at the time.

Meanwhile, the press they were getting was unswervingly good and, in some cases, from where I was sitting, hilariously sycophantic. When it came to reviewing them on tour, we had a choice. Either we sent someone along who would fawn over them again, or we could go for a more objective opinion. Which is how come I ended up going to the Norwich Arts Centre on 15 May 1991.

The first part of the evening, you already know. Ed and myself got a lift to Norwich with Philip, and we booked into a slightly chintzy hotel on the outskirts of town. With the exception of James – then the shyest member of the band – they were, if not chatty, at least amiable enough.

The gig itself was good, but sorely under-attended. The review describes the set as 'a haze of wanton energy and sketchy punk outbursts. Starting with *You Love Us*, they snap at the heels of an audience split between curiosity and approval – the parochial atmosphere of the gig exaggerated by two people pogoing at the front.'

After 33 minutes, the band walked off and the pogoers shouted after them: 'Plastic punks!'. There was no encore, but then again, I don't remember them ever doing an encore when they first started. Instead, after it had cleared of people, we sat in the hall and talked about their songs, and their vision for the band. Again from the original *NME* piece: 'After 30 minutes of friendly enough discussion and vitriol, we wind things up, for the most part agreeing to disagree. It was a good, if clichéd confrontation (maybe leaving both sides a little unsettled).'

The transcript of the interview has been printed elsewhere and yes, there are questions I asked which seem oddly irrelevant now, but there were some pertinent points too. It wasn't as if I said, 'You're crap. Now defend yourselves,' or anything. There was also no forewarning of what would happen next. Believe me, backstage, as Richey began to carve his arm open, I was as shocked as anybody was.

But people always ask me, why didn't you stop him? And there are two reasons, I think. One is that it happened so quickly. The cuts were deliberate but fast (and got faster and lighter as he neared the end). The second is: do you think he wanted me to stop him?

I don't know exactly how long we talked for after the deed was done, but it was probably about three or four minutes. Apart from the odd moment when Richey had looked down to inspect his work, we'd been staring fixedly at each other throughout (Nicky Wire has said in the past that Richey was laughing as he did it, but trust me, he wasn't). By the end, the conversation was going around in circles and Richey's arm was beginning to look uncomfortably gory. The blood from the first cut had started to trickle down his arm the moment he'd finished it (fact: until I saw the photos the next day, I didn't know what he'd written because it was obscured by the blood).

'We'd better do something about that ... you're going to mess their carpet up.'

Richey looked down at his arm, and then up again, and agreed. At least he gave a faint nod. And that was it. While he stayed put, I went to search for Philip, finding him back in the main hall in conversation with a guy I didn't know. Trying not to set alarm bells ringing, I tugged at Hall's arm and muttered conspiratorially, 'I think you should go and see Richey. He's a bit shaken up.'

Hall, a quizzical expression crossing his face, excused himself and sauntered backstage. Two minutes later he re-emerged at double-speed and darted off to find a phone or locate the nearest hospital. I found Ed, commandeered our final cigarette and stood outside the venue until it was time to leave.

No-one spoke much on the journey back to London. We listened to a compilation tape I'd made up, and then I dozed off in the back seat. Philip dropped us off in the middle of Soho, near one of those 24-hour picture processing studios so that Ed could put his film in to be developed overnight, while I trawled the mini-cab offices trying to find a car back to Brixton. When I got in, my girlfriend awoke briefly and asked how it went.

'Oh, the gig wasn't bad. Not many people there. Then we did the interview and Richey cut his arm open with a razorblade.'

'Oh. Right,' she said. Then fell asleep again.

It wasn't until the following morning that the incident started to sink in. Apart from the girlfriend ('was I dreaming or when you got in, did you say he slashed his arm open?'), the rest of the day was spent explaining what had happened. First to *NME* Editor Danny Kelly – the only man in the office when I arrived – and then to the rest of the staff as they filtered in to work. Ed arrived with the photos around noon

School jumper chic was all the rage: The Undertones with Feargal Sharkey (centre).

The Skids circa their *Into the Valley* hit. Would you buy a used haircut from one of these men?

God's lonely men: The Lurkers.
Howard, Nigel, Pete and Esso.

LEFT: the cover of the last official issue
of *A Pack of Lies*.

Drowning out the big
jets: Action Pact lived in
the shadow of Heathrow
and released two
excellent LPs in the 80s.
This was taken at the
now defunct Fulham
Greyhound, at the same
gig that I managed to
review as Julie for the
Melody Maker.

A PACK
OF LIES

ISSUE
10

Everyone's a winner on opening day

Two goal Carl inspires Blues

THE opening day fixtures of the Vauxhall-Opel League and Essex League proved a real winner for local clubs.

The top quartet, Bishop's Stortford, Harlow Town, Sawbridgeworth and Stansted all won their first games. And the Gazette's sports staff were out and about getting a first hand view of two of the day's games.

We'll be keeping our soccer coverage going strong throughout the coming season as the local sides vie for honours. So for reports, views and behind the scenes news stay in touch with Gazette Sportscene.

● BLOW it! An ... ge with Windsor & Eton's

A SECOND half hail storm threatened to grab the opening day headlines from Bishop's Stortford's two goal hero Carl Zaohhau.

With just three minutes of Saturday's Vauxhall-Opel League Premier Division game to go, referee Paul Taylor took the players off the pitch to shelter from an amazing hail onslaught.

And the freak weather left Blues fans on tenterhooks for five minutes as they waited for the restart of a game poised at 2-1 in Stortford's favour.

Windsor & Eton had pulled a goal back with 15 minutes left to add tension to a game which had previously looked wrapped up in Stortford's favour thanks to two early goals by Zachhau.

He put Blues in front after just seven minutes and added a second two minutes later to prove his undoubted eager quality.

The beavering striker, signed in the close season from Yeovil Town, chased, called and hassled for possession to begin to repay the confidence that Stortford have put in him.

The first goal was a screamer from 25 yards, Zachhau juggling the ball into the right position to unleash a super shot which flashed past Windsor keeper Kevin Mitchell like the lightning which was to appear later in the game.

His second was a thunderous shot, from close range as he struck home a rebound following a break from the midfield instigated by winger Peter Barker.

And if the two goals weren't enough there's another noticeable impact of Zachhau's presence at Rhodes Avenue.

Bishop's Stortford 2, Windsor & Eton 1
by Steve Lamacq

He's the sort of player who's not only feared by other clubs, but one who can create a buzz of anticipation from spectators every time he receives the ball.

He's not alone, of course, in Blues' current side but the limelight shone brilliantly upon him as his two early goals sparked memories of Stortford's 6-2 win over Worthing on the opening day of last term.

But as it turned out, Windsor were to prove more difficult opponents than last year's openers and the visitors battled firmly back into the game bolstering their work at the back and in midfield.

For all the inspirational ... were times ... became fully ... trated, as ... back.

Stortford ... control the ... of the b ... Barker m ... scrambled ... terval, ... having p ... ped on ... Zach ... Devon, ... action ... ing o ... pped ... from ... almo ...

goal when Windsor keeper Mitchell had to save from his own defender Richard North six minutes later.

At the other end Blues' goalkeeper Martin Taylor twice saved well, handling well in the slippery conditions, caused by the first half drizzle.

His only fumble, from a free kick by Steven Cordery, was cleared by defender Martin McCayna.

Blues' attempts to increase their lead were hampered by the weather as the rain became harder and harder, causing passes to halt unexpectedly in the wet grass, or spin surprisingly out of play.

And after 75 minutes their uncomfortable hold on the loosened when Gary ...

Andy Goodchild whose name also went into the ref's notebook.

The decision seemed to annoy the skies and a booming roll of thunder signalled the hailstorm, which led to referee Taylor taking the teams back to the dressing rooms.

Mr Taylor emerged five minutes late with an umbrella! But by then the weather had eased and the sides returned for an overlong finale which saw Blues hold onto the points.

Bishop's Stortford: Taylor, Nunn, Goodchild, Hall, McCayna, Ferguson, Candwell, Clayr Balmer.

Classic reporter-with-phone photo: the first Saturday of the season on the Harlow Gazette Sports Desk and (left) *en route* to Wembley with Colchester United.

One I took for *A Pack of Lies*. Graham Day of The Prisoners making a racket at Uxbridge University. (My career as a live photographer never took off.)

Up stares, down stares: this comes from a night on the town with Kingmaker in New York. Singer Loz Hardy was last seen on the night attempting to order a Pernod and ice ('Two cubes please, barman!').

Good advice on a Hefner badge and (below) the Teenage Fanclub *NME* cover shot descends into chaos. Do you remember those shorts? They glowed in the dark, you know. Scary.

Pull yourself together

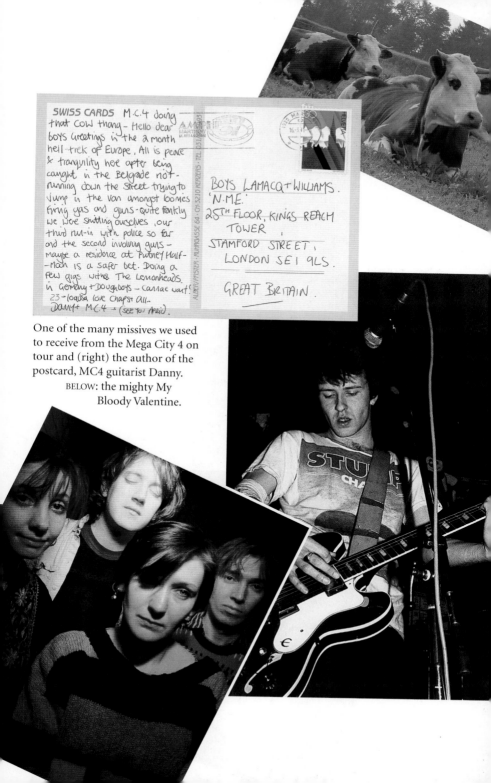

SWISS CARDS M.C.4 doing that COW thang — Hello dear boys Greetings in the 2 month hell-trek of Europe. All is peace & tranquility here after being caught in the Belgrade riot — running down the street trying to jump in the van amongst loonies firing gas and guns. Quite frankly we were shitting ourselves, our third run-in with police so far and the second involving guns — maybe a residence at Putney Half-Moon is a safer bet. Doing a few gigs with The Lemonheads in Germany + Doughboys — can't wait! 23 — lousda love Chaps! All — Danny + M.C.4 — (see you April).

BOYS LAMACQ + WILLIAMS.
'N.M.E.'
25TH FLOOR, KINGS REACH
TOWER,
STAMFORD STREET,
LONDON SE1 9LS.

GREAT BRITAIN.

One of the many missives we used to receive from the Mega City 4 on tour and (right) the author of the postcard, MC4 guitarist Danny.
BELOW: the mighty My Bloody Valentine.

The original letter that accompanied the Manics' early demo tape and (below) another terrific, all-action Ed Sirrs live shot. OPPOSITE: the now famous Richey Edwards 'mint wound' picture.

Manic Street Preachers

Dear Steve,

Heres our new demo & information ect...... I hope it conveys a sense of purpose to eradicate the desire to trip out and tune in (89) & instead fuck up & ignore "channel apathy drag". We just want to play anytime and anywhere as we just want to play live _NOW_! We have no regard for our bodies, ... We just want to waste away under speed excess and bleed to death on our own bar chord overdose. We might record this demo as a single and release it on perhaps Damaged Goods, soon, so could you consider including us in 'Rare on' or your 'turn ons'. love, M.S.Preachers X

P.S. If we do some London dates could you come?.

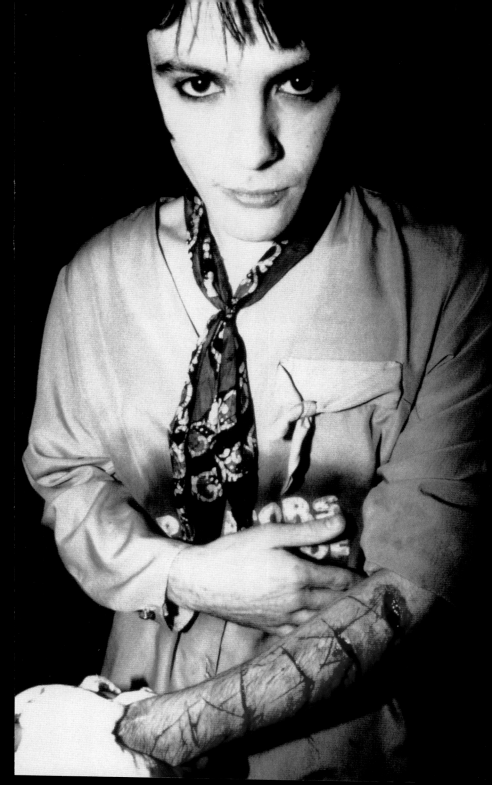

Who's in here? It's a little guy. Manic post-stagediving grin, down the front at Carter (USM) in Paris. And lurking in the background during the first Nirvana photo session for *NME* in Shepherd's Bush.

and the debate over whether we should print them or not started in earnest. To add to the unusually dramatic scenes in the office, social commentator and comedian Mark Thomas was on hand, making a Radio 5 documentary about a week in the life of the *NME*. After two relatively tedious days, he finally had a scoop (you can hear part of the programme on the CD version of the Manics' *Suicide Is Painless*).

My favourite quote came from Ed, who through the hubbub can be heard saying, 'It's a mint wound.' If you know Ed, then that's so him. But the arguments raged on around the lightbox, as people took it in turns with the magnifying viewer to examine the slides. Would the pictures prompt fans to copy him? Was it the best rock'n'roll statement of the year? Ed told me on the phone the other day that the whole question of whether or not the shots should – or could – be used was referred to IPC's legal department. I never knew that. At the time, feeling like a bit of a spare part, I wandered back to the Live Desk and opened some post.

There were two telephone calls that day that put the incident into perspective. The first was from a press officer, who hinted that Richey had done this sort of thing before; that he had a history of self-mutilation. And the second was from Richey himself. By a twist of fate, I wasn't there when he called. I was in our regular haunt, the Stamford Arms, explaining what had happened to a couple of my Live Desk team (I think, without wanting to sound too melodramatic, I may have been in a state of delayed shock. Sam Steele, then an *NME* freelance but now at Radio 1, claims I was white as a sheet). I subsequently lost the ansaphone tape with his message on it, but the gist was, 'I'm sorry if I upset you in any way but I was just trying to make my point.'

The *NME* ran with a news piece on page three – with the now famous Richey shot reproduced in black and white – and my review of the gig in the Live section. Of all the pieces I wrote while I was at the paper, this was the most difficult to construct. But some of it still stands up. This is from the conclusion:

There's no doubt that they are a thorn in the side of rock at the moment. That goes without saying. And agreed, what wouldn't we give for a new political pop band back in the charts? Someone who'd go further than just being worthy. But the fact is I'm not sure the Manics have everything under control at the moment.

The backlash was amazing. The Manics, for their part, took the incident and the pictures and attacked me constantly in interviews (but, fair play, I would have done the same thing if I was them). The famous 'mint wound' photo was also later used on thousands of posters as part of their campaign to break America.

Meanwhile, I stopped going out for a couple of days, because the incessant demands for graphic reruns of the story began to pall. The most stark reaction didn't happen until a couple of years later though. Journalist Andrew Smith travelled to Thailand with the band for a feature in *The Face* magazine. At the end of a gig he spoke with some of their fans, and reprinted snippets of the conversation in the final article.

'We understand why Richey did what he did,' said one Manic supporter. 'We have a culture of self-mutilation in this country. And if Steve Lamacq ever comes here, we will … KILL HIM.'

Bit harsh, I thought. To make matters worse, I was reading the piece on a tube train, and found myself immediately looking around for possible signs of an assassination attempt.

It's not the only feedback I've had from Manics fans down the years. Every year on the anniversary of Richey's disappearance I get a letter saying, 'I don't know how you sleep at nights having driven him to do what he did.' And I'd like to write back with my version of events, and how I don't believe I drove him to anything, but it strikes me that people like this have already made up their minds about the incident and aren't about to change. Why should they?

We only saw each other once more before he vanished. Richey and James were reviewing the singles for *NME* and I stood in the lift with them, along with Philip and (I think) Simon Williams. There was total silence as they stared at their shoes right up to the 25th floor.

But, to all intents and purposes, the Manics feud ended on the tragic note of Philip's death from cancer. It was an event which hit Richey hardest, but we were all affected in our own ways. I didn't know Philip even half as well as they did – after all, the Manics had even lived with Hall and his wife Terri for a while – but he was one of the few real nice guys I knew and probably the first close death I'd experienced while in the industry.

I phoned Hall Or Nothing to check if it would be OK to play a Manics track dedicated to Philip on that night's *Evening Session*. A hour or so later I got a call back from Nicky Wire and we went ahead with a short tribute on the programme.

Since then, I've spoken to them on a few occasions. James came on the *Session* shortly after Richey's disappearance, and in 1998 we made a programme for Radio 1 about the success of *Everything Must Go* and we went to the pub together afterwards. Nicky I interviewed for the cover of the *Melody Maker* after they swept the board at the 1998 polls. And drummer Sean Moore ... the last time I saw him was at a gig at the University of London Union, when his first words were, 'I know you don't like us, but ...'

b side

Smash Hits magazine saved my life a hundred times when I was a kid. This is what would happen. I'd have had a song stuck in my head for days, but you know what it's like, the singer mumbles at one point and you can't quite make out what he's saying, and after a while you think you're going to go insane or drop dead unless you know what it is. So I'd go to the newsagent and furiously look up the words in *Smash Hits*.

But that wasn't the end of it. How many times have you looked up a set of lyrics only to find that the band haven't been singing what you thought they'd been singing at all. Not only that, but their version is rubbish (the one in your head, the one you've wanted to believe, is ten times better than the real thing).

Smash Hits is a cruel mistress. Lyrics – forcibly separated from the bosom of the music – can look terrifically lost and lonely. There's nowhere to hide. There's a serious point here somewhere, but first, the funniest thing I have ever seen in *Smash Hits* (that's if you exclude the words to *Tatva* by Kula Shaker). During the late 70s there was a stream of chart hits which I like to remember as wally disco. It was a DJ who came up with the phrase. Wally disco encompassed all the records that sounded like they'd been recorded specifically for wedding receptions and your sister's 18th birthday party.

The epidemic of wally disco records left *Smash Hits* with a problem. Wally disco worked solely on the basis that the more words you used the harder it would be for people to sing along. Forget the mercurial minimalists of the American lo-fi scene – this is where pop music's grasp of the theory 'less is more' truly succeeded.

At the top of the wally disco heap was a track called *Dance Yourself Dizzy* by Liquid Gold. The *Smash Hits* staff must have pissed themselves as they were laying it out, but all credit to them, they printed the words in full. The opening line was:

'D-d-d-d-d-d-d-d-d-d-d-d-d-d-d-d-d-d-d-d-d-d-d-d-dizzy.'

These days I still like to know what lyrics say. But I'm less keen on finding out what they mean to the person who wrote them. I remember interviewing Damon Albarn of Blur at the time of *Modern Life Is Rubbish* and saying how great the track *Chemical World* was, because of the line 'they sleep together so they don't get lonely'. Which struck me as a harsh but true image of parts of London life. People get bored or lost and they end up in bed with someone because it alleviates the tedium. Or it stops them having to find a real solution to why they were bored or lost in the first place.

But, of course, that's not what the song meant in Damon's head. They weren't even the right words (Damon says 'stick together' instead of 'sleep together' and so the song means something else entirely). But after he told me, the song never sounded as good again.

And I've done the same with scores of other bands (though not recently). I'll have a beautifully concocted picture of what the lyrics are driving at, and Bobby Gillespie or Cerys Mathews or whoever will look across the Radio 1 desk and do one of two things. Either they smile sympathetically, or they just launch into the real reason why they wrote the track. But that's not what we want to hear. We just want them to agree with us.

It goes back to the way we personalize pop music to suit ourselves. I obviously came up with my crappy, sociology-lecture explanation of the Blur song because that's what I wanted it to mean. Either that or I'd got out of bed on the wrong side and wanted the world to be an awful place, and this made it sound as awful as possible.

I can twist countless songs around to fit me. And there are thousands of other fans who do the same. Every song on the first Hefner album says something about my life, and most of the second one as well. There's a huge chunk of *13* by Blur that could have been written about me too, though you can bet I'm not going to check this with Damon. And there are songs by Linoleum and The Charlatans and Embrace and Flaming Lips and Richard Ashcroft and they're all me as well.

If you get carried away with this fixation, you eventually find that your entire opinion of a band becomes based on how well they can archive your own life. How ridiculous is that? 'Ashcroft. Brilliant. That song about being a 30-something living in south London and the bit about getting up every morning and the first thing he does is make a cup of tea …' And so on, and so on.

I understand all this. I like imagining that I'm part of a song because I like knowing that someone else feels the same way that I do. Or at least I think they feel the same. It makes me believe I'm one of the chosen few. That makes some sort of sense to me. I've even come to terms with the fact that it's always the seriously messed up lyrics that mean the most. Ninety per cent of my favourite lyrics have to be sung either through gritted teeth or in a state of mental disrepair. In fact, some of them you can't even sing at all – you have to shout them, or snarl them, or sob them. That's OK as well. I mean, we've all known times when a pop song has saved our soul in some way.

But why, once we've found a record that is indisputably about ourselves, one that without a shadow of a doubt refers to us and US ALONE, do we go around quoting it to other people? Is it a cry for help?

'Look, don't you see what this song says about me?!'

I've done it myself. I've resorted to quoting lyrics at people in the hope that I will sound more enigmatic, and that my life will appear stranger and sexier. But I never hold out much hope that it'll work.

So I've tried to resist the temptation to quote lyrics in this book, but sod it. In this case, I'm going to allow myself to make an exception. I don't own that many books about music, but I have one which is called *It Only Looks As If It Hurts*, the complete lyrics of Howard Devoto from 1976 to 1990. Devoto was originally in the Buzzcocks but left to form Magazine and then when Magazine split he formed Luxuria.

It's the Magazine days that I like most. That's when Devoto wrote *Song From Under The Floorboards*. Help. That's me. In these lines. All over the place. Howard. You're a genius.

I am angry, I am ill and I'm as ugly as sin
My irritability keeps me alive and kicking
I know the meaning of life, it doesn't help me a bit
I know beauty and I know a good thing when I see it

This is a song from under the floorboards
This is a song from where the wall is cracked
My force of habit, I am an insect
I have to confess I'm proud as hell of that fact

I know the highest and the best
I accord them all due respect
But the brightest jewel inside of me
Glows with pleasure at my own stupidity

This is a song from under the floorboards ...

Now I'm going to have to find their live album *Play* and stick the track on and sing along to it. Then play it again – but the second time it's always louder.

The singing along thing is something else I suffer from. I can't help it. It's not so bad at home where people can't hear or see you. It's not even too bad, I suppose, if you're at a gig and there are loads of other people joining in. But it doesn't stop there for me. I find myself singing along to songs by obscure indie bands in the back rooms of pubs. Or worse – mouthing the words. I've caught myself doing it (or seen other people watching me, aghast) and I must look like a demented goldfish, gulping for life. But it's just an instinctive reaction and, so far, no doctor has found a cure for it.

NB: I have had three sets of neighbours in four years. Is there a link?

• 8
AFTER THE WATERSHED

It's been very slow going, the last two days. Julie from Wise Buddah, the management company who make sure I turn up for work on time, has phoned three times to ask, 'How's the book going?' And it's not going anywhere. It is stuck in 1990–91.

There are music papers all over the floor and old 12-inch records by the stereo, and I think I'm suffering from thousand yard stare (which reminds me. There was a band called Thousand Yard Stare who I went to the Shetland Islands with in 1991. We came home by ferry and I was violently ill for three hours). There you go. See? I'm an indie-war vet, reliving the conflict of the start of the 90s. There is a fair chance that if this doesn't clear up in the next 24 hours I'll be needing therapy. Which reminds me …

If 1989 had been some sort of dress rehearsal for the new decade, 1990 and 1991 were the real deal in my mind. I don't think any of us particularly thought at the time they were involved with setting the agenda for the next ten years. But, in retrospect, much of what happened – and many of the bands who emerged during that time – did end up shaping the 90s. There were Blur, the Manics, The Charlatans and *Nevermind* by Nirvana. There were Prodigy and PJ Harvey, Radiohead and Massive Attack.

There was so much going on that it was hard to know where to start. The way the *NME* started each week was with an editorial meeting every Tuesday around 12 o'clock. A wrapped bundle of the new issue (out on Tuesday in London, but Wednesday around the rest of the country) would arrive in the reception and everyone would charge in to get a copy. The editorial followed. It was partly a debrief, raking over the highs and lows of the previous week's issue (including endless complaints from writers who'd had their copy cut). But mostly editorials are about the following week's edition. Who's on the cover? Who's the lead live review? Who the hell can we get to do the Pet Shop Boys again?

When people ask how the paper worked, I'd try to explain it like this. Imagine taking a bunch of musicians who all liked different styles of music and putting them in a studio together, then telling them to make a record. That's what our editorial meetings were like. A lot of people banging different drums. Very loudly.

During the *NME*'s celebrations for its 40th anniversary, former writer turned TV and radio personality Danny Baker was asked to comment on his stint at the paper in the 70s. I can't remember the quote word for word, but the gist was: 'Everybody thinks their time at the *NME* is the best. We all think it goes downhill after we leave.'

Danny – you are spot on. Except you can forget Baker and the 70s, the team at the *NME* at the start of the 90s was one of the all-time greats. OK, we disagreed at length, at least once every week, and I and the LPs Editor Stuart Bailie tried unwisely to launch a Ska revival at one point, but we were good. Honest. I swear on U2's life (ha!). Alan Lewis had moved on to become Publisher, so Danny Kelly took over as Editor with the whizz-kid James Brown on Features. When Brown took off to pursue other projects, Andrew Collins replaced him. The two Deputy Editors were Brendon Fitzgerald, the indomitable leader of the subs room, and Stuart Maconie.

It was a precariously balanced but determined team. So when the paper was good, it was genuinely good, and when it was bad – when you saw another two-bit band being handed a feature on the basis of one crap single, or you saw press office hype triumphing over common sense – well, then, then … oh, it made you want to scream.

It's something that came up in conversation the other day. I was out with the long-suffering Juliet, who some days I think knows me better than anyone else on the planet.

'I was angry all the time in 1991, wasn't I?' I said, hoping that she'd say no.

'Yes.'

'All the time?'

'All the time,' she laughed. It's funny. It wasn't so much anger as journalistic indignation and petulance. We all have it at times. Because we are right and the rest of the world is wrong. And if push comes to shove then MY BAND'S BETTER THAN YOUR BAND!

'You're not so bad now,' she added. 'You don't get like that so often.'

So often. Hmmm. But that means I still do it. I still throw the toys out of the pram. I still get upset by the machinations of the industry and the rubbish groups that get signed by deaf A&R scouts. Life still isn't fair.

And I think that's why the start of the 90s is a difficult time to readdress for me. Reading some of the reviews I can see a cheeky, sarcastic, angry side of myself that I thought I might have grown out of. But I have to admit it, it's still there lurking in the background. I can still have a good row about pop music and therefore it must still mean enough to me to carry on. It's a scary, twisted logic I suppose, but it'll have to do for now.

But back at the start of the 90s the lad Williams and the boy Lamacq were, as previously mentioned, on a mission from God (at least we were if God was an indie-guitar fan and thought that all major labels were the devil). Here's an example of the highs and lows from a Singles page in August 1991. By the way, baggy Liverpool band The Farm were on the groovy train in America on the cover. The big album review was of the Paris Angels (who someone gave nine out of ten to. How we laughed).

So, Single of the Week One: Midway Still with *I Won't Try*. Single of the Week Two: *Charly* by somebody called the Prodigy (and I quote: 'a good, busy, bassy club record'). I'd actually heard the Prodge track on Radio 1's *Big Beat* show, while driving to a gig in Harlow. It's one of the few occasions I've ever pulled off the road and stopped to hear who it was by. But anyway … if those records represented my twin visions of what pop should stand for that week, then the next one was the Antichrist.

The Blessing: Flames (MCA Records)
    The very fact that the Blessing record exists means that someone at MCA genuinely believes that they will sell lots of records. If this person would like to get in touch I'll cheerfully bet them a tenner that they won't.

You might think that was a bit harsh, but there was worse to come. Not only did we not much care for the bland syrup being doled out by the major labels, we didn't much like daytime Radio 1 either. This review got me a new catchphrase that other staffers used to quote at me. And yes, I am aware of the definition of irony.

The Origin: *Set Sails Free* (Hut)
The press release of the Origin record makes a point of saying that their last single was played 35 times by Radio 1 ... just the sort of simpering thing you expect to find attached to Bands-Desperately-Trying-To-Crack-It who haven't got a following, or worse, any sense of passion. As if being played 35 times by Radio 1 is some justification for existing, or benchmark of talent. YOU TOOLS!

In my defence, I wasn't the only one ranting and screaming my way through life. After leaving the News Desk I became the paper's Live Reviews Editor and set about building a team of freelances who were as obsessed, deranged and enthusiastic as I was. That makes perfect sense to me. What makes less sense is that for a while I tried to persuade them that they all had to call me 'Guv'.

Don't ask.

Several good writers were already there (Williams, Dele Fedele, Gina Morris). To add to them, when one of the rival papers, *Sounds*, was shut down, I managed to persuade Keith Cameron (one of its best and most informed writers) to move across to *NME*. He was joined by future *Select* Editor John Harris, whom I wheedled away from *Melody Maker*, and a very tall man called Johnny Cigarettes. Cigs was one of the few writers we found from the pile of unsolicited reviews that used to clog up one end of the Live Desk.

Every music paper gets sent unsolicited material from would-be writers but, like bands and demos, the quality is usually quite suspect. If you're thinking of trying to crack the press yourself, just remember that the competition is incredibly fierce and that you need to stand out from the crowd. Cigs (all six foot of him) stood out like a sore thumb. His writing was funny and acerbic and used to take the piss out of anything that moved. I tried phoning the number he'd enclosed with the two trial reviews he'd sent, but got no reply for days.

Little did we know that he worked the graveyard shift at a petrol station near Leamington Spa, so he'd go to gigs by night, write the reviews in between serving people packets of Rizlas and Lucozade, and then sleep through the day. How can you not employ someone like that? So Cigs started freelancing, as did Sam Steele, who got her break by telling me that the paper's dance coverage was useless. After an hour of being verbally beaten up, I gave in. 'OK, then, I'll give you a trial run next week,' I told her.

'Sorry, I'm going to Goa for a month,' she replied. 'I'll phone you when I get back.'

There weren't just writers in on the team either, there were the photographers too: Tim Paton, then Andy Wilsher and, of course, Ed Sirrs, veteran of the Manics' Norwich gig. Whenever I could I went on trips with Ed as the snapper. Not only is he one of the coolest men on the planet, he's a genius when it comes to live photos. Having pioneered the all-action live shot at *Sounds* (y'know, the ones where you can almost see the guitars moving), he joined *NME*, bringing with him the air of a craftsman. His favourite phrase was, 'I'm not interested if it's going to be the size of a postage stamp.'

Ed talks like he's just walked straight out of the pages of an Ed McBain novel (he's read every single bloody one of them) and has knackered one of his knees through years of being crushed against the stage at the front of gigs. Given that he'd probably have been equally at home photographing battle zones for the *Guardian*, he was an ideal man to have on your side going into combat.

In the meantime, the Live Desk war office moved from the Stamford Arms to the Doggets Coat & Badge because (a) it had a better pinball table, and (b) we liked the barman. In the days before computer disks, the freelances used to deliver their hard copy, typewritten, to the pub. Then Simon and I would go through the Live Diary (our meticulously copied-out list of gigs that needed covering) and we'd divvy up work for the following week. I've never known a lifestyle like it. We worked incredibly hard and we hit our deadlines, but at the same time we'd be gigging most nights and falling into the pub at lunch. Either we'd discuss bands or we'd get into arguments about the direction of the paper and the rest of the staff.

It's not surprising that the war office occasionally lost the plot. Starved of sleep and wound up by the editorial policy, which of course was too safe in our view, we'd forget all reason and get into trouble. The most famous incident at the time came in the week that the Editor and his features staff decided that we should have the Beautiful South on the cover (AGAIN!). Now, on reflection, this probably made good commercial sense, because the South were popular and, in theory, sold papers. But after one particularly volatile visit to the Doggets, I think I decided that the paper should be more daring in its choice of cover stars.

The big new band at the time, just cracking the Top 40, were an Irish trio called The Frank & Walters. Let's put them on the front instead. Why no-one stopped me I'll never know, but I stormed back into the *NME* HQ and into Editor Danny Kelly's office. After a short discussion on the matter – which I lost – I think I shouted something unrepeatable and stormed back out, slamming the door behind me.

Forgetting that I was a grown-up 20-something and not a small boy who's been told that he's grounded for a week, I kicked the nearest piece of office furniture (a chair, which turned out to be made of concrete). I managed to get as far as the coffee machine in the corridor outside the office before having to sit down and take one of my DMs off. By the time I tried to put it back on, the swelling was so large that the boot didn't fit anymore. I ended up in casualty at St Thomas's Hospital.

'So, Mr Lamacq, how did you do this?'

'I kicked a chair,' I mumbled. Quite rightly, they sent me to the back of the queue and I waited three hours for an X-ray and a pair of crutches. Back home the next day, I received a homemade 'Get Well Soon' card from *NME*. It had my head superimposed on the body of a man lying prostrate in a hospital bed with a broken leg in plaster. In big letters at the top it said: 'You Tool'.

By the spring of 1990 I'd done all kinds of exciting or daft things, but I hadn't stage-dived. Even now, I've still only ever done it once. Is that a shocking admission? Maybe if I'd been a tad younger when stage-diving was invented then I'd be well into double, or even treble figures. But being in my mid 20s and scared of flying, the idea of heaving my frail body off the stage into the unknown struck me as a bit scary.

So my sole attempt came at the end of a long and difficult day on the road with Carter (USM). I'd been sent, with photographer Ed Sirrs, to review the band live in Paris. But that wasn't all. *NME* had discovered that Carter had given an 'exclusive' interview to our rival *Melody Maker*, which was due to run as a cover story. Our job was to try and sneak an interview and then run a spoiler story with a live photo on the front of the *NME* the same week.

I wasn't entirely comfortable with this. It's a journalistic trick which used to happen quite often, but I'd never stitched up a group before, especially a band I knew. Consequently, I decided that getting as drunk as possible might give me the courage I needed. This wasn't difficult. As an experiment, Carter's label Chrysalis had decided to send us to France via City Airport, the business airport in the East End of London. Ed in his shades and I in my Mega City 4 fleece stood out like a sore thumb (the drug-runner alarms lit up in the eyes of every security man we passed and we were questioned at length as they checked our bags).

Once on the plane, however, we found we'd been assigned to the business class section which meant you were entitled to as much free champagne as you could possibly handle at 11.30 in the morning. We arrived in Paris and checked in at the hotel. Then we went straight to the venue where, having made up a story about needing some quotes to flesh out the review, I got an interview and felt thoroughly rotten about it the entire way through.

It wasn't just Carter I knew. It was some of their crew as well. At one point before the gig I happened to tell the guitar tech I was thinking of breaking my stage-diving duck, and that I'd picked France because no-one would see me if I fell through the crowd and landed flat on my face. (There had been a story doing the rounds of a *Maker* writer who had leapt off stage expecting to land on a few people's heads. But the crowd had parted and he'd fallen straight to the floor.)

Halfway through the gig I managed to position myself at the side of the stage, kneeling just behind singer Jim Bob's amp. As I got up to look at the crowd, trying to pick the softest people to land on, the guitar tech thought he'd help out and gave me a firm push. All of a sudden I was on the stage, vaguely aware I was heading past Jim Bob and toward the crowd. I shut my eyes and stuck my arms out and prayed.

If you have a look at the pictures in this book, the one of me in the crowd was taken after I'd come down to earth. The smile is not one of gig-ecstasy. It's one of pure relief.

We put Carter on the cover with one of Ed's live shots. I dug out the issue the other day and it looks quite good. A few pages after the Carter piece was the only other bit of writing I'd contributed to the paper that week – a review of *Nevermind* by Nirvana.

• 9
FREAK SCENE

I can't remember exactly when it was, but some time in the early 80s I received a home-made compilation tape through the post from a fanzine in America. I can't even remember the name of the fanzine, which was based in Reno, but I remember the impact that the cassette had. I sat in my bedroom in a shell-shocked daze. It was like being in double maths, trying to learn how to multiply fractions.

What on earth was all this stuff? Who were TSOL? How great were these bands Social Distortion and the Descendents? How FAST were Hüsker Dü? What am I going to send the fanzine back in return?

The American bands seemed immediately more eloquent than the second generation of punk-inspired groups in Britain. They were more incisive and cutting, and in Hüsker Dü's case, extreme. So extreme that it took two years before I understood their appeal. They also had another major advantage over most of the punk leftovers in the UK: none of their songs were about (a) the Tories in general or (b) Maggie Thatcher in particular, who were the twin lyrical targets of 70 per cent of British bands of that type at the time. Plus, when the American groups said the F-word, it sounded like it was there for a reason. Some of the UK bands appeared to be suffering from a musical version of Tourette's Syndrome.

I'd heard the Dead Kennedys, who were the most notorious US punk group of the time, and I was aware of Black Flag. But I hadn't taken much notice of them, because, naively, I didn't believe the Americans really knew what they were doing. I thought they were cheating at school, trying to copy what was essentially a British invention. I was a bit ill-informed to be honest. I left The Ramones out of this theory because they were OK, but the rest of the bands sounded arrogant and abrupt and I couldn't be doing with them. Then the tape arrived, and with it came my introduction to hardcore – an introduction which would eventually lead me (and many others) to Nirvana.

The more I read up on the history of punk, the more it seemed like there was a huge game of trans-Atlantic tennis going on, with guitar music as the ball. The Americans invented punk and didn't know what to do with it so they served it to us. In a return cross-court volley we gave them back the Sex Pistols, anarchy, Sid Vicious and tabloid headlines. Anxious to up the ante, they struck back with the more politically driven Dead Kennedys and then, bless us, we hit them with GBH and Discharge. New balls please.

It's a cack-handed theory really, but the evolution of punk and then hardcore music has always relied on Britain and America taking a sound or a scene and then refining it into a new image. It works even better if the people in the country on the receiving end don't like what they're being given. Then they're forced to either ignore it, or reinvent it.

Back at the *A Pack Of Lies* HQ I thrilled to *1945* by Social Distortion, but it was the Descendents who really blew me off the edge of my bed. There were two tracks by them on the tape, both of which I later found on the album *Milo Goes To College* (so called because Milo the singer was, erm, off to college). They sounded desperate and edgy and had hooklines. But oddly, the bass sound was different to British records. It was more taut and tense. It was the same bass sound that later turned up on the first Fugazi album, which was another mind-blowing record.

In the meantime, the hardcore scene continued to evolve in America, watched closely by bands and fans in this country. The labels of choice at the time for many of us were Dischord and SST Records. SST had the Descendents, who after Milo's departure recruited a new singer and re-emerged as All, and Dischord had Minor Threat. Minor Threat were straight-edge (this, I think, was a comparatively new concept to Britain), which meant they didn't drink or smoke. And they looked as hard as nails. Have you noticed how the British guitar groups of the 80s looked so flimsy and underfed that they might just blow away – while the Americans came with tattoos and muscles and skinheads?

There was a definite underground community growing around these groups though, boosted I guess around this time by the skateboard kids and the first signs of American punk fashion. How much does it say about our differing approaches to pop clobber that the Americans gave punk fleeces and shorts, and we gave it the bum-flap?

It had all the criteria for being a cult scene in the 80s. It received very little press and never troubled the charts, but when the bands played in the UK they sold out wherever they went. With the exception of maybe the ever-improving Hüsker Dü, the ultra-lazy Dinosaur Jr. and the incredibly hip Sonic Youth (who have their own special place in this story), it was a music that survived in a world of fanzines and transit vans. That would all change though, from the end of the 80s onwards.

At the *NME* it was clear that something was happening in Seattle, even if we couldn't quite focus on what it was. Our pre-grunge specialist was Edwyn Pouncey, aka cartoonist Savage Pencil, who regularly filed reports on bands emerging on American labels like Sub Pop and the even-harder-to-find Sympathy For The Record Industry (who would later release an ace seven-inch by a group called Hole).

But the question was, where did the bands with ludicrous names and incredible hair fit in? It was 1989, the year of Madchester, and here we were being invaded by these nightmare visions of proto-grunge chic. It was quite exciting to be honest. As more and more British bands started namechecking cult US groups – and the gig circuit began to expand and grow again after a period in the doldrums – the American groups started turning up on a regular basis. Mudhoney, for instance, seemed to be on tour every week either with or without heavyweight labelmates Tad.

Both *Melody Maker* and the now-defunct *Sounds* leapt on the Seattle scene, and finally at *NME* we followed suit. In the end-of-year issue for 1989, Pouncey, already up to his waist in filthy guitar slurry, wrote favourably about Soundgarden (already signed to A&M after spells at Sub Pop and SST), Mudhoney and Mother Love Bone. 'But there are other huge talents to be found on Sub Pop,' he added. 'Nirvana are one with Kurdt Kobain proving himself to be a master songwriter with *Love Buzz* and *Blew* to his name.'

It's the bit about 'master songwriter' that I find interesting now (more so than the different spelling of Kur*dt's* name). Everything written about Sub Pop and the new harsher, hairier American bands of the time enthused about the noise and the frenzied sound of the Seattle groups. But songwriting? That was a new one.

For my part, Nirvana's debut album *Bleach* virtually passed me by. I had a copy. Quite liked it. Moved on. What rescued me from being a Nirvana nobody was a tape that arrived from their press officer Anton Brookes. Anton, the gentle giant of PR, knew more than most about the

American hardcore scene, having worked out of an office at Southern Distribution (who handled vast quantities of the stuff) and represented groups like Fugazi and Mudhoney.

The tape itself, badly copied onto a TDK C60, featured Nirvana's next single *Sliver* and some demos of tracks that would later go to make up their second album. *Sliver* was just pop genius. Listening back to it, it's a phenomenally to-the-point record. There's the loping bass, Kurt's vocals and then a sudden surge of guitar which induces Kurt's screaming chorus line. Other grunge records were noisier, but Nirvana's were more structured and expressive.

The single's release was delayed for weeks. I can't remember why, but I have the press release that came with it. It describes *Sliver* as 'the greatest Nirvana experience, catching the power trio in its transitional, creatively enhanced state.' Not a bad summarization, really. The final paragraph is more oblique: 'When will there be a Nirvana LP? Nobody knows. Who's drumming? It's that guy from Scream, and Kurdt says he's great … New stuff? We'll let you know.'

The confusion surrounding their future was understandable. Yes, after employing Dan Peters from Mudhoney to drum on *Sliver*, they'd recruited a new drummer, Dave Grohl. And having outgrown Sub Pop/ Tupelo recordings they were in negotiation with various new labels. As they arrived for a mini-tour of the UK at the end of 1990, Island Records were very keen, but the band still seemed non-committal. We got our interview the night after the band had played in Norwich and returned to the bed and breakfast hotel in Shepherd's Bush where they were staying. Kurt looked tired, bassist Chris Novoselic had 'one of your British colds' and drummer Grohl was rooting through a bin-liner full of dirty laundry accumulated over the past few days of touring.

I'm pretty sure we did the pictures first, so that snapper Martyn Goodacre could get away early. It was freezing cold, but he managed to cajole the group outside and set about photographing them at a bus stop, in a launderette, and on a playground climbing frame (at one point Cobain hung upside down from the frame, his legs wrapped over the top bars). Along the way, Martyn got *the* shot – the one that was eventually used as a cover picture when Cobain killed himself in 1994. It's the one with the huge eyes, staring out from beneath his fringe.

Some of these pictures can be found in the excellent Nirvana book *Winterland* – a pictoral record of the group throughout their career. Of the rest of the set, there's a particularly bizarre one of the band walking across a zebra crossing, with Novoselic puffing his chest out and impersonating a monkey. Over the other side of the road, with crap hair and an ill-fitting denim jacket, you can just about see me laughing.

There was no disguising the fact they were knackered. Back at their two-room HQ in the B&B, Novoselic retired, fully clothed, to bed and hid under the duvet for the entire interview, only poking his head out when he had something to contribute. Kurt sat next to me on another bed, staring at the floor. Grohl got on with washing his socks in the bathroom. In the corner of the room, one of those small, wall-hung TVs was showing *The Wizard of Oz*. It was all very strange.

Before talking about music, Kurt revealed that he kept turtles as pets at home in his bath. 'They have no personality at all,' he said. 'And I like that in a pet.'

But the most important revelations were about their music. Having spent the *Bleach* era concerned that their melodic side might alienate them from a punk audience, Nirvana were starting to loosen up. There was positive talk of the recent Sonic Youth album *Goo* – the Youth's most accessible record to date – and they didn't flinch when I said they could end up following the REM route out of the leftfield and into the charts.

'We're finally coming out of the drains and saying we like pop music,' Cobain added. 'So if we want to write a song like REM we'll do that, or if I want to write a song like Godflesh I'll do that.'

In the next few months the Nirvana bandwagon slowly began to roll. They signed with Geffen and went off to record *Nevermind*. And when the tapes of the album finally turned up, you could sense they'd cracked it. I'd love to be able to tell you that I foresaw the worldwide mayhem that was to follow within the next 18 months. But I don't think I did. We knew, those of us in the office who were already converts, that this was a massively important record; that the sound of it would be influential in the future; and that Nirvana had now surpassed anything previously achieved in the 'grunge' genre. But the commercial success which slowly gathered momentum over the following year was a surprise even to us. Back in the States I suspect it was a shock to some of the Geffen staff too, who hadn't exactly gone overboard with their recording and video budgets for the band.

But all this partly explains why, when the *NME* came to review it, the album was relegated to the fourth page of the paper's album section.

Mind you, it hadn't struck lucky with the competition it was up against. The other major albums reviewed in that week's issue were: *Screamadelica*, the future Mercury Music Prize-winning and highly influential album from Primal Scream; the Pixies' *Trompe le Monde* (ironically a band Kurt had a lot of time for); and *Use Your Illusion* by Guns'n'Roses.

We spent ages trying to come up with a headline for the Nirvana review, but with a deadline looming we settled for the faintly obvious NEVERMIND – THE BOLLOX! Still, that's effectively what the piece said. It's odd re-reading it now. But here's some of it:

> Nirvana do here what Sonic Youth did so emphatically with *Goo* last year – making the move from cult indie to major label with not so much as a hiccup. In fact, just as the Sonics impressed and outstripped the sceptics' expectations, Nirvana have made an LP which is not only better than anything they've done before, it'll stand up as a new reference point for the future post-hardcore generation.
>
> *Nevermind* is a record for people who'd like to like Metallica, but can't stomach their lack of melody; while on the other hand it takes some of the Pixies' nous with tunes and gives the idea new muscle. A shock to the system. Tracks like the excellent *In Bloom* and best of the lot *Come As You Are* show a dexterity that combines both a tension and laid-back vibe that work off each other to produce some cool, constructed twists and turns.
>
> *Nevermind* is the big American alternative record of the autumn. (9)

I nicked the line about Metallica from fellow *NME* scribe Mary Anne Hobbs. Mary Anne had come from *Sounds* and was loud and opinionated, and had the same musical tastes as people like me and Simon. She got the unenviable task of writing our first Nirvana cover – just as the band began to suffer under the pressure of their new-found fame.

The timing of the review might not have been spot-on, but the timing of Nirvana's arrival to a bigger, broader audience was pretty much impeccable. You could see *Nevermind* as an antidote to Madchester, the post baggy sounds of the Scream *and* to the slower, more insular music of Britain's shoegazing bands such as Chapterhouse and Slowdive. In fact, Chapterhouse were never the same again after having to follow Nirvana on the main stage at the Reading Festival that year.

NME finally featured them on the cover in November 1991. Kurt had to be gently persuaded to do the photos by his press officer, but still retaliated with, 'Look I'll do the fucking pictures, I just want to be left alone.' Despite their being slightly reticent to begin with, Mary Anne got a good piece out of them (the fact that *Polly*, one of the most harrowing songs on the album, was based on a true story, and how Chris was worried about a backlash from their original fans, now Nirvana were officially big-time).

The feature also followed them to the after-the-pub youth TV hellhole of *The Word*, which we only used to watch for the bands. Kurt swore and Nirvana did *Smells Like Teen Spirit* and, two and a half minutes into the song, the programme rolled its credits.

But here's the crux of the piece. 'Nirvana have made a more profound impact on America with *Nevermind* than Guns'n'Roses did with with *Appetite For Destruction*. And they're running all the "smack and fanny" barons out of town,' Maz wrote. 'The fantastic truth about Nirvana's new-found fortune is that there was no prior plan, no strategic media massage, no radio ass-kissing, no trading fine Columbian for favours. Nirvana have made it simply on the magnificent quality of their sound-bytes.'

That was the real point of it all. Where the Pistols had failed, Nirvana had succeeded. This was punk rock come to America, 15 years after it started bringing down the rock dinosaurs in Britain.

Nevermind was culturally important in several ways, but two were particularly pleasing. They all but ended the reign of the poodle-rocksters in Spandex trousers who had represented rock music since prehistoric times. I think that's fair.

And they brought to a conclusion the first era of hardcore, from its birth in the underground to its passing out party in the mainstream chart. It had been a long and difficult journey. Hüsker Dü had helped start the ball rolling by metamorphosing from a 30-second thrash band into a gorgeously melodic punk rock group, and they'd signed to

Warner Brothers in the process. How shocking was that at the time? I mean, Hüsker Dü were loud, but you could still barely hear them over the cries of 'sell-out' across America.

But Hüsker Dü hadn't sold out. And they made *Candle Apple Grey* and *Warehouse Songs And Stories*, and though they didn't sell in earth-shatttering numbers, they helped create a better atmosphere for bands to make the jump from an indie label to a major. Sonic Youth joined Geffen. Then Sonic Youth recommended that Geffen sign Nirvana. Nirvana made *Nevermind*.

It's a simplistic theory, I know. It doesn't take into account scores of other important groups along the way (including the Pixies, and Dinosaur Jr. with their pre-*Smells Like Teen Spirit* anthem *Freak Scene*) and bands that operated on a different and even more uncompromising level (Fugazi) but there is a line there. If Nirvana were carrying the punk torch, then they were the ones who did the final leg of the relay and crossed the line to the flash of a thousand cameras.

The trio's success also coincided with – and contributed to – a change in policy among American TV and radio stations, which finally began to embrace alternative pop culture. They were a gift for MTV. They helped reinvent alt-rock radio, which had been surviving on bands like The Cure for years. And they sent out a message to the major labels that a new sort of rock music had arrived.

Of course, having opened the doors to the underground, the American punk scene would never be the same again. The spotlight shone on the best AND the worst bands of the time. And for a lot of people who treasured the very underground nature of grunge and punk it was difficult to watch it being turned into a designer youth culture, with double page spreads on Slackers and Generation X.

It was very different to dodgy compilation tapes of TSOL.

I saw Nirvana a couple of more times after *Nevermind*. One of the nights was my friend Tall Graham's stag night, when I had to chaperone various drunkards round the Kilburn National. But Nirvana responded to the big occasion by being at their most ferocious and committed. The crowd, swelled by the success of *Smells Like Teen Spirit*, were wide-eyed and full-on. And really, that seemed as good a point as any to wish them on their way, and to return to the Falcon.

b side

Writing for the music press can be a really good life. Hang on, what am I saying? It IS a good life. You get sent free records and packed off to interview bands. You get into gigs on guestlists and go to dreadful after-show parties which are so utterly vampiric that even the band whose party it is refuse to show up. You see the best and worst of the music biz's excess and meet groups who can't string four sentences together. And for some people that's enough. More than enough. But for a lot of us – chemically imbalanced or obtuse or awkward – we have to complicate it by trying to change the world as well.

And the last thing I want to do is sound evangelical here. Just because there are people who like finding new bands and championing new talent, it doesn't make us better than the rest. If anything it makes us worse. We mood-swing and argue and sulk and behave like children – and who wants to go out with people like that? But here's the deal.

You know when you've been into something – a record, a TV show or a film – ages before your mates have? And then a couple of months later they all leap on the bandwagon and start talking about it too … And you're there, knowing that you were ahead of your time. That you were a visionary. A believer. You helped make it happen. Well, in a roundabout way that's what drives much of our relationship with new music.

It's a mixture of our good and bad sides. We genuinely want new groups we like to do well, but there is a snobbery involved which dictates that we not only want to be proved right, but we want to be first as well. We don't ask for much, do we? Everyone has their own reasons for why they champion bands, but I've noticed down the years that many of them revolve around the idea of possession. If I have seen X band 10 times and have six albums by them and you have only seen them once and have a cassette copy of their latest record, then they're more my band than they are yours. I know it sounds daft, but we all do it at some point. And anyway, I liked them before you did.

I don't know where all this reasoning leads me, but I've long suspected that my craving for going to see young upstart bands all the time has something to do with the above.

But it's not the only reason. Not by a mile.

When I started at *NME* I think I wanted to prove a point. That there was life outside the paper's then cosy little world, represented by the bigger labels and the zeitgeist-minded press officers. I wanted to cover bands who wouldn't have had a chance otherwise. And though that's still a factor – even at Radio 1 – I ditched the hairshirt years ago. These days I go to see bands because I get a kick out of groups that are raw and nervous and naive – and just occasionally exceptional.

And I know what you're thinking. Surely it's about quality, not quantity? And you're right, it is. But how are you going to find the quality if you don't go looking for it?

Sometimes it is a madness I can't control. (I had a bet one year with fellow journalist Mick Mercer over which of us could be the first to see 200 gigs a year. I started well, but faded and only did about 170. Mick, one of my journalistic heroes, simply ran out of cash.) But on certain nights it provides you (well, me) with such a rush of adrenalin that I think I might just explode.

It is not a high ratio (1:40 for a change-your-world experience, 1:4 for a really good night). But the gigs in between only serve to heighten the fervour of the great ones. And besides, I like the social side of these nights too. All the gossip and the swapping of promising bands' names, like so many sought-after bubblegum cards. There are the listeners you meet, and the arguments you have with friends over Who-The-Drummer-In-The-Support-Band-Reminds-You-Of (it's usually either (a) Matt from Dodgy or (b) someone off Eastenders).

So the way I look at it, I owe certain venues and promoters a debt of gratitude for their service. After all, it's not easy putting on gigs at the bottom level. I once saw an angry promoter chase a band down the street after they had sneaked out without explaining their failure to bring a promised coachload of fans with them. Brilliantly, she was still carrying her glass of red wine at the time.

I know I'm guilty on occasions of donning the rose-tinted specs and romanticizing about what (let's face it) are mainly just pubs with two rooms. But I think they've got character. People who use 'the toilet circuit' as a derogatory description of these venues (ones that hold 250 people or fewer) aren't looking at them in the same way that I do. They're my home turf.

I'm not mad enough to say I like everything about them. But I put up with the downsides, because I'd rather see a group highly charged and fresh than I would sit in row Z at Wembley Arena watching another bunch of jaded old troopers going through their set like worker ants.

That said, I'm not anti-glamour, or anti-big gig. Not all the time anyway. But I am anti-sitting down. I had a furious run-in once with a security man at an Orchestral Manoeuvres gig at the Hammersmith Odeon (now the Apollo). Didn't he understand that it was bad enough seeing the ageing OMD plod through their set, without being forced to SIT through it? My friend Simon has had equally terrible times at seated venues. At a Chris Rea gig (why the *NME* made him do Chris Rea I really don't know, but there you go), he sat next to a family who, between the support act and Rea himself, unpacked a picnic in row G with sandwiches and a flask of tea.

And this is maybe the point. Sitting down is something you do with your parents. Or when you're old and infirm. You don't do it at gigs, do you? Somehow, standing shoulder to shoulder watching a band, the crowd turns into one big, sometimes writhing mass. It represents the whole gang, come to see the group. And maybe that's what's really missing from the seated gig.

Standing up, battling to keep your feet on the ground, craning your neck for a better view, it's somehow easier to lose yourself in the whole gig experience. Sitting down, you are alone or part of a smaller picture (and OK, for certain gigs where you want a one-to-one with the band that's absolutely fine). But I'd rather stand anonymously in the throng at Colchester United – one part of a bigger entity – than I would sit at Manchester United. And I'd rather feel part of a crowd, which shouts as one for an encore, than be in an audience which is full of lone voices.

So I'm not anti-big *per se*. I'm not someone who shouts sell-out (unless a band deserves it) and I'm no longer the sort of person who thinks bands should pay their dues before getting a whiff of success (though paying their dues makes for more romantic copy). I just like all this.

Here are a couple of reasons why. One night I'd gone to the Falcon, then called the Phil Kaufman Club, run by Jeff Barrett. It was a Saturday, so I'd stopped off to buy some comics *en route*, before taking up a position in the corner of the bar with the latest issues of *Daredevil* and *Hellblazer*.

The headline band, who I was there to review, were called The Caretaker Race, but Barrett, who used to book the bands and man the door, popped out from the backroom and starting raving about the support band. Incredible singer. Only their third gig. How many more sweet nothings can a journalist take?

So I fell for it and ventured into the back room, and for once it very nearly was like walking through the back of the wardrobe into Narnia. There, in the orangey light (the Falcon was lit by a single lightbulb at the time), were The Sundays; gorgeous, angelic and chilling. The Caretaker Race never stood a chance after that. The Sundays went on to become the Next Big Thing and *Can't Be Sure*, their debut single, was number one in John Peel's Festive 50 in 1990. And I smile at this, because once again I happened to be in the right place at the right time.

Other bands you have to persist with more. Just over a year later a tape turned up at *NME* of a Scottish group called Teenage Fanclub, which I had trouble listening to without fainting. The Fanclub were due to play their first two London shows over the same weekend, starting with the Falcon on the Friday night. Unbeknownst to the audience though, the group had started drinking as soon as they'd got in their van in Glasgow. And by the time they arrived for soundcheck six or seven hours later they were already a bit merry.

The set was a drunken shambles. Brilliant. But an utter shambles. Halfway through, as another potential gem of a song stuttered to a halt, their singer Norman Blake asked the audience: 'Do you want us to have another go at this one, or go on to another one? Hands up for this one ...' And so it went on. The following night in the dungeonesque basement bar of the White Horse in Hampstead (no stage, so you had to grab a chair to stand on) they were sober and terrific. And I remember looking around the room, and everyone looked as if they were thinking the same. There was a collective glint in the audience's eye, and it's at those times that you realize you're caught up in something special.

And I could go with stories like this all night – like the neighbour with too many holiday snapshots – but you get the picture.

And OK, there is something worrying about the fact that I have been going to the Bull & Gate for 13 years (even more disconcertingly, until last year they'd had the same man collecting the glasses in the bar for 12 years). That's effectively two comprehensive school educations. And I haven't grown up or learnt anything much. Except:

- If a band say they're on at 9 p.m., they're on at 9.15 (or later. It's never earlier)
- If the band come from Watford, they bring a bus full of fans with them (but only the first time. Their mates mysteriously start to dwindle away after that)
- And if the band have an unnecessary keyboard player, that's because they rehearse in his/her parents' garage, or get driven to gigs in his/her parents' estate car.

But hats off to the toilet circuit: from Glasgow to Manchester; from the Leicester Princess Charlotte to the Chalk Farm Monarch. And lest we forget ... the Oval Cricketers.

• 10
(KENNINGTON) PARKLIFE

The Oval Cricketers was – and probably still is – a single, rectangular boxroom of a pub, an averagely uninviting oblong, situated two minutes' walk from the Oval Cricket ground. But I have a fond affection for the Cricketers because of two nights I spent watching bands there.

The first was three days after I came out of hospital. I'd been rushed in a fortnight earlier, suffering from the double-whammy of septic tonsilitis and glandular fever, which had come as a bit of a shock, because naturally I presumed I was an indestructable journalist who could live a perilously unhealthy lifestyle and get away with it.

Of course, I give the whole episode some romantic topspin when I deliver people the details these days. I throw in ambulances and medics running around looking worried and whispering under their breath. I've even managed to persuade some listeners that I kept the ambulance waiting while I wrote the final paragraph of a feature that had to be handed in the next day for *NME*. But at least there is some truth in all this.

As my throat started seizing up, I was working on a piece about a Welsh band called The Darling Buds. Just as I got to the end of it, I found that swallowing had become a serious problem and that's when I eventually gave in. I got a lift to St Thomas's Hospital, where a doctor shone a torch in my mouth and said, resignedly, 'If you could see your tonsils now, they'd make you want to puke.'

After a week on a drip, the medical team finally said they would release me when I could prove to them that I could eat again. The next morning they gave me a bowl of Bran Flakes for breakfast. It was like eating razorblades, but it got me to the front doors.

'Complete rest,' said the doctor, waving me out of the ward.

'Completely impossible,' I should have replied.

After getting home and being told that one of the goldfish had died, I sat around for two days watching videos before I could take it no longer. Glandular fever is bad, but gig withdrawal is worse. I pad around the house without purpose and fall into an odd stupor. 'Sod this for a game of soldiers,' I thought, 'where's the Gig Guide?' And that's how I ended up at the Cricketers to see the Prime Movers bash through their set while all my good intentions (early nights and healthy diet) went out of the window.

It's the other trip to the Cricketers, though, that's the important one. On the other occasion I saw Blur. They weren't called Blur at that point and they didn't sound much like the Blur people know now, but it really was them. As with many bands I've gone to see in my time, Seymour had come via a tip-off – in this case from a guy called Simon, who balanced working in the *NME* advertising department with playing in a band called Vicious Kiss. The Kiss had just appeared at another dimly-lit London venue, the Sir George Robey in Finsbury Park. Simon phoned a couple of days later and said, 'You should go and see the band we played with … Seymour. I didn't like them much, but they're good at what they do.'

Having tracked down a management company phone number, I got a tape and a list of gigs and then strolled off to see them (checking an old diary, it was 12 December 1989, with a scribbled note next to it adding, 'On at 8.45 p.m.'). The great thing about the Cricketers was that it was only about a mile away on the 133 bus from where I was living in Brixton. So if the band were rubbish, you could be home in 15 minutes. But Seymour weren't rubbish. They weren't anything like I'd expected either. Or, to be more precise, they didn't fit in anywhere particularly – apart from sounding strangely at times like the angular C86 band The Wolfhounds.

Cramped onto the stage, which was about six inches high and covered in gaffer tape, the four boys part bounced and part sulked through a set which was more intriguing than it was convincing. The singer hurled himself around, and bumped into the guitarist, who then looked annoyed. Meanwhile, the bassist loafed about in the corner smoking cigarettes. One of them (I'm pretty sure it was guitarist Graham Coxon) wore a blue and white hooped T-shirt, the sort that turned up again in one of the band's early photoshoots. It was all very confusing.

Among the rest of the audience that night, a small crowd of about 80 people, were Andy Ross and Dave Balfe from Food Records who had been on the band's trail for a couple of months already. Food eventually signed Seymour in March 1990, prompting the change of name to Blur and a fresh assault on the London gig circuit. I'm sure this is my memory playing tricks on me, but they must have played the Bull & Gate three times in six weeks during the run-up to the release of their first single *She's So High.*

I did my first interview with them at the start of October 1991, to coincide with the single's release, and I've followed them ever since. And this is why they take up a place in this book, because Blur are probably the one band that I feel I've grown up with. I suppose it helps that we're around the same age and that three of them grew up in Colchester, near to where I lived. But also the band's career has oddly mirrored my own ups and downs (we were both new kids on the block in 1989, we were both out of favour in 1992, both back in favour again in 1994, and both reinventing ourselves by 1997).

We conducted the first interview back in Colchester which, on reflection, was a weird choice because none of us had a good thing to say about the place at the time. I've since made my peace with the town, but then I've had reason to. There is the football club of course, which I've followed since I was a teenager and which, in a particularly miserable patch in my life, rewarded me by getting promotion to the Second Division for the first time in 18 years. And there was the night we took the *Evening Session* to the Colchester Arts Centre – a live broadcast dubbed 'Return Of Lamacq' featuring Ash and Symposium – which is still one of my favourite nights of the 90s. Tickets sold out in 26 minutes. I was speechless. Plus there are bands there now, and local fanzines and labels springing up all over north Essex, from Halstead through Colchester to Clacton.

But at the time of the interview the town was an all-too-close painful memory of squaddies and apathy and no gigs and goths in the city centre.

I described Colchester's catchphrase as 'smart casual', but Graham Coxon was even more bleak: 'When I was at school we were asked to bring in photos of what people thought of Colchester. And everyone just brought in pictures of men digging holes.'

Damon, though, did tell a great story about how his school had burnt down seven times in two years. Police eventually found that the arsonist was … one of the teachers. 'And he was still there at the time,' he added. 'Burning down the school at night and then coming in the next day and saying, "Sorry children, someone has set fire to the school again, so we're going to have to move to another building.'"

The setting for the interview was the Hole in the Wall pub (so named because it sits beside a gap in the Roman Wall). Most of Colchester's alternative and student crowd spent time in the Hole. Not many of them copied Blur and drank halves of cider and Pernod.

Damon: 'Fifteen of these and I'm away.'

The photo session followed in Colchester Castle Park, under the willow trees by the boating lake. It really was the calm before the storm. Apart from the misguided return to Colchester, Blur were just what were needed at the time. As Madchester's momentum gained pace, they were one of the few bands from around London who showed hit potential – and they were good looking and articulate. Damon sounded assured and informed: 'There are fundamental reasons why people like bands. They're drawn to them because they WANT them – whether it's in an emotional, sexual or intellectual way, they want that band. That's us.'

The next 18 months you probably know. *She's So High* was followed by *There's No Other Way*, which was a relatively huge hit for the time. It got to number eight. It's also my least favourite Blur song of all time, but it got them on *Top of the Pops*. Then came the *Smash Hits* photoshoots and the debut album *Leisure* which, despite the hit, received a mixed reaction. They didn't help themselves much by following the LP with *Bang*, a single which managed to sweep the board by not working on any level whatsoever (critically, commercially, you name it, *Bang* flunked it).

But the worst failing of *Bang* was that, once again, it didn't capture the pure abandon of Blur's live gigs. If they had a real problem at the end of 1991, it was with perception. To the casual observer Blur were just a bunch of southern middle-class idiots who'd had a big teen hit and spent the rest of the year on the razzle. They'd hit the jealousy jackpot with *There's No Other Way* and their weekly appearances in the gossip columns had started to rub people up the wrong way. And what else? The singer was arrogant, the rest of them were drunk, and their songs didn't stand up to a second listen. That summer, in a conversation with Creation boss Alan McGee, he told me: 'They're nice blokes but they've got no songs.'

In fact, they had quite a few good songs, but *Leisure* didn't sound emphatic enough to showcase them properly. Their gigs, on the other hand, were something else. Damon said around this time that if he didn't feel ill at the end of a gig then it couldn't have been that great a show. The singer, with more room to play with than at The Oval Cricketers, used to look like he'd just plugged himself into a light socket: he'd hang from the ceiling, charge round the stage and, in extreme cases, throw himself off the PA stack. The band, meanwhile, made a far thicker and fuller noise than the album suggested.

Their last live performance of 1991 was typical of all this. They played the Food Records Christmas Party at London's Brixton Academy with labelmates Jesus Jones, Whirlpool and Sensitise and stole the show. Christmas and New Year is always a time for reflection, but Blur had more to think about than most (after all, they'd been through the whole rise and fall of a pop band in less than 18 months). Upstairs in the bar afterwards, Damon seemed a little subdued, though he did introduce me to his mum and dad who were there.

We were just making plans to maybe meet up in the Hole a couple of days before Christmas when his mum, overhearing the conversation, turned round and said, 'Damon, don't forget you've got carol singing that night.' I'm not sure what his *We Three Kings* is like, but I didn't see any more of Blur for a while after that.

Great Conspiracy Theories Of Our Time: Number One. Have you ever heard the theory of Consensus Terrorism? Well, here's an example of it anyway. Blur hadn't been eaten by the good burghers of Colchester over Christmas. They'd gone away and made one of their best singles ever, the boisterous, slightly punky *Popscene*.

It should have been the record that revived not only their chart career, but their credibility rating as well. It was the first single that went close to capturing the immediacy of their live shows, but it still had a brass section to give it a hint of polish. But the record was cursed, really, from the word go. Parlophone, Food's parent label, disagreed over the choice of video edit (the better, Food-favoured version is the one with subtitles of the lyrics flashing up at the bottom of the screen). Then there was the reaction from the media hipsters and tastemakers.

Now it was Damon who came up with the concept of Consensus Terrorism, and I wouldn't be surprised if he didn't find it forming in his head around the release of *Popscene*. Hope he doesn't mind, but roughly it works like this.

If you've ever had any conspiracy theories about the music press, or radio, or the media in general, then Consensus Terrorism is the catch-all for you. Tastemaker A, probably the Editor or one of the main editorial team, hears the record and decides that he or she doesn't like it, or it doesn't fit into the musical climate of the time. Then Tastemaker B, who has been sitting on the fence, agrees. Tastemaker C, probably junior to the other two, goes along with them.

You now have three people, who wield some sort of importance, all against you, even though a couple of them couldn't really care less either way. But if you think that's bad, that's just the start. When the freelances – who haven't even heard the record yet – pile into the office and ask what it's like, they're told it's not much cop. They nod, and to join in they say, 'Oh, I always thought they'd blow it,' and they act know-ledgeable and leave with their pre-set opinion. Your record's rubbish. That night when they're out at a gig and somebody else asks them about the single, they pass on their accepted wisdom: 'Oh, it's awful.'

'Have you heard it?'

'No, but everyone who has says it's really weak.' You are now officially ALL OVER.

And before anybody stones me, I know that the machinations of the media are more complex than this, and that one bad case of Chinese whispers can't be held entirely responsible for the destruction of a group's career. But I've seen Consensus Terrorism in action (even been a part of it on occasions) and it does undermine people's confidence in a group.

So Blur found themselves in a spot of bother. The consensus view was that, despite the record's eager, edgy, excitable sound, they were going to struggle in 1992. Grunge had arrived, and the Home Counties bands, who were into baggy and shoe-gazing, were about to be swept aside. *Popscene* scrabbled to 32 in the chart (eight places lower than *Bang*) and that was the proof that the doubters needed. Blur? Blown it.

I don't know where I was when *Modern Life Is Rubbish* was released. I might have been on tour. I know I was working as freelance Reviews

Editor at *Select*, but *Modern Life* snuck into the shops while I wasn't looking. You could feel the pendulum swinging back in favour of the British bands through in 1993 and *Select* – particularly the astute Dave Cavanagh and fellow ex-*NME* writer Stuart Maconie – was quick off the mark to spot the potential in *Modern Life*.

They weren't the only ones. Over at Radio 1, Blur recorded two sessions for Mark Goodier's *Evening Session* in fairly quick succession. The second, in April 1993, featured early versions of two of the tracks that would make it onto the next album, *Parklife* (*Bank Holiday* and a curious version of the title track with Damon singing the lines later handled by Phil Daniels).

The *Session*'s support meant that by the time Jo Whiley and I arrived, we were guaranteed the first play of *Girls And Boys*, the first taster for the third album. I think we were both a bit bewildered by it (I mean, I thought they'd been listening to the Human League). What was this disco romp? This cheery singalong? This wasn't *Modern Life*. It was only when advance copies of the album arrived that the new material began to make sense.

As a result I interviewed Blur in the cramped overnight studios at Radio 1's old Egton House building and we made a big thing of *Parklife*. The reaction to the record was astonishingly good. Food label boss Andy Ross has since claimed that the good reviews were over the top because critics had felt they'd missed the boat on *Modern Life* (which by now was a great cult record). But *Parklife* was a stylish and well-executed record in its own right.

TRIVIAL FACT: The album very nearly had a different title. The sleeve was originally going to feature a fruit and veg stall, Damon revealed to us in 1999. And, on the suggestion of Food's then other half, Dave Balfe, it was going to be called *London*. I mean, gawd bless you, guv, but suicide or what?

By a stroke of luck, Radio 1 gave the *Session* an evening off the night the *Parklife* tour was due to start (there was an Amnesty International concert in its place). So on the spur of the moment I travelled up to Nottingham Rock City with a DAT machine and filed an opening night review, including reaction from the band and an interview with the support group Sleeper. The *Session* worked well as a duo at the time, because a couple of weeks later, to balance things up, Jo did a similar roving report on Oasis the night Liam Gallagher was thumped by a disgruntled punter at Newcastle Riverside.

No-one got thumped at Rock City. Blur simply went on, and Damon had the crowd in the palm of his hand from the word go. Before they played the Mile End Stadium at the height of *Parklife* fever, this was the most celebratory gig I'd ever seen them do.

With British pop music – and classic British songwriting – coming back into fashion, Blur went from strength to strength (although if Damon had mentioned Ray Davies once more, I was going to go round his house and break his Kinks CDs one by one. And as for the Cardiacs?! I've never understood Damon's taste in music). The *Parklife* album sold by the lorryload and they won awards left, right and centre. They played a huge gig at London's Ally Pally (which some sources say prompted the first mention of the word Britpop. See Chapter 15 for more conjecture). And then they went off to record the follow-up, *The Great Escape*.

Damon has talked since about becoming depressed around this time and feeling the pressure of the band's success. But no-one really noticed at the time. In retrospect, *The Great Escape* is too long and sounds a little formulaic, but at the height of Cool Britannia no-one much seemed to care. Celebrities flocked to their gigs, the broadsheets wrote features about them (thankful for some nice middle-class boys who'd done well) and the band played the aforementioned Mile End Stadium gig, which was the final nod to Damon's obsession with London's East End – a fascination which had also led me and him to join a greyhound racing syndicate.

But Mile End was the beginning of the end for Blur. Or at least it was the end of another era. If you wanted portents, what about the grey clouds and the drizzle that plagued the entire afternoon and evening? The gig was good. And the reaction to one of the new songs, *Country House*, was so overwhelming that the band ditched all previous plans and made it their next single. But the storm clouds were there all right.

I suppose that, given our history and my geographical bias, I'd always end up on Blur's side if there was a war between them and Oasis. But even so, in the week they went head to head in a race for the number one slot, I bought a copy of each of their singles (the live CD of *Country House* and a seven-inch of *Roll With It*) in an effort to remain vaguely impartial. The tabloid press were finding it hard to pick a side too. There were stories every day in the *Sun* and the *Mirror* and the rest of the national papers leapt on the story as well. We'd seen the press put pop on the front page before (everything from the *Daily Star* calling for Snoop Doggy Dogg to be thrown out of the country to 'The Secret Lives of Socialist Pop Band The Housemartins'). But there had been nothing as lasting and concerted as this since punk or maybe acid house. Britpop was part of the nation's fabric now.

As the sales figures started to filter through with two days to go, no-one wanted to tempt fate. But the Blur camp organized a 'celebration' party anyway at the fashionable Soho House in London's West End, so I guess they must have been reasonably confident. I was sent an invite, and turned up on the Sunday evening, a couple of hours after they'd officially been announced as the new number one. The atmosphere was strange. All the faces were there (Andy Ross and Miles, his A&R man at Food, the Parlophone press office, some regulars from the Good Mixer and assorted friends). But it was hard to work out exactly what we were all celebrating. Was it Blur at number one, or was it the fact that, temporarily, Oasis were number two?

Don't get me wrong. It was a nice do, and there were smiles all round, but if anything the conflict with Oasis had distracted people from the better story – which was Blur themselves. The band who were all over two years previously. At number one. Blimey.

The slightly strained atmosphere continued as Graham Coxon got pissed and then tried climbing out of the second-storey window of the bar. As someone grabbed his legs and hauled him back in (Graham trying to wriggle free the whole time), I thought that it was a good time to leave. Being a Libra, I'm not very good with conflict.

I'm aware that at stages in this book, I'm probably telling you what you already know. For instance, the post *Country House* history of Blur and Oasis has been pretty well documented. Damon gave a rather cocky interview to *Q* magazine about the relative merits and popularity of the two groups. But within a year he was eating his words as Oasis stole the show in the UK – and then found further success in the States. To coin the obvious phrase, Blur had won the battle, but it was Oasis who were winning the war.

And again, I saw a comparison between Blur and myself. Apart from the post-number one crowing, it felt for much of this period as if Blur had been drawn into a competition they didn't particularly want or need. I think it gave them a sort of personality crisis.

They began to lose track of what the band stood for. Was it a type of music, or was it how many gold discs they had compared to the boys up north? At Radio 1, I found myself slipping into the same frame of mind. The obvious comparison would be to cast Jo Whiley as Oasis and me as Blur. But that doesn't work. Jo was doing very well, but I wasn't doing anything – apart from becoming caught up in a rat-race notion that if every other Radio 1 DJ was on TV, then I should be too. And if other presenters were being offered daytime stand-ins, then why wasn't I? It was a ridiculous mindset: a) I didn't want to be on TV, and b) the idea that Radio 1 would entertain the thought of having me as a daytime presenter seemed ludicrous. But, without realizing it, I'd become unhealthily competitive (and a pain in the arse to boot).

And I don't know exactly when or why it all changed. But sometime, just as Blur stopped worrying about being the biggest band in Britain and went back to making records they enjoyed, I stopped arguing over how many times our show was trailed on air and went back to being a bloke who loves playing records for a living. All the clutter went in the bin.

Meanwhile, extricated from the war with Oasis, Blur found a new freedom which resulted first in *Blur* and then *13*. And ironically, as they stopped trying so hard to make hit records, they came up with one of their most successful tunes ever – *Song 2*. I saw them on tour at Christmas 1999 in Brighton (couldn't bear the thought of going and sitting at Wembley), when they played all their singles in order. And nearly every track has a memory attached to it now. No wonder Damon has started writing movie soundtracks – because inadvertently he's been writing one for me for over 10 years.

Mind you, I still had to go to the bar during *There's No Other Way*.

• 11
HARD TIMES

Chronologically, this is a difficult part of the story to fit in, but in October 1992 my career at the *NME* ended as quickly and almost as ridiculously as it had started. Our leader and spiritual mentor Danny Kelly announced his imminent departure to join *Q* magazine, and the paper duly advertised for a new Editor.

It's hard to sum up what happened next. I think the paper's publishers IPC knew who they wanted as their next Editor. But they interviewed some of the staff anyway. After a fortnight without hearing anything, the rumour mill went into overdrive. The new Editor was coming from our sworn rivals the *Melody Maker*! There were big changes afoot.

To be honest, I couldn't see myself working with the new boss because we were completely at odds over music. But then again I couldn't see where I was going at *NME* at all (having now been turned down for jobs as both Editor and Deputy Editor). There was talk at the time that the paper wanted to enlarge its news coverage at the expense of featuring new bands. And if that was the case, what was the point of being there? I took the only sensible route out of the situation. I went totally off the rails.

On the day the news broke, Alan Lewis spent the morning informing staff that the new Editor would be officially announced at midday. In what can only be described as a fit of pique I left his office, wrote my letter of resignation and went to the pub. At the high noon meeting, various members of staff expressed their dismay at the decision. And then, as we filed out, I handed in my notice to quit. Bless her, just a step behind me, equally piqued, was Mary Anne Hobbs handing in her resignation as well.

It cut me up at the time. And there were days when I was working out my notice when I worried if I was doing the right thing. But in the end, leaving *NME* was the best move I'd made since joining it. I'd done my stint. It was good fun and it made me happy and insanely angry all at the same time. But it was good to get out. I was £500 overdrawn and I didn't know what I was going to do next. But hey. Five hundred quid for five years of free records and a job that didn't start till 10.30 in the morning. That's not bad value.

In the uneasy weeks that formed my period of notice, I had a couple of final features to write. Amazingly, having missed out on various jaunts to the States over the past year, I was sent there twice in the space of a fortnight. The first was to interview Therapy? for their debut cover in New York – a trip that coincided with my birthday. I flew out with their press officer Andy and photographer Kevin Cummins and we met the band on the first night in some Irish bar near Greenwich Village.

Meeting bands you're going to interview for the first time is strange. There's usually a period of polite conversation as you form your initial impressions of each other. Then generally the atmosphere becomes more relaxed (unless you've really messed up or dropped a huge clanger, in which case you can feel the air chilling around you).

Therapy? turned out to be one of the nicest bunches of blokes I'd met in ages. We worked out that because of the time difference it was already my birthday in England, so they bought a huge round of drinks and we started celebrating. It was a relief to be away from London. An hour into the first session, they introduced me to their latest favourite pub challenge, Whose Round Is it Anyway? Contestants, i.e. whoever was buying the drinks, had to walk to and from the bar in the style of a chosen celebrity or pop star. Bassist Michael unluckily got Gary Numan.

If I was going to miss anything about the *NME*, it wasn't going to be raging debates over the future of pop or finishing another singles page at 3 a.m., or even the free tickets to gigs. What I was going to miss was watching the bassist of Ireland's premier new rock trio jerkily making his way back to our table impersonating a robot.

I went on tour again after I left *NME*, with the band Kingmaker. It's bit strange now, because they've had a terrible press in recent years, but I was a staunch supporter of theirs at the paper. I know some journalists rewrite their histories occasionally to make out that they only ever liked the really cool bands of the time. But, to be honest, I can't be arsed. It must hurt trying to be cool all the time – and anyway, I've liked so many groups that have been slated by my peers that it's probably an impossible task. In any case, I'm not entirely sure why they became such whipping boys in the mid-90s – but if you go back and listen to some of their stuff, it still rocks. OK, one or two of the more lyrical images were a little naive, maybe even misguided, but this was a young band who captured a lot of the feelings and contradictions of teenagers stuck in a rut with not much to look forward to. (Maybe it was the Colne Engaine punk rocker in me who identified with their dissatisfaction and claustrophobia?)

I'd first met the band properly around the time of their debut album, *Eat Yourself Whole* (an angry and angsty album that had some soaring moments on it). After writing a feature on them I ended up going to see 18 of the dates on their first massive 50-date toilet-circuit tour. And after that, their singer Loz Hardy and I used to meet up occasionally to drink and swap tapes (Loz's were always full of The Clash and Bob Dylan, mine were lessons in art-punk, like early Ultravox and Wire).

This latest tour was to promote their single *Armchair Anarchist*, the one Radio 1 wouldn't play because of its references to bombing. (Note: I'm not sure if anyone's noticed yet, but I play it once every year on the night of a certain awards ceremony, solely for the lines: 'Just the other morning, I was planning a bombing/Firstly the House of Lords … then on to the BRIT Awards'.)

Not having much money, I persuaded their management to sub me some cash to write a fanzine about the tour that they could send out to their fans. It never got written (though a couple of years later I got asked to write up the story for a book called *Love Is The Drug*). But it was a good tour. The crowds were nuts, and the support band was the then up-and-coming Radiohead. They kept themselves to themselves much of the time, although both groups watched each other at soundcheck, and one night myself and Kingmaker bassist Miles Howell stayed up in the bar of a flowery B&B near Stoke with a few of the Radiohead boys. Nice chaps. And they know a thing or two about fine wine as well.

But really all I was doing was trying to put off the inevitable return to the real world, and worrying about getting a job (the offers hadn't exactly started flooding in since the announcement of my departure from *NME*). Of all places, the *Anarchist* tour wound up in Colchester. Back where I started. From there I cadged a lift back to London in the crew van, and then spent the following two weeks trying to pursue a career as a professional gambler. I made about £7. And the Abbey National started getting shirty about my unpaid mortgage.

• 12
WAKING UP

If I hadn't got any cash out of the *NME*, at least I left laden down with some good stories. This one was told to me by a fellow journalist, and I swear it's true because he later wrote it up for the paper. (I just learnt it off by heart.)

So there's these two cultural scientists and they want to find out more about our basic attitudes to consumerism. Is there something in the human psyche that draws us to certain designs or materials? To do this, they take loan of a monkey, and the monkey sits on a stool while they hand it various objects.

The monkey's reactions, they argue, will tell us a lot about our gut instincts.

Halfway through the experiment they hand it a CD. Not the case, just the CD. The monkey looks at its reflection, looks bored and then throws it on the floor. Then they gave it a seven-inch single.

The monkey got a hard-on.

I'm not sure what this says about the human race (although I am surprised that somebody like Epic or EMI haven't attempted to recreate the experiment by playing demos of new bands to monkeys to judge their hit potential. 'If it jigs, sign it. If it scratches its bottom, pass!'). But I've ended up using this story to try to win all types of arguments – especially when I was trying to help run a record label of my own. In fact it'd probably be easier to explain the monkey story than it is to explain how a tiny indie label ended up having a number one album and putting Annie Lennox's nose out of joint in the process. But this is roughly how it happened.

During my days at *NME* I met and got to know a Liverpudlian PR man called Alan James. James looked after a series of struggling indie bands in his early days, and I suspect I was one of the few people who would take his calls. In return he was the only PR man who ever sent me records, so it was a match made in heaven.

What finally gave Alan cult status in the industry was not his growing roster of bands or his ability to squeeze even the worst of them into the pages of the press. It was his unfathomable vocabulary and phraseology. For instance, if Alan thought somebody was a bit flaky, then this person became 'a man of egg'. If they were guilty of more serious crimes against pop they were 'a man of ham'. As we started questioning his sanity even further, James's vocal dexterity became more and more absurd.

One day I answered the phone on the Live Desk and all I heard from the other end was: 'It's like chicken and cheese pies with no cheese in.' Say it in a thinly worn Scouse accent for maximum impact. He has treated us to some amazing comments in his time but this is still my favourite.

This is his description of a band's piss-poor new single: 'It's like a piece of ham sliding down a blue bucket ... but, wait, wait ... the bucket's got holes in.'

He's priceless. Not only did James's roster grow to take in various bigger and more successful acts, but he also began branching into radio plugging. I would like to think that one day he collared Simon Bates in reception and told him that Our Tune was all chicken and cheese pies, but I don't think he ever did.

Back at the *NME* we used to spend a good 30 minutes each week verbalizing our contempt for certain major record labels. I mean, what did they know? Just because they had all the money and all the office space and all the posters up around town, they were still signing groups like An Emotional Fish. Ham. Inevitably we vowed that one day we'd start a label together and show them what for, and inevitably we spent years studiously doing nothing about it. In the end, Deceptive Records happened almost by accident.

In November 1992, having walked out of the *NME*, I found myself back in Harlow, bored and broke. Sitting in the downstairs bar of the town's only venue, The Square, a friend wandered up and said, 'Anthony was looking for you the other day. He's got a tape of his new band he wants you to have.' Big Ant had been a member of, or championed, various squawky lo-fi bands in the area including the ill-fated local heroes Pregnant Neck before he'd gone on to experiment with dance music. Two minutes later, by complete chance, he walked in clutching a demo of his latest outfit, Collapsed Lung.

The Lung demo was a roughshod mix of guitars and hip-hop and tongue-in-cheek lyrics. It was also, I determinedly persuaded myself, fate telling me that I should start a label. Which is how Alan James and I, with former Chrysalis Records A&R man Tony Smith, came to launch Deceptive. The label name was nicked from the flexi-disc I'd released with *A Pack Of Lies*; the money, meanwhile, came from Tony and Alan's bank accounts.

Deceptive was set up for roughly £4000 and given a room above Alan James's PR office in a rickety building near the Elephant & Castle. The front door always used to stick and then you had to climb a couple of flights of stairs that were perennially littered with boxes left by the T-shirt company that James shared the first floor with. It became more treacherous by the week.

When Deceptive released its first single, the one-room office consisted of a chair, two phones, a desk and an old filing cabinet. When people wanted to come round for meetings Tony used to say, in a deadpan voice, 'Four o'clock's fine, but can you bring your own chair?' We often used to hold meetings at the Heavy Metal pub on the corner (so named because it used to run a weekly Rock Nite and because the jukebox would – apparently of its own accord – suddenly burst into action every half hour with some hideous Guns'n'Roses epic. You could set your watch by that jukebox).

The first release was Collapsed Lung's debut single *Thundersley Invacar*, which sold out of its initial 3000 pressing and was played on Jakki Brambles's lunchtime show on Radio 1. It got to something like 108 in the chart. By this point, I'd started work at *Select* magazine and had to juggle phone calls from penniless freelancers with desperate messages about sleeve artwork and specifications (the designer John Anonymous would phone and talk about cromalins while I listened and got a headache).

It was via *Select*, however, that I met Elastica. Stuart Maconie had been to interview some new band or other which featured Damon Albarn's girlfriend, and she'd asked Stuart to see if Deceptive might be interested in meeting up and talking about a single. I had no idea who they were, but within two weeks it seemed that everyone was raving about them. I got hold of their demo and when I heard *Vaseline* I thought, 'It's Debbie Harry.'

Now if you're anything like me, that's a good sign. Before they reformed there was a generation of boys who fell for Blondie, as much for the black and white pin-ups of Harry herself as the breathless bits of pop they used to release. Singer and Blur girlfriend Justine Frischmann didn't look anything like Harry, but when the feature pictures arrived in the *Select* office, the band looked as cool as hell. They might have shopped from a similar catalogue to the one Blur used for *Modern Life Is Rubbish*, but they looked like the Bash Street Kids come to terrorize the chart. Justine had a pair of cherry red DMs as well, which were the sexiest things I'd ever seen. Girls. Boots. Tunes. Drummer who used to be in Spitfire. It's not a concept you come across every day.

Having missed their two low-key gigs outside London, my first chance to see them was at the Falcon in Camden. Although when I say 'see them', I mean see some of them. The back room was so full that I got wedged by the PA and consequently spent the gig going deaf in one ear, while craning my neck to catch sight of anything that moved. I saw Justine and Annie and I think I caught a glimpse of Donna's guitar, but that was it.

I met Justine for the first time one afternoon in the West End pub The Spice of Life, just off Cambridge Circus. I have no idea why we picked this place. Justine claims it was my idea, but quite how taking her to a pub full of tourists and businessmen and frazzled West End shoppers was going to endear me to the new Debbie Harry, I really don't know. What was I thinking of?

Anyway, it transpired that various labels had already expressed an interest in Elastica, but Justine was wary of signing to a major because of the control they could exert over the band. As selling points go, I didn't have much to retaliate with (I was wondering how to break it to her that Deceptive was one chair and two phones). Instead I waffled on about formatting being the work of the devil and wanting to make a seven-inch single that had all the excitement of *Teenage Kicks*.

And then I did the monkey story.

I'm not sure if it was the monkey story that did the trick, but Justine organized a meeting with the rest of the group. In the meantime, having demoed material for Mike Smith, the A&R man at EMI Publishing, they finally signed a publishing deal with him in the middle of August. The night started with a meal in the West End, but because the band didn't want to sign on Friday the 13th they dragged Smith up to Primrose Hill, where they finally put their names on the contract at one minute past midnight. Smith later told me he thought it was all an elaborate hoax, and that come midnight, having got him faintly tipsy, they were simply going to roll him down the hill.

We regrouped in the Good Mixer in Camden and shook hands on a two-single Deceptive deal on 17 August. The first single was going to be *Line Up*. A couple of days later it was going to be *Vaseline*. In the end it was *Stutter* (which I thought was a nice balance between the two), and anyway I think we were all growing bored of the daily discussions over what the single would be. We wanted to get onto the exciting second level of artwork and release dates.

I couldn't get the *Teenage Kicks* spiel out of my head. It had to be a sexy seven-inch and it had to be pressed really loud, and it had to have something neat inscribed in the run-out groove. Creation had just released a Sugar single in a brown card sleeve which looked good, so I nicked that idea and told Justine we should have an illustrated colour label, because that's what The Clash did with *White Man In Hammersmith Palais*. Originally the centre of the record was going to feature a picture of a topless page-three model from a set of *Sun* playing cards Justine owned. But nobody could quite ascertain whether the *Sun* would sue us or not – so we opted for Plan B, an illustration of drummer Justin. The follow-ups would feature the rest of the band.

The decision to release the first record on seven-inch only wasn't purely a romantic nod to the late 70s which we all had an affection for (me for my early teens, them for their musical influences). As part of our attempts to raise Deceptive's profile, I'd been invited out by a sales rep from the distribution company who had taken me on a tour of shops around Derby and Nottingham. One of them in particular was fascinating. It was a dance shop in Derby which stocked all the latest house and hip-hop, but also, in a corner, had a rack of independent seven-inches. 'We don't touch indie CDs,' the guy behind the counter explained, 'but we get quite a few customers flicking through those.'

We also made the decision to press just 1000 copies, because at the time Elastica were still just a buzz-name on the London circuit and none of us wanted loads of unsold records in bargain bins. That has to be the most deflating experience for a group, doesn't it? You spend months writing and recording and you end up in Woolworths at 50p. And no matter how much your manager or your friends console you with stories about how record shops overstock on material, that feeling of being unwanted and marked down in price remains. I once read a story about a brilliant little Leeds band called Girls At Our Best who split up because they couldn't cope with seeing their LP remaindered in their local shop.

In the end 1500 copies were made (though as the favourable reviews started to flood in that wasn't nearly enough to cater for the demand). Even the band started phoning up, complaining that their mates in Brighton or Newport or Outer Mongolia couldn't get a copy. But by this time, Elastica were big news. There were lots of people who wanted a Debbie Harry who didn't look like Debbie Harry, and there were lots of people who liked the short, sharp pop stabs that were Elastica's forte.

Line Up coupled with *Vaseline* followed on the second single (with the addition of *Rockunroll* and *Annie* on the CD). Now I'm thoroughly biased here, and it was my label and everything and I love Elastica and all that … but what a terrific record. All critical faculties fail me. *Line Up* was never one of my favourites but I still play the other three all the time at home. To celebrate the release of the single they embarked on their first headlining tour and I went up to see them at the Leeds Duchess on the Saturday after it hit the shops.

There was much discussion on the night over where the record might end up in the chart. Hopefully in the Top 40, maybe even just inside the Top 30. I got the train back to London the next day and listened on my Walkman to Mark Goodier presenting the rundown. By 29 I was beginning to fidget. He kept playing records and none of them were by Elastica. By the time he introduced number 24 I was convinced that *Line Up* had charted at 41 and that Deceptive was chicken and cheese pies with no cheese in.

Then, honestly, this happened.

Goodier: 'And at number 20 it's another new entry from one of the most hotly tipped new bands in the countrsshshshshshshshshshshshsh-shshshshshshshshs.'

We were in the tunnel just outside Kings Cross. Arrghhh. Is it us? Is it us? Can't anyone make this sodding train go any quicker?

Eventually the train shunted itself out of the tunnel, and there was *Line Up*, the last 20 seconds of it. And the cheese pies were in the microwave and Elastica were on *Top of the Pops*.

They were very nervous. The entire 'staff' of Deceptive turned up in their dressing room to give them moral support, but I think we might just have made things worse (three expectant fathers pacing up and down in your dressing room and biting their nails probably isn't what you need just before your biggest TV appearance to date). Justine has also never forgiven me for my pre-show pep talk.

'When the camera gets anywhere near you,' I said, 'use your eyes. You've got really good eyes.' If you ever get a chance to see a video of the performance, note how Justine stares maniacally into the camera at every close-up. She looks like she's trying to force her eyeballs out of her sockets. It wasn't quite the alluring, sultry effect I was thinking of.

Despite this, the dates sold out and the press ran front covers and after tedious weeks of arguing over remixes and producers, the album was finished. It was released on 13 March. The same week as the latest Annie Lennox album. Lennox was tipped by just about everyone to top the chart, which wasn't surprising, because she was famous and had the might of RCA behind her. Elastica had three berks, two phones and still only one chair.

But Elastica had everything else on their side. They looked even more like a band now than in the original knockabout gang shots that had first turned up at *Select*. I've still got a picture of them from around the release of the album that's up in my front room. There's the four of them, all dressed in black, and I can't describe how it makes me feel, or what's so great about them and this picture. It just feels RIGHT. Cool isn't quite the word. Nor's sexy. But they have the look of a classic rock'n'roll group. The sort of group who thinks it's 'us against the world'.

I think that's why the pairing of Elastica and Deceptive worked, particularly in the week the album came out. It really did feel like us against the establishment. What was most touching, though, were the calls that came in during the week from people who'd been out to buy the record and wanted to tell the band and label how great they thought it was. I mean, I couldn't even bear to set foot in the office. It was too nerve-wracking. Tony was running the show virtually single-handed, although I knew about some of the nightmares he was having (is there enough stock in the shops? Will the massed ranks of the Annie army descend on Our Price on Saturday and pip Elastica at the post?).

The chart comes through to labels and distributors on a Sunday afternoon. In my more disturbed moments I'd like to change this system and make it more like the announcement of a general election result. Get the top five bands together on a stage and read out their sales figures to the cheers and derision of an invited audience of fans. Believe me, it would be the biggest draw since we put people in the stocks for blowing their nose in a funny way.

But in reality we all waited at home for the phone call (after all, there was no way I was going to risk being on public transport this time). Tony phoned around 4 p.m.

'WE'RE NUMBER ONE! WE'VE BLOODY DONE IT! IT'S NUMBER ONE!'

Not only was it number one, it was the fastest selling debut album in history (an honour later wrestled away from Elastica by the first Oasis album). But how do you follow that? I think we all had a few problems coming to terms with Elastica's success. The band was so in demand that they were constantly touring or wrapped up in promotional work. Deceptive had to go through all the tricky decisions of picking new office furniture (a second chair and a photocopier).

There were other difficulties too. By the time the Elastica album went to number one I'd joined Radio 1, and it's a grey area being a DJ and being involved with a record company at the same time. But the breaking point came when head of Radio 1 Trevor Dann was sent two anonymous letters accusing me of bias, and then the *NME* News Desk pitched in with claims that I was raking off money from Elastica every time I played them on the radio. This argument doesn't work because the cash bands get from radio play goes through their publishing company – in Elastica's case EMI, not Deceptive – so I wasn't making a penny from the airtime. To be honest, I wasn't making a penny out of the label either, but it became apparent that however much I told people this, there would always be someone who didn't believe me. After a week of mooching around and, I hate to admit it, feeling unjustly put upon, we got an accountant to draw up some paperwork and I let my share in the company move on for the princely sum of £2.30.

It wasn't just an arbitrary figure. It was the price of a pint of cider in the pub where we concluded the deal. Not exactly Alan McGee stuff, is it? I carried on as a kind of unpaid A&R consultant, bringing in Snuff, Scarfo and the brilliant but underrated Earl Brutus (whose album *Your Majesty We Are Here* is, I think, one of the best ever records on the label). But in the end there just weren't enough hours in the day to do everything. And besides, you can't skimp on the day job.

• 13
EVERYTHING FLOWS

To explain how I got a job at Radio 1, you have to spin back in time a few years. During my early twenties, I'd spent most of my time pursuing some kind of writing career and had had no time for anything as fanciful as DJ ambitions.

So by 1990 my efforts at becoming Somebody Like John Peel hadn't really got very far. My one attempt to break into radio had failed miserably when I was turned down by the local Colchester Hospital station for being too young (although I like to think it was because I was too radical for them and that it was my lack of knowledge about Duane Eddy and my reluctance to go round the wards collecting requests that was really behind their rejection).

In the end, my first steps in radio came without warning. I took a call one day on the *NME* News Desk from a man called Sammy Jacob who ranted at length about how the paper was supposed to be clued-up about indie music, but didn't even know that London had its own indie pirate radio station called Q102. To redress the situation I agreed to meet him outside Manor House tube station the following Saturday and he'd tell me more.

Sammy arrived, cunningly disguised as the sort of man who promoted 70s disco nights. He then proceeded to drive round in circles for 30 minutes (in order to disguise his route to the studio. Apparently blindfolds were out of fashion even then). And then we pulled up and parked – not outside a tower block or lock-up – but in an anonymous-looking street somewhere near Leytonstone High Road.

Inside the terraced house which was (on Saturdays only) Q102's HQ, Sammy explained how he'd started out DJing on the dance pirates and then had a road-to-Damascus conversion into indie music. Thirty minutes later he shunted me on air for an interview, pronounced my name wrong, and when it was all over said he thought I had a good radio voice. A couple of weeks later he had me doing the late breakfast show from 10 a.m. to midday.

It was both good experience and A Good Experience. The only rules were that the DJs had to pay £10 a week to keep the station on air (generally the money went on new aerials which either broke or were stolen by rival pirates) and that you never turned up at the house with a record box. You had to disguise your vinyl in carrier bags, and on no account tell anyone where the station was. Of course the threat of being busted was always there, though Q102 had a novel way of preparing for this possibility. The real owner of the house, a chirpy, no-bullshit fireman, owned two Rottweilers who used to sleep by the front door, just in case the DTI hit squad should turn up one day and break it down. If that happened, added Sammy, DJs were expected to leg it through the back garden and over the wall (presumably while various members of the DTI were chased back down the high street past the kebab shop by the two pro-pirate hounds).

Deciding to adopt a secret identity, I soon changed my on-air name (for security reasons) and adopted an old journalistic pseudonym, inspired by the TV programme *Randall and Hopkirk (Deceased)*. As Andy Hopkirk, I made every mistake that a budding DJ could make: forgetting to close the mic; leaving faders up while I was cueing a track; and, of course, that Peel favourite, playing a record at the wrong speed. But that was nothing in comparison to my near fatal *faux pas*, which was to spill an entire bottle of Lucozade over the mixing desk, putting the station off air for two weeks. Sammy gave me a very hard time over that.

It was a good time for Q102 though. The DJs were mostly drawn from inside the music industry, and so brought with them several upfront promos and new releases – which we mixed in with personal favourites.

I naturally assumed that no one could actually hear us, because we were a pirate station and our transmitter was probably run on steam. But then we started getting letters of support to the PO Box address and when the station broke into promotion, by staging a gig in Highbury, loads of people turned up. The demand for an alternative guitar station was beginning to become apparent. I had my show extended to three hours and life moved on quite happily. We even broadcast one Christmas Day when we counted down a Listeners' Top 60 all time favourites (safe in the knowledge that unless they were on double time the DTI were at home tucking into their turkey).

But the problem was Q102 could only go so far. After a couple of years it had achieved all it could as a pirate station and it finally fell apart after a heated meeting between backers and presenters, held in the front room next to the studio.

However, the foundations that the station had laid didn't go wholly to waste. As Q102 wound up, the campaign for a legal alternative station began, and the London based Xfm was born. Having just got used to not being Someone Like John Peel again, I received a call from Sammy saying we were back on air. Xfm was granted its first RSL (a restricted month-long licence) and I was handed the drivetime slot and the Saturday morning Alternative Chart rundown.

Of the two, the chart was the most exciting programme and the most nerve-wracking. What happened was that the chart itself would be faxed through on a Saturday morning from one of the major Oxford Street shops. We then scanned through it, and if we didn't have some of the records, station all-rounder Frazier had to leg it round the corner to buy them. Sometimes he nearly didn't make it back in time. 'And at number 14 ... I can hear it just coming up the stairs now ... hang on a minute ...'

My break into mainstream radio came in 1991. I'd met a Radio 1 producer at a meeting to choose bands for a co-sponsored series of Radio 1/*NME* gigs in London. The producer let on that the station was planning a new evening show, to be presented by Mark Goodier and produced by some chap they'd recruited from Metro Radio in the north east. 'Maybe you should write in and see if they want any help,' he suggested.

All I can remember is dashing off a letter which explained my role at the *NME* and that I thought I could give them some tips on the bands Radio 1 should be playing (I never was very good at this begging-for-jobs business). A couple of days later the Head of Music Roger Lewis replied and in turn suggested I get in contact with the new man on the block, *Evening Session* producer-to-be Jeff Smith.

It is Smith – alongside Goodier – who did the rest. I took Jeff for a drink one night, ranted and raved about Carter and vowed to keep in touch. Smith, for his part, went off and (together with Goodier) created a show that plugged the gaps between daytime and Peel. It was Peel himself who'd been occupying the evening slot for a time. But when he moved to weekends, the *Evening Session* started in the first week of October 1990.

'When we started, we were asked to do a show which was magazine-y – a lot of topical speech content,' Goodier revealed a year after the show went on air. 'We were supposed to go for lots of meetings to tell them what we were doing and we didn't go to one.'

What they were doing was working on the music content of the new programme. Plus Goodier still had a 'day job', which contributed to the show's perception problem. People were a little suspicious of him.

'Yeah, very much, because of where I'd come from … I used to do the *Weekend Breakfast Show*. But Radio 1 asked me to do this show because they knew I'd done something similar before. I don't blame people for being suspicious. I'd probably be the same myself, but we just got our heads down and did it.

'When we first started I think people just saw this show as the one that had taken over from John Peel, so they expected just someone else playing the same records and we had to … we sat down and thought we want to play bands which aren't getting played anywhere else.

'And we reckoned at the time EMF and Gary Clail weren't. Carter weren't. And that was the area that with a bit of help these bands might break through. Peel's still doing a good job, but his show is uncompromising and I guess our show is the compromise between what your average pop music listener will take and what Peel will do.'

I kept in touch with Jeff, off and on, while I was at *NME*. But even so I was a little surprised when he phoned me at the paper and asked if I wanted to come in and play some records one night. The segment featured four tunes (including tracks by indie hopefuls World Of Twist and Bleach) with myself and Mark discussing the future of pop.

The *Session* itself went from strength to strength. It covered much of the same ground that we did at *NME* and, like the Peel show, featured sessions recorded at the BBC's Maida Vale studios. Among the bands booked by Smith and Goodier were Nirvana in November 1991, Suede early in 1992, a whole string of Teenage Fanclub sets and two previously mentioned Blur sessions, in 1992 and then again in 1993.

By the time I left the *NME* the guest appearance had led to a regular monthly slot reviewing the week's music papers. Then they upped the ante. Mark Goodier was going to be away from the show for four weeks and instead of bringing in another Radio 1 jock to deputize, Jeff and Mark invited four young whippersnappers to take a week each.

The fantastic four were Richard Easter (who worked on the Steve Wright show), Claire Sturgess (one of Simon Bates's backroom staff), Jo Whiley (music researcher for *The Word*) and Steve Lamacq (failed gambler and part-time Reviews Editor at *Select*). All I had to do was record a reasonable demo to convince them that I could string two sentences together and play the right jingle at the right time. It was the scariest 15 minutes of my life. At Q102 the equipment numbered two decks, a cassette player and six faders. The Radio 1 desk, as it is known, had about 100 faders and 60 switches. It was like swapping the control panel of a Mini Cooper for flying Concorde.

Eight minutes into the recording I pressed a start button, and the desk went dead.

Several thoughts flashed through my mind, but 'Oh bugger' was the main one. 'I seem to have broken Radio 1.' In the studio next door Simon Bates, who had been live on air, was rushing around turning pink, while a couple of fraught looking producers gesticulated at the technical staff behind the glass partition. A minute later Bates was in my studio. 'Have you got power in here, love?'

'Sorry. I, erm, well, no, to be honest I think I've …'

Bates tore back out of the studio just as an engineer wandered in through the other door. 'Power failure,' she mumbled. So not my fault then, I sighed inside. 'You might as well go home,' she added, plodding back to the corridor.

So that was that.

They gave me the first of the four guest week deps, and on the Monday Jeff talked me through the running order. To make sure I didn't cock it up too badly, the plan was to pre-record the first 12 minutes of the first show. If nothing else, at least the start of the programme would be OK.

Unfortunately, 10 minutes before going on air, the all-powerful Controller of Radio 1, Johnny Beerling, arrived in the studio to say hello and wish me luck. 'It's part of our job to encourage and nurture new talent,' he went on, as the minutes ticked away. Jeff was about to ditch the tape – but Beerling departed with two minutes to spare.

After those initial weeks, R1 employed Claire Sturgess to present a rock show. A few weeks later Jo and I were invited back for a fortnight each. Then they teamed us up together for a further nine-week stint. By this point, Beerling had departed and a new Controller, Matthew Bannister, had arrived as the network's boss. It was soon clear that he was ready to ring the changes and, three years into the new decade, was about to start dragging Radio 1 – belatedly – into the 90s.

As the old school DJs either resigned or were released, the speculation about a new daytime line-up increased. The tabloids were tipping Steve Wright for the *Breakfast Show* and, just to make Jo and me feel a little more insecure, had Nicky Campbell down to take over the evening slot. With three weeks of our dep left, we got the call: could we go and meet Matthew.

Jo and I have talked about this since, but the way I remember it, Matthew talked a little about his plans to improve the station, while we sat like schoolchildren in the headmaster's office, averting our gaze and staring at our DMs. 'So,' Matthew continued. 'I'd just like to say thanks very much for everything you've done …'

This was it, the SACK! A brilliant career as Somebody Like John Peel cut short, even before it had started.

'… and we'd like you to carry on, if that's all right with you.'

HOLY HELLFIRE. DID HE JUST SAY WHAT I THOUGHT HE SAID?

'If you'd like to go and see Andy Parfitt, he'll talk through the details of your contract.'

There was another bit about keeping the news secret, and then we backed out of the room, issuing a stream of thank yous. Honestly, if we'd had caps to doff, we'd have been doffing for Britain. I'm surprised I didn't bow and call Matthew 'Your Majesty'. We made it to the lift before exploding and hugging each other.

It's odd looking back at this now. Matthew took quite a risk with us. I mean, we'd both had some radio experience (Jo had had a spell at Radio 5 and there was my pirate show). But it's not as if we were going to win him any instant respect. He could have gone for an easier, more reliable bet. One of the favourites maybe, instead of an each-way punt.

Because (I'll own up) when Jo Whiley and I first broadcast the *Evening Session* together we'd met twice, possibly three times – and had just one hour's rehearsal.

Actually that's not exactly true. We did have an hour's rehearsal time booked in a studio. But how do you rehearse a radio programme? I mean, we gave it a go. We played a few records and made up a few links, and then after 20 minutes we realized it wasn't working, so we gave up and went for a coffee.

Our two main weapons during our nine-week trial period were, put simply, fear and adrenalin. But mostly FEAR. We had this 'what if?' philosophy at the time. What if I press the wrong button? What if I forget what I'm saying halfway through a link? What if I say something so utterly stupid that I am booed out of the building?

The fear carried us through, and when the fear and adrenalin weren't enough we employed the ancient skills of busking and winging it. Jeff Smith, our first producer, helped. Having been there at the start of the *Sesh*, he knew how he wanted the programme to sound (pacy, informative, friendly, credible) and how to make it appear deceptively slick. The fact that after Mark Goodier's departure the show was now being presented by these two herberts, who had nothing more than nerves and enthusiasm on their side, didn't deter him at all. We were like kids at his DJ school.

'And today, class, here's how to segue a record properly.'

Much of the way the *Session* still works today is based on tips I picked up from Smith in the first two months at Radio 1. But even he couldn't save us from our own lapses of concentration. On our first outside broadcast, seven weeks into the trial run, we did a series of shows from the In The City seminar in Manchester. The mixing desk was set up in a hotel conference suite … and in my defence, the equipment was completely different to what we used back in London. But 20 minutes into the first programme I stopped the CD that was playing on air.

If there is such a thing as a HUGE silence, then there was a huge silence.

Jeff, jumping up from his seat, looked like he was about to be run over by a truck.

Not sure what to do next, I opened the mic and lied for Britain.

'Well, we've got a wiring problem with the studio here, which means one of the CD players has broken down. But never mind. Here's another tune.'

So we got by, and fluffed a few links, and helped disguise each other's moments of panic. As it turned out though, we needn't have worried that much about our early failings. Shortly after we'd been handed the show full-time we received a letter from a listener that said: 'Dear Jo and Steve. Love the show. Particularly the mistakes. They're funny. Do you rehearse them?'

We really couldn't have been in a better place at a better time. Just a couple of months after being employed to host the *Evening Session* full-time, we started 1994 with the debut session from a band just signed to Creation records called ... Oasis. For the second time in my life I'd accidentally become caught up in The Bigger Scheme Of Things: a revolution in both music and media.

Pop was changing, Radio 1 was changing. The playlist was also starting to improve, along with the emergence of Britpop and club anthems both in and outside the chart. It was hard even to identify the place from a year earlier when I'd first appeared on the *Evening Session*.

Not only did I catch a whiff of DLT's aftershave on my first visit, but while I was sitting in reception, waiting to be allowed up to the studio, the familiar sight of Simon Bates hove into view through the front door. Bates went up to reception and, proffering a carrier bag, said to the man behind the desk: 'All right if I leave this here with you? I'll pick it up in the morning. I'm always first in.'

Unfortunately the security man must have been new, or short-sighted. Because, as Bates dropped the bag and turned on his heels, he called after him: 'Wait a minute, please. What's your name?'

Bates: 'I'm BATES!'

Security man: 'And your first name?'

All the DJs who were still there when Jo and I arrived scared me witless. Except Steve Wright, who offered me a cigarillo once, and Simon Mayo, who seemed like a nice chap. And there was Goodier, of course, whom we knew. But it took me months to get up the bottle to speak to Peel.

I can't pretend we weren't still insecure about our position on the station either (after all, we'd only been offered a year long contract, and then, as far I could see, in my darker moments, it was straight back out on the street). But for some reason, it felt like we were, if not at the centre of something pretty radical, then at least close by.

b side

Annoying things bands do:

- They release the wrong singles from albums
- They 'mature'
- They split up just before you're about to see them play live
- They split up just after you've bought the album and the T-shirt
- They never play your favourite B-side or bonus track live (and if they do, they announce that 'this is the last time we're ever doing this one')
- They go through pointless image changes
- They turn around and tell you that their last album is rubbish – having spent the previous three years telling you how great it is
- Your favourite member of the band quits
- They get pictured at uncool parties
- They disappear for 18 months to write and record, just when you need them most
- They moan about money
- They tour with all the wrong bands
- They cover rock classics (badly)
- They dream up endless new ways to hurt and humiliate you.

How do they manage to do all this? And more to the point, why do we let them get away with it? I've got two explanations for this. One is that, as pop fans, we suffer from misplaced loyalty. The second is that the older and apparently wiser folk among us have simply become resigned to the fact that bands cock it up. However great they seem when they start, and however much they appear to say about your life – and wrap you up warm against the cruel outside world – they will, with a sad and stunning inevitability, let you down in the end.

My problem is that I still fall for it. I know bands are fallible but I still pray for a group (or a DJ, or a musical scene) that is superhuman and untouchable.

Mind you, I'm not as bad as I used to be. I've progressed past the stage when I carried on buying singles by bands long after I knew they'd lost the plot – why else are there so many unplayed and unplayable Stranglers singles lurking in a box under the bed? I really don't know what I was thinking of. Did I expect them to repay my faith by suddenly doing a career U-turn and returning to their old selves? Or was I simply in a state of denial?

There are two problems when bands go bad. Not only do you have to admit it to yourself … you then have to decide whether to go public and admit it to other people. Friends, enemies even. Non-believers. Oh God, the shame. It's easy to get angry or upset with a record by a band you don't care that much about (in fact it's quite therapeutic). But getting angry and upset with your favourite band is completely different. They have let you down and thrown you to the lions.

HOW COULD THEY DO THIS TO ME?

It's a shocking state of affairs but it took me until my 20s to have the strength to start admitting that groups I liked could get it wrong. I'm not sure if there was one group who forced this admission out of me, but it's more likely it was a gradual process (like slowly realizing that your suspicions about the existence of Father Christmas had been true all along).

No, I go through life an optimistic pessimist. My latest band of the moment will evolve into the best group in the world. And if they don't, well, I'll deal with it. I have armed myself with excuses now as to why bands go wrong (bad management, bad record label, bad timing, it's nearly always someone else's fault). So that's OK. We won't get fooled again.

But the scars are still there. And none of them are deeper than when bands I've fallen in love with have gone and split up. I remember the first time it happened. Graham Diss told me at school one day that The Lurkers were no more. Now, the news wasn't that much of a shock. There'd been no sign of the band for months and their last single *New Guitar In Town* had peaked at number 72 in the chart. So it wasn't such a big surprise. I think what hurt was that they hadn't had the decency to tell me. They told Graham Diss – and he wasn't even a proper Lurkers fan. He'd just written a crafty letter to their label Beggars Banquet asking for news and freebies and they'd sent him a letter saying, 'The Lurkers are no more, but here are some badges to make up for it.' Badges!

And there was I, a fully paid-up member of the Lurkers Flan Cub – their little joke (cringe) – and I didn't know. This was as bad as finding your girlfriend in the arms of another. Not only had The Lurkers, the object of my infatuation, split up, but they'd been unfaithful in the process. I went all trembly at the knees.

And yet, when they came crawling back, reforming first in 1980 and then 1989, I forgave them both times. The first time they had a new singer; the second time they were led by original bassist Arturo Bassick, who softened the blow by phoning me at the *NME* out of the blue and asking if it was true that I'd been a long-standing fan of the group. Well, yes actually. OK, can you write the sleevenotes for the new live album?

As part of this deal I made them come and meet me in the *NME* pub, much to the amusement of the rest of the staff (the idea that the young gun A&R scout was entertaining a bunch of old punk rockers was all too much for them). But for me, it was like an apology. They turned up and bought drinks and told stories about the old days. They even admitted the second album sounded wet, and quite rightly blamed the American producer for it. And I finally put the incident with the badges behind me.

But this is why I can sympathize with anyone who's gone through a similar experience. For instance, the band Symposium broke up just after I started writing this book, and within days of our announcing the split on air, I was inundated with letters and e-mails from upset fans.

Each one wept with the same phrases: 'How could they do this?' and 'Tell me it's not true'. Well, I'm sorry, it is true. It's harsh and it hurts, but time is a great healer and you'll get over them.

What does all this say about our relationship with bands – particularly in our teens? Does it say that some of us are too obsessed for our own good? Or does it say that bands are rubbish? That's right. Pop groups are rubbish.

For once, take note of the Gallaghers, and please, PLEASE don't put your life in the hands of a rock'n'roll band.

• 14
SHAKERMAKER

On the Thursday night of Radio 1's Sound City festival in Glasgow, Danbert Nobacon of anarcho-punk pop band Chumbawumba walked naked through the bar of the Forte Crest Hotel. I guess it was around 2 a.m. He must have marched past about 50 late-night drinkers (made up of other bands, managers, press officers, roadies and journalists), and do you know what happened? None of them batted an eyelid.

Now I've been thinking about this a lot recently, and the first assumption I come to is that, to put it bluntly, no-one really cared about a naked member of Chumbawumba (possibly because the band had always been considered a little eccentric by the rest of the rock fraternity). But being a theorist, there's an alternative explanation that I'd much rather believe. I'd like to think that this was the week that rock music was about to change for ever and that the man to change it wasn't going to be Danbert Nobacon.

One group who had already set the wheels of change turning had already been and gone – in fact, they'd left Glasgow a few hours earlier. The other man responsible for changing the course of rock music was thousands of miles away in America. Together, however, they were the ones about to make the week's headlines. Enter Oasis, exit Nirvana. Apologies to Danbert.

It was at the small but famous Glasgow haunt King Tut's, situated just around the corner from the Forte Crest, that Creation records boss Alan McGee saw the nascent Oasis for the first time, supporting future labelmates 18 Wheeler. And it was back to Glasgow that the band came for their first live appearance on Radio 1 and their first major interview for *NME*.

This was the week when everything fell into place for Oasis; when you knew that they were really going places. I'm sure, in their own heads they were practically superstars already, but if the rest of the media needed any convincing then here was the proof. One guerrilla raid on

Glasgow, one gig and one amazing interview in the course of a few hours set them up for the rest of 1994. Their art of timing was immaculate.

Having been serviced with a single-track promo of *Columbia* at Radio 1, the new *Session* producer Christine Boar leapt on the 12-inch and booked a session by the band at our Maida Vale studios. It was broadcast in the first week of January 1994 – that key time when pundits and fans alike are looking for new bands to champion for the year ahead. In fact, not only did the session run, but *Columbia* made the R1 playlist, guaranteeing it coverage throughout the day.

It didn't take a massive leap of faith to follow up the station's support by booking them for Sound City, Radio 1's annual live music festival. Sound City has evolved a good deal over the years, but in 1994 it was still in its infancy. Previous Sound City festivals in Norwich and Sheffield had featured some bizarre and eclectic choices of bands. And 1994 wasn't much different (M People, the Inspiral Carpets, Therapy?, Urban Species).

For Jo and me, Sound City was a completely new challenge. Having started to cope with the idea of broadcasting on national radio, we were now faced with the prospect of introducing bands on stage, live on air. Now, this may not seem like the most frightening prospect in the world – and I'd certainly rather compère a gig than sit in a dentist's chair for an hour – but it's not that easy either. You have a producer talking to you through an ear-piece; you have a crowd in front of you; and you have the devil on your shoulder trying to make you slip up and say the F-word.

On top of that, you are among people who believe that if you're not in the band, then what are you doing on stage? We've all seen roadies who love running on to the stage and finding problems to deal with (the drum mic is an inch too far to the left or there's a speck of water by the singer's foot which needs mopping up in case they slip on it). That's OK. I can forgive them. It's sad, but it's their problem. But anyone else is just in the way.

And this time it was me. If you've ever been to a Radio 1 live event, you might notice that I try to get on and off the stage as quickly as possible. Sorry, don't mean to be rude, but I don't want to outstay my welcome. In Glasgow, there was a delay before the Inspiral Carpets came on and I had to hang around as people threw empty cigarette packets at me. Inspirals keyboard player Clint Boot very kindly defused the situation by starting up a chant of 'You thin bastard! You thin bastard!' That did the trick.

I was incredibly lucky though, because I had some friendly faces from the *NME* hanging out in Glasgow through the week. And that helped with the nerves. Williams was there, photographer Roger Sargeant, Keith Cameron and John Harris, the man with the plan. He was there to interview Oasis.

NME had first interviewed them just a few weeks earlier, for the paper's On section, but in the same way that the Mondays had made the press an occupied zone in 1989, Oasis were already a band who couldn't keep out of the headlines. In between the last interview and this one they'd played an astonishing gig at the tiny Water Rats venue in London. And they'd been refused entry to Holland because of their drunken behaviour on the cross-channel ferry.

It was this incident that had created a rift between the Gallagher brothers, exposed to great effect by the *NME* piece. It was such a charged confrontation that highlights even turned up later on a single called *Wibbling Rivalry*. On it you hear the tension twixt the brothers with Harris in the middle refereeing. Every time he thinks he's got them to return to their corners, they're at each other's throats again.

It was riveting.

Oasis announced their overdue arrival in the same week that Nirvana's Kurt Cobain made his tragic exit. The morning after Oasis's radio appearance and the Nobacon No Clothes incident, news began filtering through from the States that Cobain had committed suicide at his home in Seattle. To all intents and purposes, the grunge movement as an energetic, creative force died with him.

The problem with bands like Nirvana is that they bring with them a handful of groups who all sell a few records, but are, in all honesty, worthy runners up. They are good team players but they're not captains. They're not big or strong enough to shoulder a movement, at least not without the movement reinventing itself (grunge, having licked its wounds, has made something of a comeback with the Smashing Pumpkins, not to mention the Foo Fighters. Mind you, it was Foos leader and former Nirvana drummer Dave Grohl who announced at a gig last year that 'grunge can never die, because grunge was never born').

Cobain's suicide sent a shiver through the industry. We knew all the stories. Kurt and drugs, the tough love therapy, the cancelled gigs, his unhappiness with the rock star status he'd acquired. But we had never imagined life without him.

As people gathered in the foyer of the hotel, ready to leave for home, the news started to spread around the room (late risers had seen it on TV or heard the first reports on the radio). Everyone looked stunned. Simply unable to cope with the bad news and a hangover at the same time.

As it did sink in, the full impact of Cobain's death started to hit home. There were the vigils in Seattle, the conspiracy theories – and his friends back in London, including Anton his PR, who were too cut up to even talk.

Kurt had gone, but what the hell happened now? However much he had tried not to be the voice of a generation, it was his human and fragile side – his anti-star role – which had made people believe in him all the more. No-one else could capture that. I don't think we even wanted anyone to try. He left a gap that nobody could adequately fill. And if no-one could replace him, then thanks a lot, but we'd prefer to remember Nirvana and grunge as they were, rather than what it would be like populated by understudies.

Our American infatuation had gone into decline and then ended in the saddest way imaginable, and we'd need some time to grieve before going back there again. Instead, people started looking the other way. To a band whose songwriter claimed that *Nevermind* and *Never Mind The Bollocks* were two of the greatest rock albums ever made – but who could also provide a link to the Roses and The Beatles.

After all that American angst, it was time for some British rock'n'roll.

• 15
COMMON PEOPLE

Looking back, it's obvious that Britain had begun to lust after a music scene all of its own, but explaining how it finally fell into place is another, much trickier matter.

Yes, a lot of what was happening in the UK from 1991 onwards was a reaction to grunge. But not everything that Britain was touting as the Next Big Thing went down a storm. And there were several false starts before Oasis and co strode forth into the chart in 1994.

The first difficulty with Britpop is picking a start point. But for the sake of argument let's stick a pin into the spring of 1993. Suede had already arrived – dubbed the 'Best New Band In Britain' by the *Melody Maker* in 1992 – and Blur's rehabilitation into a cred-pop band had begun as well. In April, *Select* magazine ran with the first Britpop-style cover, featuring Suede's Brett Anderson on the front, dressed in black leather and superimposed on a Union Jack. The cover line was: 'Yanks Go Home. Suede, St Etienne, Denim, Pulp, The Auteurs and the Battle For Britain'.

As a concept piece it spoke volumes about the changes in critical opinion at the time. Inside it ranted: 'We don't want your plaid! We want crimplene, glamour, wit and irony.'

What's the old adage? 'Be careful what you wish for, some of it might come true'? Luckily it wasn't the bit about crimplene.

Unwittingly, though, *Select* had hit on something here: the dress up/dress down phenomenon which you can trace right back to the start of rock'n'roll. If one scene prides itself on looking smart, the next will want to be scruffy. And if the two ever meet? Well, then you get running battles on Brighton beach.

I've watched this since the 70s. For glam rock you dressed up and had long hair, for punk you dressed down and went short and spiky. After the perceived scruffiness of punk came the suits of the mod revival and the 2-Tone ska bands, not to mention the walking flower arrangements of the new romantic movement. In the 80s there was the post-rocker look of the Midlands grebo bands, followed by the smarter, hipper, new casual

baggy style of the Madchester scene. Post-baggy you had grunge ...
and after the plaid fad of grunge came the first wave of Britpop.

A month after the Yanks Go Home cover, Suede's debut album arrived,
which I found myself reviewing in my new role as the magazine's Reviews
Editor (in response their PR company enclosed four cans of cider with
the review copy of the record). We gave the album four out of five – not
for the free cider – but because at the time, it was a genuinely refreshing
record. There were, as various critics pointed out, elements of David
Bowie, but I think I also compared it to the first Adam & The Ants album
mixed with the plotlines of various Dennis Potter plays. Whichever way
you called it, though, it was a decidedly English-sounding first outing. So
much so that when Suede played one of their first gigs in Scotland, Brett
Anderson told the *Evening Session* that they were petrified for their lives.

'This really tall punk with a mohican stood at the front of the gig all
night, and between songs pointed at us and shouted, "You effete
southern wankers".'

In the same year Blur released their second album, *Modern Life Is
Rubbish*, complete with a series of press shots which had captions like
'British Image Number 2'. In the photos, the previously bowl-haired
pretty boys had swapped their pop image for Fred Perrys, DMs and
cheap suits. Was there a theme here?

If there was, then there wasn't any time for it to solidify. Britain became
impatient and, in an attempt to outgun its punky American counterparts,
came up with the short, sharp shock of the New Wave Of New Wave.

If anything reveals how desperate the UK was for its own guitar
movement, then it must have been the NWONW (even the concept of
selling a whole new scene based on two or three bands is very British.
You don't find it anywhere else in the world's media. But then the rest
of the world is bereft of weekly papers and the music scene doesn't move
as quickly as it does in Britain).

The NWONW – a title poached from the short-lived late 70s/early
80s British rock scene dubbed the New Wave Of British Heavy Metal –
was a frantic, speed-fuelled attempt to launch a handful of bands at the
chart and reclaim the guitar baton from America. Come to think of it,
baton makes it sound like a race. Maybe a better sporting analogy might
be the Ryder Cup. Instead of playing the Americans at golf we could
challenge them to a duel of rock genres.

The groups involved with NWONW weren't all bad as far as I could see. We even got in there early and played a demo by one of them, S*M*A*S*H, on the *Evening Session* to general thumbs-up all round. But in the end I think their repetitiveness and lack of subtlety undermined them. Maybe S*M*A*S*H were even too overtly political for the time (their best single *I Want To Kill Somebody* included a hitlist of Tory MPs).

As well as S*M*A*S*H, there was These Animal Men, and Elastica got lumped in there too. But the NWONW wasn't a strong enough or broad enough platform for all the bands that started to emerge through 1994. At the *Evening Session* we played a white label seven-inch from Backbeat Records by some new group called Supergrass, who all my mates were raving over. And for a time, it felt like each week brought a promising new debut record. There were Ash, Echobelly, and Gene, whose limited edition first single even made the Radio 1 playlist.

The response from the listeners was terrific. On the crest of the New Wave, Radio 1 decamped to the movement's spiritual home on the south coast for a week of *Evening Session* shows called 'Brighton Rocks' (I know. Imaginative, aren't we?). I have several poignant memories of this week. The most ridiculous is being sent out by Radio 1 to compile a five-minute feature on the pubs of Brighton and arriving in the final one to find Bob Grover, singer with original new wave group The Piranhas, hunched in a corner.

It was a curious week of gigs. The Fugees flew in from America to play (supporting Transglobal Underground). The Prodigy also appeared, as did Brit-rap acts Kaliphz and Honky. But the rest of the live bands were the ones that had crashed ashore on the New Wave – some of whom would later become the sandcastles of Britpop. Elastica led the way, but during the week there were also sets by Shed 7, Sleeper, Gene, Echobelly, These Animal Men and Lush.

Oh, and it rained every day.

To my knowledge no-one really coined the term Britpop until around the start of 1995. I'd like to be more specific, but I can't find anyone who knows or who'll own up to it (any offers?). By then, with all the pieces laid out in a jumble on the floor, Britpop started to fit together like a jigsaw. If you take Blur and Suede as the corners (they're the easy bits to start with), then Elastica fitted in between them. Having slotted

Justine and co in, then many of the bands who followed snapped into place quite quickly. Supergrass's *Caught By The Fuzz* had a similar feel to Elastica's debut *Stutter*. Then there was Ash, who toured with Elastica, and the 60Ft Dolls, who garnered some of their early attention through their links with old friend and Elastica guitarist Donna Matthews. Other groups fitted together because of other factors behind the scenes. Either the same people signed them, or the same press officer plugged them.

Even the difficult bits, that when we started didn't seem to fit anywhere, all of a sudden fell into place. There was Radiohead (who in jigsaw terms were a difficult piece of sky). And there were the oddly shaped pieces that you pick up and put down and come back to later. The misshapes. Which is why the last important piece to go in was Pulp.

Everyone will have their own defining Britpop moments. But for what it's worth, these are mine:

- The *Parklife* Tour
- Pulp going to number 2 in the chart with *Common People*
- *Country House* vs *Roll With It.*

Of these, if I had to pick one point in time when you knew the world had gone (Britpop) mad then it was the release of *Common People*. Interested parties within the music industry had already become aware of the buzz surrounding the track, long before it hit the shops. It had been promoed to alternative clubs some weeks ahead of its release, to a surprisingly good reaction (indie clubs are notoriously conservative when it comes to new music, but *Common People*, which had already been played to death on Radio 1, was an exception).

The day before the chart was unveiled I was guest DJ at Nottingham Rock City and Mike, the resident DJ, was frothing with excitement over the news of its possible chart position: 'It's number two midweek … Number two!' Number two was a big deal. Number two was almost unbelievable. Number two was notice that the lunatics had taken over the asylum.

Here was the band who had spent years selling 22 copies of each record they'd released finally selling 80,000 in ONE WEEK. And that singer, who we'd always said was going to be a star, now really was GOING TO BE A STAR.

But there was more to it than that even, because Britpop – a scene which thrived on the best and worst English excesses – had succeeded in producing one of Britain's favourite and most romantic phenomena: the victorious underdog.

Pulp were a band who had succeeded against the odds. If you look at the rest of the Britpop groups, including Oasis and Elastica, they'd had a relatively straightforward career. Sure, Oasis had put in the graft, rehearsing day in, day out at the Manchester Boardwalk, and Suede – another of Pulp's peers – had lived off tins of cold baked beans in various damp Camden flats before their break had come. But Pulp had been trying to crack it for years.

My introduction to them came via Dave Bedford at Fire Records, who gave me a copy of one of their old singles, *Little Girl With Blue Eyes*, just as the group were about to re-emerge on to the London circuit in 1991. A few weeks later came their new single *My Legendary Girlfriend* – an *NME* Single of the Week – and then a few of us trooped out to west London to see them play at a venue called Subterania. Subterania was a bastard to get to, and it seemed like every indie gig there was barely half full, but the record was good enough to warrant a live review so I bowled up, not sure what to expect, and then Alvin Stardust walked on stage. Or at least, it was someone who posed a little like Alvin Stardust, but it couldn't have been Alvin Stardust because he had brown cords and glasses on. The review of the gig went like this:

Pulp provide another lucid, sometimes eccentric view of music. Out front, singer/satirist Jarvis Cocker sashays around the stage, part Elvis Presley, part John Travolta.

'It's a bit like playing on somebody's fireplace here,' says Cocker. 'I don't know if you can see, but it's all tiled around the stage. You could put a couple of horse-brasses up on the walls, give it a bit of atmosphere. Until then, here's another song.'

The disco-boogie angst of *Countdown*, the next single in June, is followed by the climatic current 45 *My Legendary Girlfriend* – complete with cock-up in the middle. It's very grand, but it's top entertainment.

I remember the cock-up. I saw Pulp about three times around this point and every night Nick Banks would launch his drums into the final part of the song, eight bars too early – and every time he did it, Cocker turned round, shook his head and stared at him. Could have been part of the act, for all I know.

But although *My Legendary Girlfriend* earned them a lot of praise in the press, and sold in the region of 1500 copies, Pulp's career still managed to hit the skids again. There was a falling-out with the record label, problems with management and all kinds of drama until they found their way. But Pulp were so endearing that however badly they were doing, someone always seemed to turn up who had faith in them.

I'm not sure what to attribute this to. Was it Jarvis's charisma? Pulp's music? Or was it just that they all thought this band deserved a break? Whatever, Pulp secured the services of one of London's leading music PR companies (who were so convinced of the band's future that they did their publicity for free). And then they met Geoff Travis. Travis had set up the legendary indie label Rough Trade and later signed The Smiths. He helped re-energize Cocker, and Pulp's prospects of fame.

The band signed to Island and recorded *His & Hers*. And in April 1994 they had their first Top 40 hit with *Do You Remember The First Time?*. With bands like Suede and Blur around, Pulp no longer seemed to be as out on a limb musically as they had been (prior to their association with Britpop, the only band that had come into their orbit was a spangly, futuristic group called World Of Twist who'd had a couple of minor hits at the start of the 90s).

Not only that, but Jarvis was running up the star ladder two rungs at a time. As we cheered him on, he appeared first on BBC TV's *Pop Quiz*, where he shocked everyone with his extraordinary knowledge of both credible and cheesy pop trivia. Then, after Pulp had been to America and narrowly lost the Mercury Music Prize to M People, he hosted *Top of the Pops* and famously introduced the number one band of the week with the words, 'Take That ARE Top Of The Pops'. From that show onwards, every presenter was told to finish the show with the same phrase.

His & Hers had made it into the Top 10 of the album chart, and Pulp went about their business working on a follow-up. The starting point was *Common People*. Stop me if you've heard this one before, but the story goes like this. Having sold some records in the Notting Hill branch of Record & Tape Exchange, Cocker immediately reinvested the money in an old Casio keyboard.

A few days later, fiddling around with the Casio at rehearsal he played a tune to guitarist Steve. 'After we both stopped laughing,' Jarvis told me once, 'he said it sounded like *Fanfare For The Common Man*. And that's where I got the idea for the words from.' They first recorded *Common People* for a John Peel session in the autumn of 1994 and then went into the studio where they spent a week recording it for release.

As they came to the mixing stage, however, Jarvis decided the track wasn't sounding right. There was something missing. The problem was, it didn't sound chuggy enough. Unable to conjure up the right explanation, he went to his record collection and selected the chuggiest record he could find. He sat producer Chris Thomas down and played him ... *Mr Blue Sky* by the Electric Light Orchestra.

Can you imagine how bewildered Thomas must have been? Here's a man who's worked with the Sex Pistols, The Pretenders, and some of the biggest names in rock, being told that the track they've sweated over for days on end should sound more like the invention of ELO – an opera-obsessed 70s rock orchestra led by Jeff Lynne, a man held together by a beard and dark glasses.

Thomas did the trick, though, and Jarvis added some acoustic guitar, and – bingo. Pulp had *Common People* in the bag.

The next problem was persuading Island Records that they should release it straight away. The label was wary of putting out a single without the entire new album being finished and ready to go. But Cocker was convinced that at last, after years of hanging around on street corners, Pulp were finally in the right place at the right time. Blur and Oasis had just had huge hits. The record buying masses were ready. Island concurred and Pulp went to number two.

'We used to have a rivalry going between Food records and Savage & Best (Pulp's PR company),' Andy Ross from Food told me a while later. 'You could see one of the windows of their office from ours, and we used to stick up midweek chart positions of our bands versus theirs.

'When *Common People* came out, I got a fax with Pulp's midweek on it and rang them up to congratulate them. I said, "21, that's really good." I didn't realize the one was really an exclamation mark.'

FOUR SKINNY INDIE KIDS

Just as the world of high finance has a base in the square mile of the City of London, Britpop developed its own centre for movers and shakers. Except the high powered execs and bright young things of pop weren't in the east London commuter zone. They were all in Camden.

The centre of the pop economy was in a square mile around Camden Town tube station with the Good Mixer pub to the west, Dingwalls and the Monarch to the north, the Falcon to the east and the Camden Palace with its Tuesday night Feet First club to the south.

Camden was the big noise. It had been through sporadic periods of notoriety before, but nothing like this. The invasion of bands and fans and tourists that took place through 1995 was so huge that Britpop even drove some of the Camden old guard out of the borough altogether.

Among the groups to flee were Gallon Drunk – a stylish band of bluesmen – who, ironically, were the group who had first made the Good Mixer semi-famous in 1992 when they did all their interviews there. But that's jumping ahead of the game. Camden's first flirtation with fame in the 90s was centred more to the east, where Jeff Barrett was promoting bands at the Falcon. Apart from early gigs by the Mondays and the Inspiral Carpets, the Falcon became one of the two breeding ground venues that played host to a handful of infectiously noisy local groups including Silverfish and Th'Faith Healers. If anything, these bands were British grunge even before there was American grunge (so you can imagine the complaints from the neighbours). Together they were shouty and hairy and their followers used to do a strange lunging sort of dance, which involved tipping themselves backwards and forwards from the waist in a bastardization of headbanging.

In fact, it was at the Falcon that these bands got their nickname. One night, while watching Silverfish, we worked out that the dance was 'less Lambeth walk, more Camden Lurch'. BINGO. Having had features on both the Healers and Silverfish turned down at *NME*, we went back in with news of the new Camden Lurch scene and within minutes had been commissioned to write a two-page spread about it. Never mind that Lurch was really only three or four bands (if you included Milk and Sun Carriage), it was a good way of squeezing Camden and its underground culture into the paper. Sadly, they didn't use the suggested headline, The Chords of the New Lurch.

The other fan-based venue at the time was the Hampstead White Horse which had a series of nights running called the Sausage Machine. It was the Sausage Machine which finally spawned a new record label called Too Pure, which signed Th'Faith Healers and later PJ Harvey and Stereolab. Together with the nascent Wiiija label (based in west London, but spiritually at home in Camden) there was a feeling that something was happening here. Wiiija had Silverfish and then signed Therapy? from Northern Ireland and the noise-mongering continued.

Meanwhile, back in Inverness Street, Gallon Drunk released a gloriously embittered single called *Some Fools Mess* and we did the follow-up feature in the Good Mixer. I couldn't believe the place. The feature even started with the line, 'Somewhere in Camden there is a pub that time forgot ...' There was an old seven-inch jukebox on the wall, two old men in the corner, and Gallon Drunk in their vintage suits playing pool. It was like stepping back in time 20 years.

But that was the appeal of the Mixer. Not only did it seem like the most eccentric pub in London, you could always get a seat, and it had a good jukebox. The same things appealed to the staff of Food Records who moved in round the corner in 1992 and then the PR firm Savage & Best (whose clientele included Suede, Pulp and the fledgling Elastica), who arrived next door to Food in 1993. Both firms were to become synonymous with Britpop; both drank in the Mixer. In fact, both used the Mixer for business.

Savage & Best used to take their bands there to be interviewed, while Food were in another corner chatting up potential new signings. Embarrassingly, I barged in on a Food Records A&R meeting once by mistake to hear Dave Balfe grilling a group called Three And A Half Minutes about their manifesto for making it.

As the Mixer's notoriety spread among journalists and bands, the pub started being namechecked in the music paper gossip columns. Through 1993 and 1994 the clientele began to change. Not only did the numbers grow, but the type of customer started to change too. Out went the drinkers who were living off the proceeds of their last trip to Record & Tape Exchange. In came the daytrippers with their HMV carrier bags, who wanted to finish off their shopping spree with a couple of hours of celebrity-spotting.

The Square Mile – and the Mixer in particular – was happy to oblige. Blur, Elastica, Pulp and even Morrissey drank in the Mixer in 1994, while Noel Gallagher moved into a flat in the area in 1995. The Mixer became the trading floor, the home of the hustlers – it was the FT Index of Britpop (Blur up four, The Bluetones up two, Thurman down six). To add to the packed crowds doing business in the Mixer, the Dublin Castle, around the corner in Camden Parkway, became the venue of choice for the A&R scouts of the day.

Camden venues go in and out of fashion, not because of the décor or the drinks they serve, but because of who's booking the gigs. By 1995 a guy called Chris Myhill, previously a booker at the Bull & Gate and a man with a good ear for a new band, had taken charge of some of the gigs. And the Castle, which had spent years as a home for no-hopers and covers bands, became a good hunting ground for talent.

Monday nights in particular were an A&R hot ticket. Just like the days of Dingwalls' Panic Station, I used to leave work and head straight up there (prior to the start of *Lamacq Live*, the *Evening Session* used to finish at 8.30 p.m. so I used to arrive halfway through the first band). Along with Myhill, the Monday Club Spangle nights were organized by Simon Williams and Nude Records A&R man Dave Laurie. Of the bands they booked, several went on to get record deals or end up on the *Evening Sesh*.

I spent a lot of these Monday nights trying to come up with a collective noun for A&R scouts. Well, when you're stuck in a corner, waiting to see the next band, there's not much else to do. But there they'd be, gangs of A&R staff turning up *en masse*, trying to find the new Blur or new Oasis. They hunt in packs, you know. If you have any ideas, pass them on (a chequebook of A&Rs? A confusion? What about a rash?).

Among the gigs which attracted huge industry interest were The Bluetones and a band who, legend has it, formed in the pub just two streets away … Menswear. Menswear were the first product of the Good Mixer and the huge success of Blur's *Parklife* LP. They were hugely endearing. To me, they were the first band to form out of the audience and walk straight on to *Top of the Pops*. But that was the mood of the Mixer and pop music in general in 1994 and 1995. It felt like anything could happen. If you could blag and hustle and charm and stand up straight for half an hour, then there was nothing you couldn't achieve.

Britpop ran on self-belief. And when the self-belief started to run thin, the cocaine kicked in to replace it. I'm not a drug-user myself, not because I have a conscientious objection to drugs, but because I have genuine doubts that my skinny frame and addictive character would be able to handle them. I might be a kid in some instances, but I'm grown up enough to know that I don't live the healthiest of lifestyles and taking drugs might just finish me off. But coke – which was on the increase everywhere during the 90s – hit Britpop very hard. It's difficult to be specific without getting wound up in libel actions regurgitating old tabloid stories, but there are records from the later Britpop era which have all the hallmarks of being made on coke. And they aren't very good. I bet they sounded great in the studio at the time though ('LISTENTOTHISSSSSS!!!'). And I bet all that nonsense of employing orchestras and string arrangements sounded massive and classic and world beating at 2 a.m. But, in reality, it was a clear sound of some bands losing the plot.

Meanwhile, back in the Square Mile, life was becoming odder by the moment. One day Menswear were just five blokes who you used to see in the pub, the next there was a drawing of them pinned to the wall of George & Nikki's Restaurant in Parkway (George & Nikki's was a Britpop haunt, serving roasts and fry-ups which earned it the nickname School Dinners). The walls were always covered with pictures of TV celebrities. Proper famous people. Then one day there was a hand-drawn picture of Menswear amongst them, brought in by an adoring fan.

That must have sent tremors of nervous energy through the trading floor back in the Mixer.

• 17
STREET SPIRIT

In the bowels of Radio 1 there is a man called Phil Lawton and a basement library which houses the station's archive. Ever wondered where the mastertapes and DATs of your favourite sessions go after they've been broadcast? Phil has them, lovingly filed in aisle after aisle of shelves and drawers.

I mention this because it was Phil who I went to with a sketchy list of highlights from the past few years of the *Evening Session* … and it was Phil who lent me some tapes which jogged some memories. So thanks, Phil. But, erm, I've got some more for you to look up.

Through 1995 and 1996, the *Session* was stuffed with interviews and sessions featuring virtually every likely alternative/dance outfit who meant anything (and some, with the benefit of hindsight, who didn't). Some of these are as clear as day. Others – well, I'll get back to you after Phil has been to work.

1995

JANUARY: Simon Williams (*NME*), Gina Morris (*Select*) and Dom Phillips (*Mixmag*) with their tips for the top. Also reports back from the *NME* Brat Bus tour.

JANUARY 19: On Campus at Sunderland University with live sets from Terrorvision and China Drum. We always looked forward to doing the On Campus nights. They were an occasional series of live gigs from student unions around the country, where we'd get to do the show out of London (good), and get to put on a couple of bands (also good), and then bond as a team after the show by getting hammered (dangerous). China Drum, who I've always had a soft spot for since their debut single *Simple*, gave us a guided tour of Sunderland in a mini-cab. Don't remember much about the gig, but remember Jo drinking Tony from Terrorvision under the table.

FEBRUARY: Interviews included Louise Wener from Sleeper, Belly and a chat with dEUS who also played acoustically in the studio. We also had each member of Elastica in, one at a time for four nights running, asking them questions about the other members of the band. If you remember the TV show *Mr & Mrs*, it was something like that. Among the snippets of trivia we forced out of them were the facts that the favourite group of Annie the bassist was The Clash (or The Stranglers); guitarist Donna was a huge Brookside fan; Justin the drummer didn't bother with underwear; and one of singer Justine Frischmann's uncles wrote the Benny Hill theme tune.

FEBRUARY 7: Launch of Sound City in Bristol with The Bluetones and Gene. This year's Sound City was to be in Bristol, which we launched with a warm-up gig featuring two of the bands who we'd first played on the *Sesh*.

FEBRUARY 23: On Campus in Liverpool with Echobelly and AC Acoustics. I remember this for two reasons. One, Jo and I had agreed to DJ afterwards. That meant that after the gig had finished we spent the next hour behind the decks trying to work out which Pulp tune was the most dancefloor-friendly. Also, just as we had done in Sunderland, we hung around the following day to take part in a Radio 1-sponsored pop quiz. The *Evening Session* team came fifth (still, would have been much worse without Whiley's knowledge of Roxy Music).

MARCH. Another four-nighter interview with Radiohead to mark the release of *The Bends*, the album that was to take them to a new level of fame. There were veiled comments about how difficult it was to record, and how the constant touring, provoked by the global success of *Creep*, had taken its toll on them.

Johnny Greenwood: 'It's like writing a play and then having to tour it for too long.'

Thom Yorke: 'We got to the stage of becoming acutely paranoid in the studio. There were times when we could have walked out of the studio and just given up there and then.'

Other interviews featured Apache Indian (who was a very nice fella), James Lavelle from Mo Wax Records and Martin Carr to trail ahead to …

MARCH 23 On Campus in Cardiff. The Boo Radleys. The Boos, on the back of their biggest hit *Wake Up Boo*, played live, less than a fortnight after scoring their first Top 10 hit.

APRIL 17: SOUND CITY: I've mentioned Sound City before – the previous year's event in Glasgow – but Jo and I were novices in our first year, and I think this was the week when we really started feeling part of the team. Sound City was in Leeds, which was a good setting for a start. The audiences were friendly and the line-up of bands was impressive (a whole week of gigs by the likes of Garbage, the Manics, Sleeper, Ash and Fun Lovin' Criminals – not to mention up-and-coming tykes like my new faves Scarfo). On the first day, a Bank Holiday Monday, Jo and I made a guest appearance on the Roadshow alongside Mark Goodier, the only time I've ever bounced onto the stage and shouted, 'Hellloooo LEEEEEEDS!'. Bouncing is the key to roadshows. The sprightlier the DJ looks, I've spotted, the more the crowd *gives it up* for them. In my new bouncing-sole cherry red DMs, I must have looked like I was walking on propelled by an invisible space-hopper.

One thing I remember about Leeds is that Ocean Colour Scene didn't want me to introduce them on stage. This answers the question, 'Do you ever fall out with groups?'. Well, patently, yes. The Scene, I was told by one of their pluggers, were still miffed by a review I'd given them years earlier at the *NME* when they were right at the start of their career.

They were about to be signed, but I gave them a bit of a savaging ('horribly average' and 'does OCS stand for Office Cleaning Services?' and such like). Obviously they weren't going to countenance the presence of such a non-believer on the same stage as them. Mind you, what did they think I was going to say? 'Make some noise for the worst band in the world …'?

But apart from that, Leeds Sound City was one of the most enjoyable I've ever been involved with – partly because Jo and I had been passed fit by the Live Music Outfit.

When Radio 1 put on these live events, there is a huge behind-the-scenes team who, over the years, have become part of the *Session*'s extended family. There are Sam Cunningham and Andy Rogers, who oversee the general running of the show, and there are the sound producers, such as Miti and Big Simon Askew, who mix the groups' sets to air. And then there are all manner of other people, responsible for on-stage sound and techy stuff I don't understand.

And now, when I turn up to present an outside broadcast, their faces are familiar and friendly and reassuring, no matter what chaos surrounds us. They are also incredibly good at standing around. Sorry, standing *their* round.

Back at the hotel afterwards, knackered but still too churned up by the adrenalin that drags you through a show, there is the post-gig ritual of beer and sandwiches and bad gags and piss-taking. Leeds was a perfect example. We'd start at the aftershow party – a small affair for a few fans and bands and crew at the Town & Country Club – and then head back to the hotel. And the gang – which is effectively what it was – grew bigger all the time. Controller Matthew Bannister, never shy of pitching in, joined us for a couple of days, while another night we stayed in the bar being entertained by John Peel until it was nearly time for breakfast. Every time he finished another Noel Edmonds story, or the one about the Radio 1 Fun Day Out, someone would refuel him with another red wine.

The following day we were out putting together Leeds-related packages for the show. Jo, naturally, did the origins of Goth; I ended up doing a feature on curry houses with Terrorvision. Not playing to type at all, then.

PS: There is a CD featuring tracks recorded during the week, which I'd completely forgotten existed until I found it in a shop the other day (had to buy it for posterity). It's called *Uproar*.

APRIL 26: Paul Weller plays live on the show. They made a TV trailer for the *Evening Session* out of this, cutting together clips of Weller reheasing at our Maida Vale studios – and Jo, producer Christine Boar and me preparing for the show back in the studio.

Christine: 'Paul Weller live. Apparently he's in a good mood.'

Me: 'Paul Weller in good mood shocker!'

Cut to Weller laughing.

MAY 4: I'm on holiday for a week. Jarvis Cocker co-hosted the show with Jo (one of the best co-hosts ever). I got a tape of this from Phil and it's a brilliant show.

Jarvis: 'That's Bernard Butler; it's out on the 10th. Two days after VE Day. And he's playing the Hanover Grand soon … Watch out for them bouncers at that place. I had terrible time the last time I went there.'

And again (after playing *White Man In Hammersmith Palais* by The Clash): 'I went to Hammersmith Palais the other night, but it's like Hitman and her. I was very disappointed. Coming up next, the Stone Roses.'

MAY: We also did our first interview with Supergrass, plus the return of Teenage Fanclub. Oh, and Black Grape. I wasn't quite sure what to expect from Shaun Ryder. I'd never met him before, but he turned up with Kermit, fresh from the pub around the corner, carrying a pint of Guinness. Their promotions girl even returned the empty glass afterwards.

Ryder (on the end of the Mondays): 'The last three years of the Happy Mondays was like a relationship where you were going to bed with someone and not having sex. I always thought we could fix things, if we just had some time off. But people were more concerned with Big Dollar than music. I did fight for the Mondays to stay together, go away for a year and come back, but everyone else wanted to finish it.'

'So how did you get together with Kermit?' (formerly of the Ruthless Rap Assassins)

Ryder: 'Well, it was just me and him. We didn't have any friends left. No-one would talk to us.'

'Have you swapped musical influences? What does Shaun play you?'

Kermit: 'Rod Stewart.'

Ryder: 'Early Rod! When Rod was a mod.'

JUNE: Jo's turn for a holiday, so we phoned round to try to find some guests and no-one was in the country (or at least, that's what they said). Instead, I came up with a new phone interview. 'If they're not in Britain, then they must be on tour, or something. So let's phone the bands up and ask them, "Where are you right now?"' (see next chapter for more details).

Guests in the studio – who *were* in the country – included the Chemical Brothers (chatting and mixing), J Mascis from Dinosaur Jr. (not chatty) and Prophets Of Da City.

JULY: We'd played a couple of records by a band called Perfume who we both liked and it became a running gag that Mick their singer shared his birthday with Jo. Without her knowing, we got hold of Mick and set up Whiley live on air. She was interviewing him over the phone from his rehearsal studio – or at least that's where he claimed he was. In fact, he was standing outside the studio door. Halfway through the interview he walked in, carrying a birthday cake. Candles and everything.

Other July highlights included a series of last-half-hour mixes (from David Holmes, Fluke and the team at the dance magazine *Volume*, among others), plus interviews with the Roses, Garbage and Peter Buck from REM, recorded at their gig at Milton Keynes Bowl.

AUGUST: A whole bunch of stuff. Jo interviewed Ash (bassist Mark Hamilton was so nervous he had to leave and Jo started again with singer Tim Wheeler); there was me with Money Mark; and a Charlatans interview made up entirely of questions we'd received from listeners. Oh, and the big Blur interview plus the first play of tracks from *The Great Escape*.

SEPTEMBER: Manchester In The City. Britain's answer to the CMJ or NMS Seminars in the States where representatives of the music industry come to talk shop and watch showcase gigs by unsigned bands. This year was spiced up by the KLF premiering their film *The KLF Burn A Million Pounds*. I was live at the centre of the seminar, standing in a corridor in the conference hotel, while Jo was back at Manchester BH. One night she got a desperate call from somebody back at Radio 1 in London. 'Jo, there's a Noel Gallagher in reception! We've told him you're not here, but he wants to speak to you.' Noel had just finished his contribution to the charity album *Help* and had brought in a DAT to debut on the show. By the miracle of modern technology we played the track out down the line from London.

OCTOBER: Guests included Green Day, Menswear, Jarvis on the phone again, John Power from Cast and Brit-Rap outfit the Kaliphz. Then, just as we'd gone to the spiritual home of the New Wave Of New Wave, we now decamped to the spiritual home of Britpop.

OCTOBER: CAMDEN LIVE. Another week of live shows – this time from the Camden Underworld. We'd only been set up for about five minutes when a tramp started pissing against the side of the OB studio.

NOVEMBER/DECEMBER: Sleeper, Kim Deal on the phone and Chris Evans.

Chris Evans. There's a name writ large in Radio 1's recent history. Though in fact this wasn't where I met him. In between working for *NME* and doing a stint on Q102, I helped out on Gary Crowley's Sunday afternoon show on GLR. No-one used to be in at GLR at the weekend, so you could learn how to edit tape and mix in one of the spare studios. And after a while I started contributing a weekly London Gig Guide.

If Crowley – before the days of Xfm – was the indie sound of Sunday afternoons, then Chris Evans was the anarchic wake-up call of Sunday mornings. I only heard about the final six months or so, but it was one of the few radio programmes I've ever taped (it was basically Chris, and a few listeners who'd been invited in to the studio, having a good time). Some of the features like 'Personality Or Person?' later reappeared on his Radio 1 *Breakfast Show*.

So this is how I met the soon-to-be-rich-and-famous Chris Evans.

The studio door opens. Evans bounces in. 'Can I borrow one of these?' he asks, cadging a cigarette.

'Sure.' We had some short conversation about the lack of chinagraph pencils in the building. And then he was gone. Nice chap.

His arrival at Radio 1 had a more profound effect. Having spent a year as part of a station that was constantly berated in the press for losing listeners, the staff at Radio 1 had adopted a kind of trench mentality. Before the benefits of Matthew Bannister's changes had started to emerge, the atmosphere was tense and occasionally gloomy.

Evans changed all that. There was a certain amount of resentment at his show being produced by his own company, and at how he often flouted the playlist rules and so on, but in his first year there he had the place buzzing. Or at least he did on the *Sesh*. It was like watching your team sign a new striker who immediately started banging in the goals left, right and centre (he struck the first on his opening morning when he played *Welcome Home*, the new theme tune for listeners who were retuning to Radio 1).

I've tried not to use too many music–football analogies in this book (though there are quite a few, I can assure you), but this one seems appropriate somehow. I've stood on the terraces at Colchester and watched as we've sunk down the table and the home crowds have dwindled. And I've been there again, when a new bunch of youngsters have broken through and the entire team seems to respond. But it's not just this image that makes me think of Evans.

I can tell who the most talked about DJ at Radio 1 is just by having a drink in the Drury Arms before the game, or bumping into people in the queue for the gents. As soon as Evans started, everyone wanted to ask questions about him or talk about something he'd said on air during the week. It was during one pre-game drink that someone said, 'You should get him on your show,' and promptly collapsed laughing.

Not a bad idea though.

There were other good reasons to be seen alongside each other at the time. Evans, on the *Breakfast Show* and *TFI*, had started championing several bands we'd played on the *Session*. He even used to phone up during the programme and swap stories about records we all liked. For a time, *Breakfast* at 7 a.m. and the *Session* at 7 p.m. were like the bookends of the day. So when Jo took another break, we broached the idea with the bosses, and Evans said yes.

Me: 'It's Lamacq and Evans and that was Black Grape. Chris, have you come tooled up?'

Chris: 'I have come tooled up … I've got two bags here. I've got a Tesco's bag and a Crispin's Food Hall bag. And in this bag, because you've got to have respect for the *Evening Session*, I've got half a bottle of warm cider, ten Embassy Regals, and for some reason there's bits of card ripped off the top of it, don't know why. I've got a copy of *NME*, *Viz* and *Marxism Today*. And that's it …'

'And you've also brought some records with you, which we're going to play, and here's the first one, and why?'

'Oh, it's The Pursuit Of Happiness and it's called *She's So Young*. This is simply the best pop song I have ever heard in my life. It was never a hit. By a Canadian band. But it's also got the best gap. The best way to get anyone to listen to the radio is to stop talking … [pauses for three seconds] And then everyone goes, "What was that?". Stuart Copeland from the Police once said that the most important beats are the ones you don't hit … and I think that's quite profound as well. And in this song, there's a beat they don't hit.'

'Aah. But is it a better gap than the one in *Should I Stay Or Should I Go?* by The Clash?'

'Steve, it just doesn't compare. Just wait till you hear it …'

Apart from the warm cider and the gaps in records, Chris did his 'Personality Or Person?' quiz on the phone with Andy Cairns from Therapy? (where celebs are asked questions about everyday life, to see if they've turned into a personality or they're still a person). We also did a phone-in about the biggest band you've seen in the smallest venue. And if I remember right, Chris gave away his £100 fee as the prize. One of the most riotous co-host shows I've ever done.

Just as an aside, the co-hosts were an idea which started when either Jo or I went on holiday and the one left behind got lonely. But even after Jo departed, we kept doing them, because they give guests more room to stretch their legs and air the best bits of their record collections. We've had so many co-presenters during my years on the *Sesh* that I feel like a cab driver: 'I've had them all in that chair y'know. That Zoë Ball. Ant'n'Dec, they were nice fellas. Fatboy Slim, that little Tim fella out of The Charlatans … knows his music he does.'

Zoë's appearance provoked raised eyebrows at Radio 1. She hadn't made her radio debut at the time, and the suggestion from some quarters was that maybe she wasn't hip enough for the *Session*. But we all thought she'd helped make *Live & Kicking* a good Saturday morning programme, so we went ahead anyway. In the end she was ace. We did the programme, then hailed a cab straight off to north London to see the Fun Lovin' Criminals at the Kentish Town Forum. Having hung around at the aftershow for half an hour to catch a word with Huey, we finished off drinking at a late-night kebab and booze den called the Marathon Bar. Three months later she was on the *Breakfast Show*. Now, I'm not saying there's any connection, but …

b side

Ten lost features from the *Evening Session*:

- 30 MINUTE MENU. Half-pinched from an idea in a newspaper, the 30 minute menu was just that. Pop stars would pretend to be in an *Evening Session* kitchen and, between records, act out the preparation of their favourite meal. Amongst others, Jarvis did a nice pasta dish, aimed at penniless students (he even brought the ingredients with him) while Asian Dub Foundation did a home-made curry.
- THE SESSION JUKEBOX. This was one of mine, I'm afraid. You could call up and pick a track from our jukebox selection and after we'd played it, we would replace it with a song of your choice.
- WHAT'S THE STORY? Launched just after the arrival of the second Oasis album, this was our first attempt at a slot which answered listener's letters.
- SMASH OR TRASH. Jo Whiley plus guests in a reworking of the classic Radio 1 reviews slot Roundtable. Jo hosted Smash Or Trash on a Tuesday which meant, on Thursdays ...
- NO BIG DEAL. Smash Or Trash except with demos instead of singles and A&R guests instead of pop celebs.
- FANTASY FESTIVAL. And the post just kept coming and coming. One of the few features we've ever dropped and revived later because of its popularity. Easy idea. Pick the seven bands you'd have playing at your ideal one day festival (one can reform for the day, and you are allowed one dead pop star). You could also add any of your own embellishments, i.e. venue, food stalls, entrance restrictions. We had a lot of people wanting to ban those jester hats – and, in extreme cases, people over a certain height.
- WHERE ARE YOU RIGHT NOW? I came up with this while Jo was on holiday – to cover for her absence. I'd tried to book some guests from bands to co-host the show but they all appeared to be out of the country. 'OK then,' we thought. 'We'll phone them.' We got Martin

Carr, pre-gig in a restaurant in France; and Richard Ashcroft, by his own confession, naked on a hotel balcony in Australia (the first and only full frontal radio interview I've ever done).

- DO YOU REMEMBER THE FIRST LINE? Do you know how hard it is coming up with competition ideas? This ran for months though. Very easy, fill-in-the-first-line-of-a-song-and-win-some-CDs gambit.
- TOUR BUS TEST. A two-minute grilling of bands on the *Session* tour, including essential junk food of choice, highlight of the group's set and what's the most difficult song to play and still look cool.
- GENRE GRAVEYARD. A fortnight-long revisitation of classic tunes from famous – and infamous – musical genres of the past few years. Remember grebo? The New Wave Of New Wave? C86? All those and more.

• 18
KING OF NEW YORK

It's years ago now, around the time of Madchester, but one afternoon, in a massive hotel near Times Square, Factory Records boss Tony Wilson offered the American record industry out for a fight.

Not a physical one. Not a punch up on the sidewalk between a gang of British indie labels and some well turned-out American corporate execs. This was a fight over creativity and invention. This was about artistry and honour. This was the cheeky, small boy on holiday, goading his American cousin over his lack of culture and subtlety.

It's folded now, but there used to be an annual music event in America called the New Music Seminar (NMS). At night, New York's venues used to rumble to the sound of bands trying to impress record labels and journalists, and by day there would be a series of crushingly dull discussion panels called 'A&R of the Future', 'Breaking New Territories in the Southern States', and 'AOR Formatting for the Under 50s'. And all the seminars had guests sitting on a top table and all the guests were high-powered execs called Brad and Bill and Hank.

Representatives of the British industry used to go to NMS – as they still go to its latter-day equivalents South By South West in Texas and CMJ in New York – to try to work out how the hell you sold records in the States. The Americans flocked from every state to see who could talk the loudest and give out the biggest number of business cards in a week. I'm surprised that there isn't a bell that sounds every so often in the background ('Brett Guzzelwitz has hit 100 cards today! Let's hear it for Brett!'). And yes, this is stupidly cynical, and smacks of xenophobia, but during our lives we will all have American friends we like, and business acquaintances we hate.

Over the years I've met some extraordinarily nice folk in the American music and media game (but even they would admit that if you want to find the brashest, loudest, grossest, scariest creations of the biz, then America's the place to go. The PR girls and the pluggers, well, some of them really are straight out of *Spinal Tap*). At times in the 80s and mid 90s, you even got the impression that the American industry was like a National Park, set up to protect some of the ghastliest creatures of the 70s.

And this was what had got up Tony Wilson's nose. The Americans were slow and out of touch. Worse still, they weren't buying any of our records (the Stone Roses had recently returned from America with their tails between their legs, and Wilson's Happy Mondays weren't faring any better). So, Wilson (a respected man, who later set up his own British version of NMS – In The City) went to New York and called his discussion panel: 'Wake Up America. You're Dead'.

The hour-long session started very positively, if a little dully. Wilson and his guests explained how Britain was in the throes of the house invasion (which ironically had come from Chicago). Britain was cross-fertilizing dance and rock genres and had bands that were real and fell into their record label offices after 24 hours' clubbing. It was exciting and the scene was changing. But what was happening in America? Wilson argued that the USA was ignoring the most exciting music on its own doorstep (again, the house producers and scratch DJs) in favour of adult-orientated rock dinosaurs.

What turned the mood of the room was a sudden outburst by actor Keith Allen, co-opted on to the panel by Wilson and determined to shake some life into the proceedings. Acting out a role as a drug dealer – and eulogizing over the effects of ecstasy on music – Allen riled up the onlookers to the point where some of the hip-hop representatives at the back of the room were ready to end the discussion physically.

And as the arguing turned to shouting, and the shouting turned to swearing, I wasn't there. I was supposed to be there (to cover the panel for *NME*), but after 10 minutes I'd snuck out to meet an old friend from Brixton who had a flat nearby and was going to put me up for a couple of days.

When I heard about the panel's chaotic finale later that night at a gig, I went white. I was usually very conscientious about the job – but now I was going to have to explain to the headmaster why I'd been bunking off. I spent a day working on good excuses … and then, wandering around the seminar's reception area, I came across a stall which sold cassettes of all the panels. 'Can you do me "Wake Up America. You're Dead" by tomorrow?'

'Certainly, sir. That's the most popular one this week.'

Tony Wilson had been in the game long enough to know about the friction between labels in Britain and the States, but I was a novice. I couldn't believe some of the stories that A&R people began telling me about how transatlantic politics affects the careers of new bands. Was I really that naive?

Try this, for example. It's going back five years (so the system may have changed, I'm not sure). But one A&R man told me that each year his label invites their counterparts from America over to Britain so that they can sit in a huge boardroom and play each other tapes of their recent signings. The American reps yawn through the British bands, so, having got the hump, the British reps do the same to the Americans. Later in the year, the Brits go to America – and they'll repeat the whole process (except with the UK going first). The truth is … they really don't like each other.

But there's something else here. I don't think they understand each other either. There is a complete clash of cultures at times. When the British band Five Thirty were being entertained for the first (and I think only) time by their label in America, one of the staff took them to a table-dancing club. As they sat and fidgeted, they heard one of their own songs come over the PA and cringed with embarrassment as various scantily clad ladies stripped off to the accompaniment of their song, which the A&R man had slipped the club some money to play. They returned to the UK, incredulous.

Numerous other bands will have a hundred other stories like this. And to be fair, there are scores of tales of British bands embarrassing themselves in America and treating their labels in the States in a pretty shitty manner. But every time a band talks about breaking America, I think of all this and wonder whether – having paid for the ride – they'll want to get off halfway through.

The British bands of the 90s – our *Evening Session* favourites – had their own share of ups and downs. Radiohead's *Creep* was a huge anthem which turned them into an overnight success story in America. But it also dubbed them 'that Creep band' and when *The Bends*, their second album, arrived, defiantly un-*Creep*-like, they suffered commercially.

Elastica and Oasis both did well. But Suede, Pulp, Blur – the most English of the Britpoppers – all struggled, just as countless other Brit bands had struggled before them. Never believe one of those headlines that says 'X BAND TAKE THE STATES'. They've been to the States. I'll give them that. They may even have played 10 dates in key cities. But in most cases America refuses to be taken anywhere. It's stubborn like that. It's big and immovable – and doesn't have much time for our sensitivities and our subtleties. But, of course, there are exceptions.

At the time of writing this (mid-March 1999), there has been a flood of optimistic stories about how well British bands are starting to do in America. Supergrass, Catatonia, Travis, Gomez, they've all been tipped to do well (by the time this book is released, you'll know how they've fared). But just maybe the surviving anglophiles in the States have finally forgiven us for sending them over a string of bands at the start of the 90s who moaned and whinged and finally cut their tours short and flounced back to Blighty.

Industry insiders also tell you that you need to spend months in America, touring and doing promo, before you stand any chance of success. So if you take that argument to its logical extreme, then the bands best prepared for America are the ones ready and willing to pay their dues. For some British groups, who've done one UK tour, had one front cover and been made into deities overnight, this reality comes as a terrible shock.

Back in the mid 90s, with Britpop sales booming, America didn't matter so much to people for a while. So what if our bands weren't making it there? Let's face it, even the American groups we were championing couldn't get arrested in the States. And they live there.

And that's true. Perversely, in the middle of the Britpop era, we got behind a series of unlikely American bands. First Rocket From The Crypt, then two groups who went on to make the Top 40 with their very first British releases. The first came early in 1996. I'd been employed to make a corporate video for EMI (I know, all very Alan Partridge and I've never done anything like it since). The job involved interviewing members of staff so they could explain the different departments of the company to new recruits.

Down in the offices of Chrysalis, I bumped into their Head of Press, who told me about some new American signings they were going to launch in a couple of months time. She gave me a CD and it lay around at home for a couple of days and then I played it ... and it was so out of step with what was going on in this country that it was brilliant. And that's how we tripped over the Fun Lovin' Criminals. The *Session* did its own edit of *Scooby Snacks* for the radio, and we banged it in the programme the following night (even before a release date was set. In fact, the label went with *The Grave And The Constant* as the first release, but by August 1996 they followed it with *Scooby Snacks* which hit the Top 40).

Very sweetly, when Huey from FLC was in town prior to the release of their second album, he called to say, 'I want you to have the album from us. Not from the record company. I want to deliver it to you in person. I'll come round your house ...' He never did. But it was a nice gesture. And they've repaid our support on several occasions over the years. But already there was a theme to the American groups who were popular in the UK. Apart from Green Day (massive on both sides of the Atlantic), Rocket From The Crypt didn't mean much in the States, despite signing a massive record deal, and the Fun Lovin' Criminals couldn't even get arrested outside of their own apartment.

The same was partly true of our next tip. We saw out 1996 with a curious album that arrived in the post from America one dour, rainy morning. I remember it was pissing down because the record seemed to capture the mood. I was on a mailing list for Geffen Records in the States (a result of having met A&R man Mark Kates who was the guy who signed Elastica in America). Geffen gave us Weezer, who shone for a time, and then some band called eels. Bear in mind, I had absolutely no idea who they were, or where they came from, or why they were signed. I hadn't got a clue that singer E had already released two solo albums, or that some radio station in New York or LA or wherever had been playing them so much that they'd started to attract attention from various labels.

I knew ZIP. And sometimes that really helps. British bands, with their press packs and their A&R buzzes, come with all manner of preconceptions and emotional baggage. *Beautiful Freak* just came out of the blue. It was one of my favourite records of the year.

And it probably sold 14 copies in America.

America-related trivia break: It's cheeky, I know, but when we have bands playing live at our Maida Vale studios, there's a button in our studio which lets you eavesdrop on what's going on (without the band knowing you're listening). Just before crossing to Green Day's debut live appearance, Jo and I listened in – and they were playing along to all the records on air. You should have heard their version of *Kandy Pop* by Bis.

Me: 'So you've been recording the session today … is this new material or stuff you can find on the album?'

Billie Joe: 'Two of them are on *Insomniac*. It's the single *Brainstew* and *Jaded*. And also two others called *Do Da Da* and another one called *Good Riddance*, which is previously unreleased.'

Me: 'You're not going to do what you did last time, which was to record a brand new song and then get the engineer to ditch it?'

Billie Joe: 'Yeah, he erased everything. Actually, that's when I found the title for the song. I was going to the bathroom and that's where I saw the words Armitage Shanks and that was what we called the song.'

Me: 'You named a song after a toilet?'

Billie Joe: 'Yeah.'

• 19
FOR THE DEAD

Having felt poorly for months, Britpop was finally taken to hospital in 1997. The poor thing. People were fighting over its will, even before it had passed away.

Still, it had had a good life (smoked 60 cigs a day you know). I didn't go to the funeral. I hate music scene funerals, they're a bit of a mess. You get a bunch of critics turning up who you haven't seen for ages ('Sorry we had to meet again under such unhappy circumstances'), then the vicar makes a speech about how Britpop or grunge or Madchester will be sorely missed, and then the record company execs shove off back to the house, nick the free food, and probably go for a round of golf.

As Britpop lost its fight for life, it left a lot of people very upset. The major labels had invested in countless groups who did very little apart from burning a hole in the corporate cashflow. And there was uproar in the press. I've never seen anything like it. Not only was Britpop a goner, but several experts claimed it was the end of rock'n'roll, full stop.

Here, have a nice of cup of tea and a sit down.

You wouldn't find this sort of hysteria in other industries. Farmers see crops fail because of bad weather – and agreed, some of them will sell up and try their luck elsewhere – but you don't get headlines saying 'Farming's All Over' or 'Is Farming Dead?'. Crops succeed, crops fail, crops succeed again. (I've suddenly realized you can take the farming analogy much further. Is the changing in trends just a form of crop rotation? Plant grunge one year, Britpop the next. Should come up a treat. And as for genetically modified food ... well, have you seen those pictures of Marilyn Manson?)

The problem with Britpop was that it had got out of step with the laws of supply and demand. At the start, there was a handful of bands who hit the charts and as the weeks flew by the appetite for British guitar music grew and grew. As the first wave of bands disappeared to make new albums, they left a gap in the market. All those hungry new Radiohead and Elastica fans and nothing to feed them.

BING! The industry went bonkers. The majors started running around signing anything that moved (or, in some cases, anything that breathed or could hum in a cockney accent). On a bigger scale this time, it was a repeat of the A&R feeding frenzy that followed in the wake of the Happy Mondays and the Stone Roses. You could almost see the A&R men in their cars, zipping north on the M62. 'Last one to Manchester is a cissy!' By the time some of the labels had picked up on what was happening, they were left scavenging for bands in bins outside the Boardwalk.

The Manchester music regulars became so miffed by all this, that someone even started a fanzine called *If You Have To Dial 061 You're A C****.

I'd like to, but I can't blame the major labels for everything that started to go wrong in 1997. Some of the bright young things who were signed in the initial 18 months of optimism simply didn't flourish as expected (because there will always be groups who, for whatever reason, never fulfil their potential). And anyway, some of the indie labels had gone just as barmy.

But by the time the Britpop leaders returned to the fray, there were simply too many groups looking for too few places on the playlist or picture stories in the press. The business plan was all to cock; the supply outstripped the demand. Overnight we were faced with a Britpop mountain (caused by whatever the pop music equivalent of an EU grant is). Scores of bands were left rotting by Camden market.

And here again I'm grateful that I was never in a band – particularly one whose career went off like a firework (after all the explosions and bright lights, you're left with cinders and the smell of burnt gunpowder). Do they live in fear of those four little words: where are they now?

All the bands who flitted and strutted through the *Session* studios as bright young things, and later as bona fide *Top of the Pops* starlets ... Menswear, Northern Uproar, Echobelly, Sleeper ... where are they now? I know there is a school of thought now that says that 99 per cent of these bands (and the rest) were, frankly, cobblers. But still, in the context of the time, they commanded big audiences and sold shedloads of albums. Some of them even made some cracking records.

But you know when you meet a boy/girl who you used to go out with (or desperately wanted to go out with)? One who you lost sleep over, fretted about and tried to impress with a new haircut? Then a couple of years later you meet them and you can't understand what you got so worked up about. I mean, they're not that *attractive*, and they've got a funny laugh or their feet are too big ... well, it's not very different with bands.

I've managed to 'stay friends' with some exes and there are groups who I still get along with even now, because we've changed or I've maybe become more tolerant. (Mansun are one, and then there are Gene, who I've always had respect for because they've been through the mill but have always acted in a pretty dignified manner for a pop band. They were always more human than some of their peers.) But it doesn't end there. Late at night, if pushed, I'll confess to still having schoolboy crushes on 60Ft Dolls and the second Sleeper album (a very sexy record in places).

Yet the truth is that there are records and people who don't stand the test of time. And in 1997, as Bob Dylan would have said, the times they were a-changing.

There were some dreadful mistakes and miscalculations being made, though. Faced with stiff competition, labels turned the Top 40 into some kind of arms race.

They started releasing records on multiple formats, and then discounting the price of them to make them more appealing than the rest of the pack. They spent thousands on co-op ads with the major High Street record stores (a co-op is a deal that gets your record high profile space on the shop's racks and mentioned in the store's advertising. There are deals to suit all budgets. Unless you're a breadline independent label, in which case you're stuffed).

The money didn't seem to matter at the time, though. British music was the talk of the town, and the bank accounts were looking healthy. But the majors were well on course to outspend their income. And when the audience woke up and realized that some of the identikit Britpop groups weren't really going anywhere, that's when it all came to a grinding halt.

As a brief aside here, it's always puzzled me how the big companies deal with plummeting record sales. Around this time, there were scare stories about album sales falling – and Playstation games and other

Blur "Modern Life Is Rubbish"

A1. FOR TOMORROW   4.18
2. ADVERT   3.43
3. COLIN ZEAL   3.14
4. PRESSURE ON JULIAN 3.30
5. STAR SHAPED   3.25
6. BLUE JEANS   3.53
7. CHEMICAL WORLD   4.02
8. INTERMISSION   2.27

23-03-93

See Over For Side B Details...

Parlophone

Spray paint as an offensive weapon: the born-again Blur in British Image mode.

The promo cassette for Blur's second album.

SCHOOL OF ART

Art for art's sake. This would have made a good record sleeve, I think. Pulp rediscovering their art school roots.

elastica

0023

You've no idea how long we took stamping the numbers on these sleeves. The first (and now quite rare) Elastica single, *Stutter*, with a painting of drummer Justin on the label.

Big boots, no knickers. Elastica pulling their Last Gang In Town pose around the time of their first two singles: (left to right) Annie, Donna, Justine and Justin.

Whatever happened to that Jacob's Mouse T-shirt? Pulling moody faces, Lamacq and Whiley in the old Radio 1 studios in Egton House. The jingles behind us are for *Steve Wright in the Afternoon*.

Our first Radio 1 promo postcard. In the absence of a studio, this was taken in a corridor in the basement of Broadcasting House.

'Excuse me, how do you get this thing to move on its own?' Fatboy Slim, aka Norman Cook, always manages to play records that complement his shirt collection.

Liam Gallagher and Oasis playing live on the *Evening Session* from BBC Maida Vale studios. Jo and I were in a vocal booth opposite Liam, while the audience scrambled for a view from the balcony. OPPOSITE: the ad for The Verve's *This Is Music* and the laminate for their incredible Haigh Hall gig.

Say 'Arrgghhhhhhhh'. Good dentistry shots of Darren Hayman from Hefner and Chris Martin from Coldplay. LEFT: Idlewild bassist Bob does his helicopter hair trick.

Taxi for Noel Gallagher. Coming to the end of the infamous Oasis interview in the all-new R1 studio where we now do the show. BELOW: you don't have to be mad as a snake to work here, but most of us are. Some of the recent *Session* team: (left to right) Sam Steele, Louise Kattenhorn, Joe Harland, Simon Barnard, Jane Graham and The Thinker.

leisure gear climbing. Yet at the same time, faced with accusations that CD albums were (and still are) overpriced, the majors never once tried to tempt audiences back by lowering the cost of CDs in shops. Oh, there are mid-price reissues and special offers from time to time, but nothing that isn't calculated.

Back in the Square Mile in Camden, there was panic on the dealers' floor. It was like the Wall Street crash or the collapse of the Hong Kong Bank (and of course everyone was looking for a Nick Leeson to blame, so you had to watch your back the whole time). Just as one sniff of a rumour about a fall in profits can send a company's shares plummeting through the floor, just one whisper of a disappointing midweek (a Salad or a Marion) sent a band's reputation reeling.

How many times did you hear the phrase, 'So and so. They're all over,' in the summer of 1997?

But it wasn't all over. I'm mixing my metaphors again, but music can be like the tide going in and out. It went out on the NWONW, but it still left Elastica behind, so that was OK. And it went out on Britpop, but there was still Oasis, Radiohead, Blur and the return of The Verve – striding barefoot up the beach when they'd previously been considered all washed up.

The critical and creative tide of Britpop might have been slipping out to sea again. But if the tide was going out here … it must have been coming in somewhere.

I've referred to Manchester countless times in this book, but it's important to point out the contribution to pop of Glasgow as well. If Manchester leads the way with mainstream alternative pop music, then Glasgow, on countless occasions, has controlled the underground. In the 80s it had Postcard Records and Aztec Camera and Orange Juice. Then later came Creation Records, McGee, the Jesus & Mary Chain and Primal Scream (not to mention the Soup Dragons, who later scored huge hits on both sides of the Atlantic, and the influential Pastels and Vaselines).

Away from Camden, Glasgow (well, Scotland in general) was full of all sorts of great, life-raft bands. If Britpop had been played out in the mainstream, mostly by the majors, then the latest wave of Scottish groups were defiantly independent. The year 1997 gave us the gorgeous

Lazy Line Painter Jane, confirming the arrival of Belle & Sebastian, who had already released an album. Then there were Mogwai, The Delgadoes and their Chemikal Underground label. In their own way all these bands were a reaction to Britpop and Camden, though some were more vociferous than others. Mogwai (perhaps the My Bloody Valentine of their generation?) even went as far as producing BLUR ARE SHITE T-shirts, which emphasized how poorly Blur translated north of the border and how indignant Mogwai appeared to be about the whole Cool Britannnia chart crusade. The shirts created something of a storm at the time – though the irony is that Blur's guitarist Graham Coxon probably pays homage to as many cool American bands as do the Mogwai boys.

Which is another thing. Is it just me or is Scotland the nearest link Britain has to the American underground? London's famous Rough Trade shops might have all the imports, but it's bands like Mogwai who have publicly shown their devotion to Slint or Ariel M, and it's Scottish groups like the Vaselines (later Captain America), the Pastels and Belle & Sebastian who have caught the imagination of American underground audiences and bands (not least Nirvana, who covered the Vaselines' *Molly's Lips*).

So, Glasgow and its surrounding estates and outposts became a haven for people who cornershopped for pop, rather than doing the big Tesco's superstore thing. And though not all the records made the *Evening Session*, round my house it was like the early 80s all over again. Then one afternoon, at Radio 1, the big one turned up. It arrived in an anonymous brown seven-inch mailer and I got so excited when I heard it that I had to run next door (and I mean run) to play it to producer Claire. It went straight into the following day's programme and became the most consecutively played single on the *Sesh* of all time. We played it every night for two and a half weeks. It was Arab Strap – *The First Big Weekend*.

The only other record that's come close is *Rockerfella Skank*.

• 20
PUNK DA FUNK

I know this might come as a shock to you – unless you grew up in a small corner of Essex – but I used to run the Equinox Disco. Well, co-run actually. It was Carl Daw, the electronics whizzkid from my physics class, who actually did most of the graft. For a start, it was Daw who bought two turntables from a Tandy catalogue and then set about making them look like a proper Citronic Disco unit. I was very impressed. Two decks and a mixer (like the ones they used to advertise in the back of *Record Mirror*).

We spent another afternoon making and painting two light boxes – the sort of sad-looking traffic light affairs that you find at wedding receptions – and then we were ready. We had our own mobile disco. Stuck for a name, we trawled through Carl's record collection, looking for something snazzy to provide us with inspiration. Sadly, as all his singles seemed to be by Jean Michel Jarre, we were limited to the French pioneer's output of Oxygene or Equinoxe. But hey, I reasoned, we could always change it later.

But that's how the Equinox Disco started (we dropped the final E, I seem to remember, which would make for a good gag here, but you're probably ahead of me on that one). Before long we were out every fortnight playing wedding receptions, youth clubs, friends' parties – and even my old primary school. The decks used to break down at least once every three gigs, and the speakers blew one night, but it's not as if we were expensive or anything.

In retrospect, this was the first time my DJing ambition had got the better of me (although I rarely said anything over the mic, apart from 'last orders at the bar'). To add to the pile of Jean Michel Jarre records, we put the cash from the gigs back into collecting a stunning array of dodgy compilation albums and a few 12-inch singles. All of a sudden, though, I found I'd turned into a musical schizophrenic.

These days when, happily, music is far less tribal, this condition isn't a problem. In fact, it's a positive advantage. But back in my teens there were endless drawbacks caused by an allegiance to more than one brand of music. How could you be punk, for instance, if you had a Chic record at home? How could you be a sensitive indie-type interested in poetry and Joy Division when all you could recite were a list of varying beats per minute (Donna Summer *Hot Stuff*: 138, Edwyn Starr *Contact*: 132 … and that's just off the top of my head).

I've kept remarkably quiet about my dance addiction over the years but every so often it just blurts out. Did you know that the amazing *Shame* by Evelyn Champagne King (another record that I bought on a family holiday) was the biggest selling 12-inch of 1978? Or that before they had a hit with *Oops Upside Your Head* the Gap Band released a better record called *Baby Baba Boogie* (my first ever import purchase from a shop in Bournemouth)? Oops. Damn. There you go, you see. I suppose the reason I've decided to get this off my chest is that, like all those 80s indie bands who jumped on the dance bandwagon with appalling baggy remixes, 'there's always been a dance element to my music'.

So, while we're in confessional mode, here are two words: Norman Cook.

It was an accident, OK, and I wasn't ready for it, and oh, well, I suppose you should know this. But Norman Cook is Mystic Meg and I am the man in the lottery syndicate who one day pockets his colleague's cash and then spends it on beer instead of buying a ticket. And well, you can probably guess the rest.

It had been a quiet fortnight at the *NME* and the only feature I was due to write was a small introductory piece on a new and much-tipped Scottish band called the Trashcan Sinatras. Their press officer duly sent me a cassette of some new songs and I duly listened to it at home one morning, scribbled down a few questions and then put the kettle on.

In the background, the Trashcans' songs ended and the tape flipped over automatically, to reveal something very un-Trashcans-like indeed. Instead, the tune on side B was a loping, mellow dance number with a girl singing prettily over the top. Must be a cock-up, I thought. Actually, hold on, whatever it was, it wasn't the Trashcans, and it was quite good.

On further investigation, the only words printed on side B were Beats International. Who the hell were Beats International when they were at home? What were they doing lurking on the flipside of a tape of The

Next Big Thing from Scotland? The impertinence of it!

Back in the office, the phone call to the press officer went something like this:

'Thanks for the Trashcans stuff. By the way, who are Beats International?'

'Oh, that's Norman Cook's new thing.'

'Wwwhhaaattttttt?'

Norman Cook? One time bassist with The Housemartins? Impossible. Does not compute. Syntax error. The last time I'd seen Norman Cook in the flesh, he was bouncing – and I mean really bouncing – around the stage at the Hammersmith Clarendon. The Housemartins had started life as one of the fanzine world's favourite groups (the ace Cool Notes had written about them all the time, including the band's Adopt A Housemartin scam where fans could offer floorspace to the group to kip on after dates on their first tour). They'd gone on to have number one hits, but then, at the height of their fame (just after the tabloids outed them for being middle-class lefties) they split, publicly and somewhat acrimoniously. There had been stories of the four members wanting to go off in different musical directions and there had always been rumours that Cook was a soul boy at heart, but nothing had quite prepared me for this.

'I think we should do something on it,' I spluttered. 'Let me see what I can do.' And so the tape went round the office. Cook, it transpired, had stayed with Go! Discs Records (home of The Housemartins and also new signings the Trashcan Sinatras) and was ready to make a comeback. The feature was commissioned and I ended up on a train heading toward the south coast.

Cook lived one station short of Brighton (there's probably a gag here too) in a house that boasted not one but two playrooms. The first was indeed full of kids' toys; the second, a small boxroom upstairs, was full of shelves weighed down with 12-inch singles and old vinyl LPs. This is where he had been since The Housemartins split.

'Rocking backwards and forwards on a stool in the living area of his new house – upstairs there's a small home studio and a Scalectrix – our Norm's got a new "bonehead" haircut but has held on to his boyish smile,' the feature ran.

Cook revealed he'd worked on numerous dance remixes since The

Housemartins split. But had he felt insecure at any point since the band broke up?

'Yeah, definitely, because of the switch to dance music and because I thought people might think I was jumping on the bandwagon. But then when I started doing a lot of remixes, most people buying the records didn't know I was in The Housemartins. Or they didn't know who they were.

'I take your point about being a white bloke moving into dance music but this is what I've been interested in ever since I was 14. And after a while doing the remixes – and seeing people dance to them – I realized I'd almost rebuilt the whole track, and that gave me confidence to make my own records.'

The new one by Beats International (the loping reggae one featuring guest vocals by ex-Grange Hill actress Lindy Layton) wasn't a conscious effort to take reggae back into the charts. But it was designed to halt a landslide of incorrigible headlines.

'I suppose it was a reaction against the pun "From Housemartin to Housemaster", because I don't like house music. I went to the Hacienda on a Friday night, the big house night, and it all sounded the same. It was so stark. Maybe I'm getting old and that's what the kids are into, but not me. I'm sick to death of all these bleedin' Italian records.'

Instead, *Dub Be Good To Me* was 'an attempt to do something completely unhip.'

'The bass line on the single, that's an affectionate tribute to The Clash. It's like tipping my cap to them because they were a huge influence on my growing up both musically and politically.'

That's all it says in the feature, but during the interview I tried to get him to admit that the bassline was a direct sample from The Clash's *Guns Of Brixton.*

'No,' he said, 'it's a re-creation of the original.'

Oh, all right then. Don't really understand much about this sampling business (which in 1990 I didn't. Despite being three years on from *Pump Up The Volume*, sampling culture was only just starting to blow up a storm, with legal suits pending all over the show). That's when he hit me with this.

'You should get out of the indie guitar ghetto, Steve. Dance music's where all the new ideas are happening.'

Hmmmmmmmmm.

By the time the feature hit the streets, *Dub Be Good To Me* had started to be played on the radio and subsequently went to number one. That was the last I saw of Cook for ages (apart from a surreal live appearance with Freak Power at T In The Park one year where Cook was dressed in a Ken Dodd hat and a flamboyant long orange overcoat). I hid the ticket out of the indie guitar ghetto under my bed and forgot all about it. After all, he'd never be able to pull off another shock like that.

By Christmas 1996, with the music scene becoming restless, it was obvious that the mainstream needed freshening up.

It was a time of upheaval for me too. Lisa I'Anson was leaving the lunchtime show and, having been a hit with her *Saturday Social* programme, Jo Whiley was approached to take over while I'Anson took maternity leave. The original plan was that Mary Anne Hobbs would replace her on the *Session*, thus reuniting the *NME* Two for the first time in four years. We got as far as trailing Mary Anne's arrival on a show over Christmas, but just before the change around, Chris Evans quit the *Breakfast Show* and there was a snappy rethink. Mark and Lard moved to breakfast, Mary Anne took over their late-night slot, and I was given the nod to go solo on the *Sesh*.

If that wasn't scary and foreboding enough, just two weeks before Jo left the show, I split up with the Better Half after seven years. And then I promptly contracted conjunctivitis. For the first two weeks after Jo's promotion I was doing the show with one contact lens (if your tour dates were printed in anything less than 14pt, I'm afraid you were knackered).

Partly by luck and partly through judgement, we tried to galvanize the new *Session* into action by broadening its musical horizons. Big Ant had already started tipping me off about some new dance and hip-hop tunes, and the more I looked around, the more the maze of dance music led me into new and often dead-exciting territory. Other people had been here before. Having exhausted their interest in guitar music, people had been cross-fertilizing rock and club culture for years (Underworld, for instance, whose *Born Slippy* was the perfect crossover tune). Plus, the band that the tastemakers were talking about at the time were not your average indie-thrash band, but a duo who had grown out of an indie thrash band. It was Bentley Rhythm Ace. Armed with this scant amount of knowledge and £50 from the cashpoint, I found I'd caught the record-buying bug again.

One of the records I bought in a spree at HMV was *Punk Da Funk* by Fatboy Slim, which I'd never heard but thought might be worth a go because (a) it was on Skint and (b) it had the word punk in it. What a sucker, eh? I loved it. It had a sample of the *Big Match* theme tune on it and we played it the following night. I played it at the wrong speed mind you, but if you listen to it, it sounds better at 45 anyway.

A day later a man from the promotions company came on the phone.

'Heard you played Fatboy Slim.'

'Yeah, good record.'

'It's Norman Cook's new thing.'

'Aaaaaaaarrrrghhhhhhhhh.'

And the rest, as they say, is history.

NB: There is a pay-off to this chapter. Having conquered most of the known world and married Zoë Ball, Norman Cook has also sold millions of records across the globe. At the *NME* Awards in February 2000 he won the Best DJ prize. After presenting him with his trophy, I shook his hand. And I thanked him for his advice. Doh!

b side

It is difficult getting off with someone at a gig. It's not impossible, but it's not easy either. The odds are stacked against you.

It is loud, and if you've been anywhere near the front, you probably smell. There's the time factor as well. You'd have to get to the gig pretty early and put in a determined effort to meet someone, chat them up, and then snog them in between bands and trips to the bar before the end of the night. I think this is one of the reasons why fans of guitar music finally owned up to liking clubs.

The first indie club I went to was a Thursday night shindig called Syndrome in Oxford Street. During the height of its fame at the end of the 80s and the early 90s, it became a haunt for bands and journalists as well as fans. There were so many chummy pop stars hanging out there for a while (Blur, Ride, Lush, all the shoegazers and the Camden Lurchers) that it became dubbed 'The Scene That Celebrates Itself'.

But, having made the leap from gigs to clubs, we had a problem. What were the rock fans going to dance to?

It was Madchester and the Mondays and then the Primals and even the KLF who came to the rescue (people who had all come from a rock background themselves). Then there were the 12 million baggy groups and remixes of indie tunes, tarted up to sound vaguely housey. It wasn't exactly an adventurous playlist – though the Syndrome's DJs mixed these tracks up with fantastic old classics by people like the Violent Femmes – but you had to start somewhere.

Besides, different people want different things from dance music and club culture. And it's only by experimenting that you find out what they are.

Journalists and A&R scouts and MDs are always getting asked this: 'What do you look for in a record?' (the subtext: is there a magical formula I can follow to get rich quick?). I'm sure we've all developed polished answers over the years, but mine is a little vague. I can tell you it's not a great hookline, or an amazing guitar solo, though I'm a sucker for both. But what I really like is CLEVER. And that's what's so fascinating about some dance and club music to me. CLEVER.

Someone asked me the other day, 'If you could be in a band, which one would you be in?' to which my knee-jerk answer was the Chemical Brothers. 'And why?'

'Well, they're nice blokes … and well, they're CLEVER.'

And by this I don't mean they can recite Camus while building their own computer blindfolded with one hand tied behind their backs. It's a different sort of CLEVER. It's wit and invention and attention to detail (and, if you can manage it, a sense of humour and a sense of the absurd too, though not necessarily on the same track). I'm struggling here, aren't I? Oh, look, it's just CLEVER.

And the thing about Fatboy and *Surrender* by the Chemicals, and the extremes of drum'n'bass and all the other dance music I like, is that, in their own ways, they're all CLEVER. OK, I know Norman Cook has lifted some of his hits almost lock, stock and barrel from old soul records, but you have to admire him for his choices of samples. That's the clever bit.

Plus, in their construction, the best hip-hop rhymes are clever, the scratch DJs are clever (what wouldn't you give for just one afternoon's tuition from DJ Shadow, whose set at Oxford Sound City made me want to cry with admiration) and the best remix engineers are clever.

So through 1997 and onwards there have been all manner of clever bastards dealing out records to the *Session*. The Propellerheads, Death In Vegas, DJ Shadow, Blackalicious. And we play tracks lent to us by Pete Tong and Tim Westwood and other DJs around the station. It's a mash-up of crossover tunes and white labels (the *Session* was apparently the first show to play Oxide & Neutrino's number one *Bound 4 Da Reload* — another 12-inch I bought out of curiosity in a trawl round the West End).

Norman Cook and Paul Oakenfold, meanwhile, among numerous others, have revived the late 80s trend for putting remix topspin on rock bands (Cook, famously, with Cornershop and Oakenfold with bands such as Mansun). Meanwhile, (punk) rock fans have become increasingly attached to their links with hip-hop.

But there was one particular night in 1999 which to me summed up how much the barriers have come down between dance and rock music, and how, in effect, the late 90s had gone full circle back to the late 70s.

There is still dance music I don't understand, or I don't get, or I simply don't like (trance, ambient ... the sound of dripping taps). But drum'n'bass, that's the kiddy. I can go a bit of speed garage if it comes to it as well, but give me an ear-piercing, rattling drum'n'bass 12-inch any day. I couldn't work out why I liked it (not that you need a reason for liking something. My compulsion to over-analyse doesn't stretch that far). But it just sounded exciting.

How on earth could you dance to it, though? Have you heard how fast those beats are?

In the end, curiosity got the better of me and I went to a Fabio & Grooverider night in Glasgow as part of the BBC's Music Live festival. And for the first time in ages – gigs included – my heart wouldn't stop pounding. Not only were the tunes good, but the crowd were mesmerizing. My actual train of thought went like this: You don't dance to the drums, you dance to the bass. It's reggae speeded up. I like reggae. That's why I like this. I have been a twit for two years.

Not all of this is strictly factually correct, of course. You *can* dance to the drums and the leap from reggae to drum and bass is quite a long jump. But before I could get any further with the reasoning process, one of the audience came up and tapped me on the shoulder.

'Steve? All right? Always listen to the show. Hey, can I give you a demo tape?'

'What is it? Like this?' I asked, pointing at the PA.

'No, guitar band ... we like a bit of this though. It's like reggae speeded up.'

And in a flash, half of me was standing on the vibrating club floor, knees and shoulders bending around another tune; and the other half of me was a small kid again, listening to The Clash and Misty; to the punk rock The Ruts and reggae supergods Steel Pulse. And as a diversion, it was a good road to go down.

• 21
HAPPY

We squabble over whose idea it was, but between us (Matt Priest and Jason Carter from Radio 1's marketing team and me) we came up with the idea of taking the *Evening Session* on tour.

Mark and Lard had just been on the road with the *Breakfast Show* and their covers band The Shire Horses, entertaining the student masses of Britain. So when it came to planning live events for the *Evening Session* for 1998, the idea of taking the team on the road for a week was virtually staring us in the face. What was more exciting was how we'd do it.

It took an hour of brainstorming to plan, but by the end of it Matt and I had the blueprint. We'd hire a proper, Starcruiser-style sleeper bus and build a studio into it. Then we'd put a tour together with three bands and follow it around the country. Sleeping on the bus.

I was grinning from ear to ear. Sleeping on the bus. Like a band on tour. Really travelling around the country SLEEPING ON THE BUS.

'Who's sleeping on a bus?!' said producer Claire. 'Couldn't you have asked us first?' Claire has a selection of faces she pulls, depending on her level of disapproval or disbelief. The news about Sleeping On The Bus earned one of the best ones. It's the one grown-ups give you when they think you're behaving like a child.

'Go on, it'll be great.' Erm … oh dear. I appear to have gone insane again.

In my own head, the idea of the *Evening Session* tour wasn't based on Mark and Lard's at all. It was fuelled by a week I'd spent on tour with the band Therapy?. Back in 1996 I had the same agent as the band and after a drunken night at a gig in London, we'd dreamt up the idea of me DJing between bands on their next set of UK dates.

The tour started with two nights at the Shepherds Bush Empire and then we were off for another six days. I learned all you need to know about tour bus safety and etiquette in about ten minutes from Roger Patterson, their tour manager. For future reference the advice was:

- Always sleep with your feet facing the direction of travel (that way you won't break your neck if the coach stops suddenly)
- Don't use the toilet
- Try not to get a bunk too close to the recreation area. People in bands will stay up all night drinking and watching videos and keeping you awake
- Don't leave half-drunk cans of lager where they'll come a cropper as the bus goes around a roundabout.

And that's it. I mean, really, these are the only rules. As soon as you step on a tour bus, the rest of the outside world's normal codes of conduct go out the window. Don't tell the Sex Pistols, but this is as close as anyone gets in the music industry to anarchy.

So by November 1997 we had the concept. All we had to do was book some bands, and book them sharpish, so we could get the tickets on sale before Christmas.

Travis were on board immediately. They'd just had a minor hit with *Happy* from their debut *Good Feeling* album, but also they'd endeared themselves to the *Evening Session* a month earlier in New York. We'd taken the show to the States to cover CMJ – the big annual college radio festival – which every year embraces a handful of 'showcase' gigs by British bands anxious to attract attention in America.

Travis played two shows. One was a terrifically upbeat set in a bar in the middle of nowhere. The other was their proper Seminar show where they shared a stage with, I think, Mansun. The second gig was swamped with people from their American label, one of whom came out with one of the most extraordinary sentences I think I've ever heard. Now I know American radio pluggers are meant to have a sense of the absurd about them (see Spinal Tap's Artie Fufkin for more details), but having worked the room, the guy sidled up to Fran and, putting his arm around his shoulder, said, 'OK, Franny, great gig. Now let's go shake some hands and kiss some babies.'

On the whole Fran didn't look like a man who wanted to either shake hands or kiss babies, but he followed the plugger anyway.

So Travis were in (because they were nice, quite gregarious chaps, and because if we needed any babies kissing, then we had the man for the job). To co-headline, we plumped for Catatonia. And I pay respect here to the judgement and terrible singing of then *Session* assistant Hannah Brown. It was Hannah who had started regaling the office with renditions of Catatonia's single *I Am The Mob* – and the enthusiasm rubbed off. The more I listened to it at home the better it got. On the back of that I wheedled myself an advance copy of *International Velvet* and that was it. Done and dusted. I'm hit and miss with my predictions, but there was a track on it called *Mulder and Scully* which was going to be the next single, and that was a nailed-on Top 40 record. No mistake.

Besides, it felt like Catatonia's time. They'd managed to hide in the corner during Britpop, and now all the scuffles had died down, they'd taken this as their cue to re-emerge. They had a cracking album up their sleeves – a mixture of hooklines and sensitivity – and they had Cerys Mathews, who was Nancy from *Oliver*.

It's strange putting this on paper now, three years down the line, when both these bands have suffered the sort of public backlashes that inevitably come with success and over-exposure. But back then, as 1997 wilted away, they felt like the natural progression to what had gone before in the past three years.

Idlewild, meanwhile, were something of a curveball. Their bassist was bonkers and their singer took his shoes off during their set. No-one had warned me about that. I'd been on my way to the Garage in Highbury one night to see a group called Astronaut, but having half an hour to kill I popped into the Hope and Anchor in Islington on the way. The band first on, Idlewild, had released a seven-inch which we'd played a couple of times on air, so it made sense to see what they were like.

And that was about the only thing that made sense. The singer leapt around like a maniac, removed his shoes, grappled with his hair and pogoed until his head hit the low ceiling. The rest of the band, in scraggy T-shirts and hair all over the place, made an angular pop racket. The audience, all friends of the headlining band, looked on bemused, but applauded politely at the end of each song. It was like watching Seymour all over again (by coincidence the only other music industry people in the audience that night were Matthew from Food Records and the group's future manager, Bruce).

I saw them again at the Garage, this time with Simon Williams.

Me: 'Great aren't they, but do you think people will get it?'

Si: 'Nope.'

Me: 'No, me neither.'

I booked them for the tour and Simon released their next single, *Chandelier*.

Now I'm not a connoisseur of tour buses, but, boy, did ours look impressive. It was silver and had 'Evening Session' in huge letters down the side. It was like the stories you hear of boys buying their girlfriends cars for Christmas and parking them outside the house. 'Steve, we got you this ...' WOW. You shouldn't have. Can I sit in it?

The bus was hired from a company called Nova Travel, who also supplied Brett, the driver. Brett's opening speech was a virtual dictionary definition of life on tour: 'Only one rule. No dumping. Every form of vice and sin is fine, but no dumping.'

And it was in this playground den that we went to work. And it's here that you'd expect a blow by blow account of all the testosterone and tomfoolery, but if there's one thing I've learnt about touring – it's that retelling the stories is the hardest and most unfulfilling part of it all. Touring comes with several in-built mechanisms for ensuring that it remains just that little bit elite and mysterious. Namely – the in-joke! The short-term memory loss! The stuff that you do that's so out of character you'll never want to tell people about it until you're on your deathbed.

And anyway, who's really interested if every story you tell either starts with the line 'It was really funny, right ...' or finishes with 'Well, I guess you had to be there.'

I think this is why bands who've just come off tour are listless and irritable and make no sense. Apart from suffering from the obvious lack of attention – let's face it, no-one cheers when you walk in the pub like they do when you walk on stage – they have nothing to say. Nothing that connects them to the real world. All they have is a bunch of crap jokes, a few stories about their guitar technician and his underwear, and an impressive array of service station nik-naks (come on, hands up).

Not only that, but my most vivid memory of this tour was the journey across the Snake Pass from Manchester to Leeds, which isn't very rock'n'roll, is it? All it was was a gang of mates on a bus telling stories and talking nonsense as Simon Mayo crackled out of a transistor radio and we gazed at the scenery. Maybe it was something to do with the fact that, by then, we felt comfortable enough to rip the piss out of each other mercilessly. Maybe it was just sleep deprivation kicking in. Who knows? Everyone on the bus probably does, but I'll be buggered if I can explain it.

For the sake of future pop historians, though, here are the more accessible highlights.

DAY ONE: Glasgow Barrowlands. Belle & Sebastian (all 108 of them) record a live acoustic session in our studio on the bus. Meet Fran Healey's mum. After the gig Travis try to break into our bus because they've run out of beer and they think we have a secret stash. They do this in the dead of night in their pyjamas.

DAY TWO: Manchester. *Melody Maker* arrive to do a feature. Tell them that we had to saw two seats out of the bus to get all the studio equipment on board. They describe conditions on the coach as 'like being in a U-boat'.

DAY THREE: Leeds. A day off for the bands, but we take the bus into Leeds and park outside the venue, the Duchess, where the Pecadilloes are playing. Burn an incredible amount of money in the pinball machine and after the gig get woken up by a posse of drunks trying to rock the bus about.

DAY FOUR: Birmingham. Fuzz Townshend, ex of Pop Will Eat Itself and now Bentley Rhythm Ace drummer, turns up and busks on the bus. This entails a very long percussion solo on a drumkit we've made out of various bits of debris we've found on the bus (eight empty Pringles tubes and a Tupperware container that used to have some spare fuses in it). Post gig, hold an impromptu aftershow party on the bus with Fuzz, Cerys Mathews and assorted fanzine writers. Halfway through, we spot one of Idlewild trying to snog someone in a bush.

DAY FIVE: Newport. Roll out of bunk to find Radio 1 soundman looking down at me, laughing. Go and check in a mirror and understand why. Best gig of the tour. Am given a pair of Welsh flag boxer shorts by Cerys (just one example of the underwear she's been bombarded with for the past week. Thinks. Does this make her the new Tom Jones?).

DAY SIX: London. Home. Bored.

A year later we did it all again, this time with 3 Colours Red, Muse and American all-girl band the Donnas. Only this time, it was all boys. The staff on the show had changed (Claire and Hannah moving on, and Rhys Hughes, Simon Barnard and Joe Harland joining).

Rhys 'Chunky' Hughes was used to touring. He's been in bands, you see, not that he liked talking about them. NOT MUCH. Every town we pulled into, Rhys would crane his neck around and peer out the window to see if the venue we were going to was one he'd played before ... Actually, that's a terrible exaggeration. But then, the second *Evening Session* tour was all about exaggeration.

It is a strange thing, but people on tour play to character. Loud people are louder, sick people are sicker, and messy people are even messier. On the second tour, without even thinking about it, the boys from the *Session* – me included – played out our real-life roles with a certain panache. Simon needed to sleep more than ever and looked like he might break when he eventually raised himself from his bunk of a morning. And Joe, the efficient one, was unbelievably more efficient and organized than ever – except on the day we drove to Sheffield and his thirst got the better of him. Fortunately, it was Saturday and a day off, and after starting on the Bacardi Breezers in Manchester we arrived in Sheffield, where Joe climbed onto the roof of the bus to sunbathe and promptly fell asleep.

The two of us ended up going to see dEUS and Ten Benson at the excellent Leadmill, though when the gig finished and the Step On club began I lost him again. Getting up onto the stage to survey the room, I spotted him in the middle of the dancefloor, headbanging to The Offspring.

For my part, I did everything I always do (go to bed too late, get up too early, eat nothing but curry and crisps – though not together obviously – and wash them down with Hooch and cider). If I wasn't such an exaggerated character on tour as the rest of the team, then that was simply because I do all this at home all the time anyway. It's not like I've been let off the leash or I can break all the usual house rules of where I live, because there aren't any rules.

But in some cases I think that's why people go barmy on tour. It gives people a chance to behave in a way they can't at home or in an office. So, scarily, although people talk about bands being juvenile on tour, I'd hazard a guess that the characters they portray on the road are probably closer to the 'Real Them' than the parts they play in polite society. And if that's true, then that's quite frightening.

Mind you, I can think of one thing which is MORE frightening. And that was producer Rhys's snoring. Rhys had come to the *Session* from Mark and Lard's *Breakfast Show* via a stint on Simon Mayo's programme. His most recent stint on tour had been as bassist in The Shire Horses who, along with his girlfriend, had completely failed to warn us about the noises he makes while he's asleep. AND I HAD THE BUNK OPPOSITE HIM. You know in cartoons, when a character is snoring so heavily that the sheets on top of them rise and fall in time with their breathing? That was Rhys.

But despite this, we got on terrifically well (along with Alan and Kev the on-board Radio 1 engineers, who are always the funniest part of any outside broadcast. Years of setting up sound for everyone from live sport on Radio 5 to *Sunday Night Is Music Night* have imbued the Beeb's technical staff with a sense of humour second to none).

This time around we invented a feature called the Tour Trauma League Table, giving and taking away points depending on how much of a turbulent time the bands were having on the road. The Donnas won it, despite Joe's loyal attempt to win bonus bravery points for the *Session* team by climbing out of our bus and on to the roof – as we sped down the motorway. He'd have made it as well, if the rest of us hadn't grabbed at his legs.

This is my funniest moment of the 1999 tour though. Simon had been given the task of taking the Donnas shopping in Manchester. The only problem was that it was pouring with rain. So, as the band sheltered on the Oxford Road steps of Manchester University, Simon (who had failed to hail a cab) spied a bus coming down the road and darted out to the edge of the kerb to make it stop.

Unfortunately, the Donnas hadn't a clue what he was doing. And Simon had neglected to tell them. The bus stops, Simon jumps on, and then just as he turns around and the doors close behind him, he sees the Donnas, standing exactly where they were, looking at him like he's run away. The bus pulls off and he gesticulates at them, hopelessly (four damp, teenage Americans in an unfamiliar city).

Five minutes later, having jumped off at the first stop he could, the next they see of this man from the BBC is an out-of-breath, out-of-shape, skinny, short-haired indie-bloke running back up the street ... still waving at them.

Later in the year I went on tour again. But this time it wasn't with a band. This time I WAS the band. And I know I've said all the stuff about not being a frustrated musician, and never wanting to be on stage. But honestly, this was different.

When I joined Radio 1, my friend Tony Smith suggested that we get a booking agent and see if he could fix me up with some DJing dates around the country. Tony used to drive, and we'd turn up at student unions and indie clubs and play some records and I'd mumble into a mic and shuffle about looking embarrassed every time I cleared the dancefloor.

But with some practice and experience I started to find it is possible to mix records, rather than just segue them, just as it is possible to clear a dancefloor and refill it ('If you're any good,' Jez from the Utah Saints once said, 'you don't worry about clearing the floor because you've got records up your sleeve that will pack it again').

In the spring of 1999, I went to said gig agent – a chap called Jim Morewood at Helter Skelter – with the idea of maybe taking a week off work, and doing a tour of student unions during Freshers' Week. Jim thought this was possible. In fact, Jim's been very good to me over the years, and he has only really cocked it up once. It was his suggestion that I did an NUS conference in Reading.

The theory was right enough. Every year the NUS puts on a weekend of showcase gigs, so that the various ents officers from around the country can cast their eyes over some of the groups that agents are trying to promote in the following term. If I was DJing, who knows, they might even book me. That was the theory.

The reality, though, was that on the coldest, wettest, most thoroughly miserable day of the year, the gig took place in a marquee outside the Reading Uni building. Every time a band went on, a handful, and I mean a handful, of people would wander in, take one look at their breath frosting up in front of their faces, and head steaming back to the sanctuary of the bar. Meanwhile, I had to DJ on a door-sized raised platform to one side that, thanks to the rain, was surrounded by a small moat.

I've never let Jim forget this. Nor has my current driver Liam, who isn't a driver, but has wafted through life doing various jobs (including running a gym where he worked with Geri Halliwell). Liam is lethal. He could poke a student's eye out with such deft precision that you'd think he'd been trained by the SAS. In fact, dressed in his combats and woolly hat, you'd think he *was* one of the SAS. Anyway, Jim came up trumps with the tour and we set off for the opening date in Bath. It was the coldest, wettest, most miserable night of the year. And when we arrived, we were shown the marquee.

This tour taught me a lot about what it must be like when you're a new band on the bottom rung of the circuit. Liam and I stayed in small B&Bs (mostly twin rooms to keep the cost down) and had to work out our journeys so they didn't clash with rush hours that turn into traffic jams, which in turn sap your patience and resolve.

We'd already noticed other similarities between ourselves and the lives of other bands on tour. We have our own in-jokes that nobody else understands (mostly quotes from the film *Mars Attacks* or various editions of Chris Morris's radio show *On The Hour*); we have our favourite service stations up and down the M1; and we're so hyped up after a gig that to go straight back to the hotel and hit the sack is absolutely unthinkable.

We're also affected by the same outside factors too, like being at the mercy of the promoter's fly-posting budget, or being given maps to the venue that were drawn in 1975, 18 years before a new one-way system was introduced. But, of course, it's still a tour – and, at 10 days long, it's not enough to send you insane. I think I could do two weeks without seriously damaging my health, but how bands manage four-month-long treks across America, I'll never know.

The Bath gig wasn't that bad in the end. But the hotel was a warning of what was to follow. It was chintzy and stuffy and we couldn't get the kettle to work. The phone went in the morning at 8.30 or something with the landlady inviting us to breakfast.

'Now, are you sure I can't tempt you?' she said.

Liam, who'd taken the call and isn't spectacularly good in the morning, thanked her very politely and said no. 'You know what she's done,' he joked. 'She's got all the guests in the breakfast room and told them there's a Radio 1 DJ in the hotel. They're all waiting. "Is he coming down? Phone him again!"'

AKDAKAKAKDACKDACK. As they say in *Mars Attacks*.

And once again, I'd love to crack all the jokes we had over the next few days but even I can't remember why some of them were funny. I do know one thing though. As the tour went on, via Guildford, Wolverhampton and Exeter, our sense of humour became crueller and crueller. On tour, the funniest things always seem to be those that involve other people's misfortunes. After four days on tour, trust me, intellectual gags are out the window. What we want is more people falling over or banging their heads.

And you become prone to sporadic fits of giggles. I burst out laughing in a café in Aberystwyth and couldn't stop for hours. Hysteria maybe? I suspect all this is the child in us beginning to reconquer the mind that it lost to maturity as we attempted to grow up. It's either that or the realization that we haven't grown up at all.

• 22
HIGH NOON

By the time the Gallagher brothers prepared to release their third album, *Be Here Now*, they were the most sought after band in Britain.

Radio, TV and the press were fighting over any little scrap of Oasis news or information, and behind the scenes there were endless negotiations over which TV channels and radio stations would get the 'exclusive' first play of tracks from the record. For the promotions team who were working Oasis, it was a delicate balancing act – not helped by the fact that a copy of the first single from the album, *D'Ya Know What I Mean?*, had leaked out to a local radio station in Scotland.

The pluggers had promised the first play to Radio 1, but were caught on the hop. It wasn't their fault, but it mucked up their carefully laid plans. At the *Evening Session* we were told we'd get the album first and could play as many tracks from it as we wanted. A day later, the plan changed. We could have three tracks one night and another five the next.

Then on the day we were ready to broadcast the first three, Oasis's people called to say that I had to talk over the start and end of every track – or better still drop a Radio 1 jingle in the middle of them. Now, I could see the management's point here. They were scared of bootlegs of the songs creeping out to Camden market and across to the States before the album's official release. But then again, I've never believed that these badly copied advance tapes actually damage sales that much (the major labels will take me to task on this, but you can make your own minds up). Besides, there was no way I was going to play a jingle over the middle of a song. It just wouldn't sound good.

We'd already promised listeners that they'd be able to hear the album in its entirety, based on the original plan. Now we had to go on air and backtrack, play the three tunes we had been delivered, and promise the rest on the following night.

Come the next day, the remainder of the tracks failed to show. According to the plugging company, Ignition (Oasis's management company) were unhappy that I hadn't talked over the tracks enough.

I'm still not sure whether this was bootleg paranoia gone into overdrive, or whether there was more to it than that (pressure from Oasis's American label Epic maybe?). But I ended up back on air, apologizing to listeners again for not coming up with the promised goods. We got a further two tracks, but that was it. It was all very messy.

Unlike the follow-up, *Standing On The Shoulder Of Giants*, Oasis didn't do that much promotion for *Be Here Now*. Interviews were out of the question. Then, at the end of the campaign, a rumour went round that Noel wanted to break his radio silence. It might happen tomorrow, we were told, or next week. Who knows. Are you interested? Considering the grief that had gone before, I suppose we should have just gaily waved two fingers at their radio plugger and gone back to our pile of demos.

But despite everything, the letters from Oasis fans had far from dried up, and anyway, Noel Gallagher is a good interview. He's funny and he doesn't dry up on you. He'll try and get one over on you maybe, if he's in a cheeky mood, but he's never dull. We hadn't reckoned on him turning up with Liam though.

This was a bit of history. The brothers hadn't conducted a high-profile interview together since the *Wibbling Rivalry* showdown for *NME* back in 1994. The news of Liam's appearance spread like wildfire around the Radio 1 building. By the time the brothers arrived in the studio a small crowd had already formed behind the glass partition that separates my studio from John Peel's. Frankly I was scared witless.

Noel and Liam loafed in and I shook hands with Noel. Then I put my arm out to shake hands with Liam, and he just stared at it.

'You're shaking, man. Why are you shaking?'

You should be standing where I am.

As they sat down, Liam carried on: 'So, who are you shagging then?'

'Sorry?'

'Who are you shagging at the moment?'

Me: 'Well, no-one. Sometimes you're so busy in the music industry you don't have time to have a relationship … that's what I find.'

Liam: 'Are you saying me and Patsy are fucked?'

The CD machine that's playing is counting down the minutes and seconds on the track that's on air. It says 1 min 27 secs, as Liam gets to his feet again and offers to punch me out.

Noel: 'You've took it the wrong way, man. Sit down.'

Me: 'I didn't mean *you* don't have time, I'm saying that when I'm working flat out, that's when a relationship suffers.'

Liam: 'Right. Cos anyone says that me and Patsy ain't going to make it, I'll take them on.'

The CD starts to fade.

Me: 'It's the *Evening Session* and that was *Fighting Fit* by Gene.'

Listening to the interview for the first time in nearly three years, they sound far more wasted than I thought they were at the time. The interview starts politely enough (there's some small talk about the band having just returned from America).

Then comes a fairly innocuous question about the B-sides for the forthcoming single *All Around The World*. And then Noel lurches to one side and says: 'We've actually recorded a cover of *Street Fighting Man* just to piss Keith Richards off because he's been slagging us off.'

Piss I can handle. I don't even notice it whistle through the air. Then, from out of the corner of my eye, Liam starts to fidget.

Liam: 'Can I just interrupt here?'

Noel: 'Interrupt away.'

Liam: 'All these slags coming out of the closet at the moment right … before we go any further, I'm going to shoot me mouth off to them right …'

Noel senses the danger even before I do. Standing up, he produces a wodge of cash from his trouser pocket. 'All that says you'll shut your mouth. Go on, what is there? £85? And a platinum credit card.'

Liam: 'No, I've got my own, man. Listen right, all these old farts [he draws the word farts out, so it becomes more of a sneer], these old farts who get out the day centre, they've got a problem with Oasis. And I ignore all that right because I dig their music, but at the end of the day they all must want a scrap right and I will offer them all out right here on radio. So if you want a fight right … Primrose Hill Saturday morning, 12 o'clock. I will be there. I'll beat the fucking living daylight shit out of them. And that goes for George, Jagger, Richards and the other cunt who gives me shit.'

Noel: 'So in answer to your question, yes, we have just been to America.'

There is a sort of unwritten league table that deals with swearing on air at the BBC. The first time I knew about this was when Menswear were recording a session for us, and asked the engineer how much they had to censor the lyrics to their song *Stardust*. Without a flicker of emotion, the man at the mixing desk looked up and said, 'Shit OK. Fucker no good.'

What about the C-word though? A producer had once told me that one C was as bad as five Fs – in which case we were already scoring bad boy points left right and centre. Except no, maybe no-one had noticed it. Maybe that was the rant out of the way. Maybe not. Bugger.

Me: 'Who's hurt you most out of those?'

Liam: 'Oh, fucking hell, it's got to be Jesus Christ hasn't it? But no, listen, no-one's hurt me right, because I still dig their music. But at the end of the day it's getting childish innit? It's like being in the playground, and I left the playground years ago. Now they want to be pushed onto the fucking swings.'

Me: 'Do you think they say these things because they've been goaded into saying them by the press?'

Liam: 'I think they're jealous and I think they're senile and they ain't getting enough fucking meat pies in them.'

Not sure why, but I make a thoughtful 'mmmm' noise here.

Me: 'But does it bother you? Because you're bigger than that.'

Liam: 'Yeah me, personally, I'm bigger than that, but they obviously want a scrap. And I will beat them up if they want a fight.'

Noel: 'SHUT UP, man.'

Liam: [sounding a little hurt] 'What? I told you I was going to say that.'

Noel: 'NEXT QUESTION.'

And so it continues. There's a celebration of the recent tour – including two dates in Aberdeen which they rate as among the best of their career – and their appearance at Knebworth. Then it's on to the changes in their audience, and the relationship between the brothers on stage.

Noel: 'When he turns to me and goes, "Are you mad for it?" That's what it's all about.'

Me: 'OK, we'll be back with Noel and Liam after this from Laidback ...'

Noel: 'He's getting thrown out after this ...'

We both tried. Producer Claire Pattenden and I both asked them if they could cut out some of the swearing. Noel was contrite, Liam seemed put out. Claire tried again, but Liam got up from his seat and looked suddenly very menacing. He wasn't having any of it.

Claire: 'I'm the producer and asking you to tone it down …'

Liam: 'Well, I'm the fucking singer in Oasis and I'll have you and your family.'

It's live radio. There's no delay mechanism. We have the two most famous rock stars in the country in our studio – possibly a bit pissed. I suppose we could have pulled the plug on them there and then, but at the time I never felt that was an option. Besides, this was the most animated I'd ever seen them. Who knew what might come out of the interview?

On my tape copy of the show, the tracks are edited out, but the next bit happens like this. I back-announce the Laidback single and Noel talks about the hype surrounding the release of *Be Here Now*, blaming it on Creation. Liam falls silent. Then there's a minor verbal skirmish over whether it's the best record they've made to date, and I ask if it's the end of an era.

Noel: 'Yes, definitely.'

Liam: 'He's right there. You're on the ball Steve. You cleaned your teeth this morning. Flossed them, maybe?'

Noel: 'We always said the first three albums were part of one big one. It's the last Oasis album of the 90s. I'll say it to the kids now, there ain't going to be another Oasis album in the 90s.'

Liam: 'We're going to kick in, in the Millennium … The next one – am I too far away from the microphone? I don't want you shouting at me. But the next one's going to have more colour in it. That's what I think. If I've got anything to do with it.'

Noel (laughing): 'But you haven't.'

There's a Captain Beefheart track – chosen by Noel – and then we're into the news. I'm surprised we didn't get a mention ourselves. Hundreds homeless after flood in India, but fucking hell, you should hear what's happening on the *Evening Session* …

We come out of the news with a Paul Weller song, and discuss the brothers' favourite bands of the moment. Among them are Ocean Colour Scene, Travis and, of course, The Verve, led by Richard Ashcroft.

Noel: 'When he got on a stool and played a few songs before we went on in New York, including *Bitter Sweet Symphony*, now they are songs that do actually touch you … But I will say [slight pause] drugs do work.'

Me: 'That's something you've been quoted as saying before.'

Liam: 'Either that or he's got a shit drug dealer.'

The pair dissolve laughing.

Me: 'Is it good to have The Verve back, then, so you've got someone to push you?'

Noel: 'Listen, right …'

Liam: 'He asked me the fucking question, will you calm down … It's nice to have them around.'

Noel: 'There's only one person that's going to push Oasis on, and it ain't going to come from any particular band. It's to do with us. Now is The Verve's time and that's the end of it.'

Liam: 'I disagree [sounds hurt]. It's our time.'

Noel: 'Well, whatever. Richard is a genius. And Nick McCabe is one of the best guitarists I've ever seen. And even when we supported them years ago they were a great band then. And circumstances worked against them. I was the happiest man in the world when they went to number one with their album … He's not writing those songs for him. He's writing those songs for me.'

Me: 'How do you mean?'

Noel: 'Because he's got to be a better songwriter than me, and then I've got to be a better songwriter than him. And that's what it's about.'

Me: 'OK, we're going to play another of the records you've brought in … DJ Shadow.'

Liam: 'Who's he? Is he a boxer?'

Noel: 'Well, he's a shadow boxer.'

Me: 'That's such a terrible gag. We'll play this. DJ Shadow and High Noon.'

The DJ Shadow record kicks in … Not going too badly now, is it?

Me: 'Talking of people who inspire you – do you still inspire each other?'

Liam: 'Well, Noel inspires me, I don't know if I inspire 'im.'

Noel: 'Yes he does. He knows he does.'

The sound of their voices has changed. They're more echoey. Not because they've moved away from the microphones, but because there are smoke alarms in the studio and the pair of them have been puffing away since they arrived. To avert the alarms going off, we've got the studio door held open by a chair.

Me: 'Has your relationship changed over the last year?'

Noel: 'Yeah. Of course it has, yeah. He's got more paranoid because he thinks the whole world is against him.'

Liam: 'And you're full of shit, because I don't think that at all. No, he inspires me more than I inspire him. Me mum inspires me, me wife inspires me, me little stepson inspires me. Bottles of lager inspire me. You inspire me, Stephen, when you pay the time to listen to me.'

Me: 'But what is it? Is it the mood of the people around you that picks you up?'

Liam: 'No it's just people who can be arsed and who've got a brain and clean their teeth in the morning. People who actually listen to you and don't chop down everything you say. But listen right, this chap hasn't been bed-friendly over the last couple of days.'

Noel: 'Bed-friendly? [starts laughing] What's bed-friendly? You ask my wife, I'm totally bed-friendly.'

Liam: 'No, I'm on about bed-friendly. Nothing to do with your wife. Anyway what was the question?'

Then the conversation collapses again. There's a question about the Oasis photo exhibition which was running in London at the time. Liam is definitely attempting to say something, but all Noel keeps repeating is 'ShutIT. SHUTTTITTTT.'

Liam: 'I don't get anything out of the *expedition*…'

Noel: 'Expedition? Where did you go marching to? The South Pole?'

Liam: [smiling] 'Shut up, man.'

Me: 'Apart from not being bed-friendly, you seem to be getting on really well.'

Liam: 'I'm about to knock the fucking cunt out.'

Noel takes the mickey out of Liam about the expedition slip-up.

Me: 'That's playground behaviour, picking on your brother on air. I'm going to play another record.'

Noel: 'I'm allowed to! I'm allowed to!'

Liam: 'Wait a minute, hold that record because I'm going to knock the cunt clean out.'

Noel: 'He hasn't got a good enough lawyer to knock me out'

Liam: 'I thought we were getting on all right till we came here.'

Noel: 'We were getting on all right. We do get on all right.'

Liam: 'But you've got a pen in your gob and it's pointing my way.'

By this point we'd opened the phone lines to take questions to put to the band. Far from being inundated with complaints, the enquiries (by both phone and fax) are piling up. Claire brings a bunch into the studio and we start on them after the next record.

Me: 'Here's a question from one of the listeners … "Will you start writing classical music when you get to 50 like Paul McCartney?"'

Liam tears into this one: 'Is Paul McCartney composing classical music? Because sitting around with a bunch of old lesbians doesn't sound classical to me. So no, we're not going to get into that pile of shit.'

Then Noel gets defensive after I ask him about his visit to 10 Downing Street for one of Tony Blair's soirées at the height of Cool Britannia ('I didn't go there to represent some shitkickers in Dagenham, I was going there for me').

Then we play *There She Goes* by The La's.

Noel: 'You have to understand right that when that album came out in 1989, everything was groovy and dancey and baggy. The climate was dance-rock-indie crossover and that was the first Britpop album.'

Question from a listener about married life.

Liam: 'I believe in marriage and I believe in family. I'm going to buy a dog next week and I'm sorry if that pisses people off but I'm an old fart [does the fart/sneer thing again then brightens up]. No, I'm enjoying it. I wanna have kids, yeah, next year I reckon. Don't know. I'm going to have a bang at it.'

Will you be a good father?

Liam: 'I'll be the best father in the world, yeah. I'll be shit at paying the bills, but …'

Me: 'Has it made you feel less responsible for your brother?'

Noel: 'He can look after himself. He's my younger brother right … How old are you?'

Liam: 'Twenty-five. And you didn't get me a present you cunt. Oh, you did, you did.'

Noel: 'Yeah I did. He's 25, I don't need to look after him. He's a bigger man than I am.

(Liam mumbles something in the background about not needing anyone to look after him and, 'Don't speak for me, you cunt.')

Me: 'Why?'

Noel: 'Because he has to deal with his life and he has to deal with someone like me. But he's still a knob.'

Me: 'We'll play another track. This is what you wanted to hear by Travis.'

Off air, while the CD plays, we turn the volume up full-blast and Noel sings along at top volume.

Me: 'When was the last time you wanted to run away?'

Noel: 'Gonna do it. We don't need a break, but I think people need a break from Oasis. Once we've toured this album, we have to sit down and think where we're going.'

Bubbling away there's a disagreement over what Oasis should do next. Noel says they need a break. Liam – by now drifting off mic – wants to 'get down to some serious work'. Noel claims Liam loves being in the limelight. Liam disagrees. Vehemently. Liam wants to make another record.

Noel: 'Well, I don't [sounding suddenly very miserable]. Work's become boring, mate.'

Me: 'Suddenly you seem a bit down about it.'

Noel: [drawing audibly on a cigarette] 'Yeah. Everything that led up to Knebworth was really special. Really exciting. Now we've become just another band.'

Liam: 'No we haven't. I don't know what band you're in …'

Noel: 'We're going to take time off and regroup …'

Liam: 'We're going to sit down and change the face of OUR music and like …'

Noel: [interrupting] 'Blah, blah, blah, blah …'

Liam: 'Well, see you later then …'

There is tense silence, as Liam stares at Noel and Noel stares at the floor and then I hurriedly hit the Death In Vegas track *Dirt*. While the record's on Liam walks out. Claire, meanwhile, has been taking calls from various members of the management. They don't want us to pull the plug, but we need to give out some sort of warning about the bad language.

Dirt finishes. Ridiculously, we've played the radio edit. Might as well have gone the whole hog and played the sweary version. After it ends,

Noel explains why he likes DIV, and I say, 'It's Thursday night, the *Evening Session*, and if you're offended by any of the language on tonight's show … turn off. That's our advice.'

Noel laughs.

Me: 'Here's another question which has come in. Has Liam ever written any songs and will Oasis ever record one of his tracks? Would you like him to write something?'

Noel: 'I would do, yeah.'

LONG CONTEMPLATIVE SILENCE

Me: 'And do you think he'd be good?'

Noel: 'We're talking about something I've never heard, so I don't know.'

Me: 'Does the responsibility of being the leader of the band ever get you down?'

Noel: 'Well, yeah it does because, you see it's like now. I always said that the first three albums were like one big rock'n'roll album. And I don't really want to go and do the same thing again, because that would be boring. It's not that the BAND have become boring or anything like that … [lowers voice] it's sort of not exciting any more. And HE would disagree, and I'm sure he's about to bound through the door at any second …' He's not. Liam Gallagher, we deduce, has left the building.

Me: 'Is it harder on you?'

Noel: 'Well, we are the establishment, I understand that. And I don't know what I'm going to write next time, but if I can't do something that excites me, then I could possibly never do another album. But I need, mentally, time off. I could go and start to write another album next Tuesday afternoon, but it wouldn't mean anything to me, and I don't want to do that.'

Me: 'What do you do when you get down about it?'

Noel: 'Well, I'm quite lucky because I've got a lot of friends in different forms of music. And I chat to them and they've got different ideas … and it's not like we're going to go and do a dance album. But I've said this since 1994, that the first three albums are part of a set and then it's going to change. And that's the most exciting thing. I don't know what the next album's going to sound like. And nobody else does.

'I want him, when I play him the demos of the next album, I want him to tell me he's not going to sing it because he thinks it's naff. And I'll think, "Well, we're getting somewhere now."'

Me: 'What was the band's reaction to the last album when you played it to them?'

Noel: 'Well, as long as 'e likes it … When I'm sure about something, I'm really sure about it. And then I only need him to say yes, you are right. He can sit there and say, "Oh, I'm just the singer," but it's his band … [and again more quietly] It's his band.'

Me: 'You're getting …'

Noel: 'I'm getting old now, Steve …'

Me: 'Are you? Are you mellowing?'

Noel: 'I'm getting fatter.'

Me: 'But you're giving Liam more credit than you've given him before.'

Noel: 'Well, no … um, yeah I suppose I am.'

Me: 'Where's that come from?'

Noel: 'I don't know … [first he sounds like he's about to cry and then he bursts out laughing]. He's got a good lawyer.'

Me: 'We'll play The Verve. This is *Lucky Man*.'

After The Verve there's a chat about complacency, the music scene and Noel's proudest moments.

Noel: 'One of the best things I've ever done is *Setting Sun* with the Chemical Brothers. We're stuck in a rut of being this five-piece rock'n'roll band. Stick it in the Marshalls, blah, blah, blah.'

Me: 'You sound like you're unhappy with the last record.'

Noel: 'I'm not unhappy with the record. Not at all. I think the songs are great songs. But I'll never record songs like them again.'

Me: 'OK, we have to wrap things up. It's the Sex Pistols. I read somewhere – it was in the *Sun* newspaper I think – that this is your favourite album of all time.

Noel: 'Well, *Never Mind The Bollocks* I think I bought when I was 12, and it's still the most dangerous rock'n'roll record of all time.'

Me: 'Noel Gallagher, thank you very much.'

Noel: 'Thank you.'

The show ends on *Pretty Vacant* by The Pistols. Immediately we've come off air, there's a freelance photographer (employed by the Radio 1 press office) standing by to take a picture of Noel and me. Noel says: 'You might get the sack after that …' Then it's all smiles for the camera. After Noel leaves, Claire and I and a couple of others decamp to the Stag's Head, where Gary the landlord has already pulled me a pint of a cider.

'Oh, mate,' he says. 'I was really feeling for you. I had it on in the pub, but then I had to keep turning the volume down when they started swearing.'

For what it's worth, I thought it was a revealing interview. It was the first time Noel hinted that *Be Here Now* had been hurried and sounded like it was the end of an era. Liam said for the first time publicly that he was going to have children with Patsy. And Noel (exclusively) revealed that there wouldn't be another Oasis album until the year 2000.

But of course, you can't swear like this on national radio without there being some kind of furore. The following morning I stopped at the corner shop as usual, and gingerly picked up the *Sun*. Sure enough: front page. '4 Letter Oasis In Radio 1 Shocker. Full Story Page 7.'

My stomach started to twist slightly. There on page seven, alongside pictures of the brothers leaving Radio 1, was the full story. 'Foul-mouthed Oasis brothers Liam and Noel Gallagher caused outrage last night when they unleashed a torrent of four-letter filth live on Radio 1.'

Good intro. You have to admire the subs on the *Sun*. Whoever had put the story together had done a brilliant job on it. As I skim-read the rest of the piece all the key words were there: 'disgraceful', 'often rambling tirade', the references to drugs and the threats to Mick Jagger. It hardly seemed real. They'd even managed to get the necessary quote from an outraged lorry driver and another 'appalled' parent whose 13-year-old daughter 'heard the Oasis row'.

But it was the penultimate paragraph that really caught my eye. 'Lamacq apologized for the swearing towards the end of the one-and-a-half-hour show – the most foul-mouthed pop broadcast since the 1976 TV interview which made the Sex Pistols famous overnight.'

Quietly I was quite pleased with that. I've never set out to provoke a band to swear, or to offend the good folk of middle England. But given the circumstances, at least we were in famous company. Even if it did suggest I'd stopped being Someone Like John Peel and become Someone Like Bill Grundy, the idea of causing such an extreme reaction excited every punk rock gene in my body. I never once believed it (the Pistols were on prime-time TV, for heaven's sake), but it was nice that someone had given us decent context.

The problem was, I doubted very much whether the BBC would be as pleased. After the *Sun* I saw the *Mirror* (front page as well, but the full story and pictures included one of the posed BBC studio shots with me and Noel. What was that expression on my face?). The other tabloids had run with the story on inside pages as well, reflecting varying levels of indignation. One outrage creates another. Even the *Evening Standard* weighed in with a story peppered with quotes from a member of the clergy claiming that this was the sort of incident that was indicative of the declining moral standards of Britain's youth.

I wanted to be able to say, 'Yeah, right. What planet are you on then?' But the level of press suggested this wasn't a time for frivolity.

I imagine there was an inquiry, but if the bosses were angry or disappointed in me, they did well to shelter me from any adverse reaction. I found out more from reading Simon Garfield's book *The Nation's Favourite* a year later than I ever knew at the time. Obviously Andy Parfitt asked for my side of the story and what we'd done to calm the situation, but he could have been far more abrupt with me than he was. I think Andy and the station handled everything really well.

In the meantime, the Oasis show went on to be the most bootlegged radio programme I've ever been involved with.

23

HISTORY

Noel and Liam were definitely right about one thing. It was good to have Richard Ashcroft around. I was a late convert to The Verve (so late that most of the pre-The days are a bit of a mystery to me). By the time I saw the light it was at their final gig at the T In The Park festival, just before they split for the first time. Ashcroft was spellbinding that night. He'd been wandering around the compound behind the *NME* tent for about two hours before they played. A tall man with a languid walk. He looked completely dislocated from the world around him.

When they finally got on stage, the tent was heaving with people. And for their part, The Verve were just really lovely. I know lovely's not a word you associate with rock critiques, but it was ... lovely. The sound was big and tense and impassioned, but at the centre of the storm, it was almost as if Ashcroft was swimming to shore after finding himself shipwrecked. After they'd finished, he walked off the ramp at the back of the stage, barefoot, like he was walking on to the beach and away from danger.

When they reformed and the tapes started circulating of *Urban Hymns* it was clear they'd picked up from where they'd left off. Except they were even better (at least in some ways. Early fans doubtless missed the layered, claustrophic rolling sound of their first records, but The Verve were song-based now, which for me made them more spiritual).

I can't remember whether it was before or after *Urban Hymns* was released (possibly before), but they played a gig at Hammersmith Palais. This couldn't have been better for me. The Palais doesn't book many gigs. In fact, it's been so long since I've been there that they might have knocked it down for all I know. But in my mind, it's like a church, where I've only worshipped on a couple of special occasions. The first was The Ramones supported by The Prisoners (the night I bumped into Leigh from The Price on the balcony who said: 'If the Prisoners start with *Melanie* I want you down the front, sharp.' They did and I was).

The Verve gig was a hot ticket. After their split and subsequent lengthy absence, their legend had grown and grown. But it wasn't the new breed of fans that made the night so special. It was the followers who had arrived, vindicated for having faith in the group through all the bad times, that really made it a night to remember. The crowd reaction was extraordinary. By the end of the third song, the sea of applauding hands went right from the front to the very back wall. It was as if everyone felt part of some huge congregation – but at the same time, there were people lost in personal worship (one man just to my right didn't open his eyes for the entire gig. He stood and swayed and applauded and seemed to be plugged directly into Ashcroft's mind).

Following the success of the album, their audience grew by the week, culminating with one enormous celebratory gig. The Haigh Hall show was to be their equivalent of the Stone Roses at Spike Island. I remember it, because it's one of the few times when I've actually felt part of a major event.

I got the 13.05 train from Euston to Wigan, and the compartment I was in was virtually reserved for members of The Verve's congregation. Opposite me, there were a couple of guys making their way to the gig from Eastbourne. Both former punk rockers (with a preference for Slaughter & The Dogs and Stiff Little Fingers), they hated outdoor festivals but thought The Verve were top. They also predicted that the heavens would open mid-afternoon and that we'd all be drenched long before the band arrived.

Behind them, I remember there was a troupe of younger fans whose stereos all leaked *Urban Hymns* and who spent much of the journey discussing the merits of the Super Furry Animals and Spiritualised and singing Travis songs in just the wrong key. I was late, so I got a cab at Wigan station driven by a 40-something-year-old guy who couldn't see what all the fuss was about. 'They're not really from Wigan at all. They're from Skelmersdale, aren't they?'

'They went to college in Wigan.'

'Yeah, but they lived nearer Skelmersdale. They're more Liverpool.'

More Liverpool than what? Anyway, at least he thought the weather would be nice. He turfed me out, about a mile from the site, amid scenes of absolute chaos. To get to the gig you had to walk down a winding country lane, which probably sees about six cars on a good day. Not with The Verve around, though. It was like a leafy Wembley Way, beer bottles strewn on the verges, and merchandise men trying to flog their wares on every corner.

And when you arrived it was through a gate at the top of the hill, which gave you an incredible view down to the stage at the foot of the rolling bank. All the BBC staff (radio and TV) were parked up to the right of the stage. This was a comparatively easy show to do. There were no pre-gig interviews to record. All I had to do was run through the script and work out a few links. Even had time for a bottle of beer with Cas from Delakota in the hospitality tent. The only pre-gig excitement was when a gang of ticketless fans charged the backstage gates and scarpered for the safety of the main arena.

The only difficult moment is the point just before the band go on stage. The record on air finishes, and you have to try and capture the scene you can see from the side of the stage. You're not sure exactly how long you've got – two, maybe three minutes, it depends on how much the group dawdle around.

I described the scene as best I could, feeling a little awestruck. The field was full to the back of the hill. You could just about make out a few expectant faces at the front. Just as I was beginning to fill for time, the cheers began. As with all these big gigs, it's the front few rows of people who catch sight of the group first – then the roar spreads through the crowd like a forest fire.

The gig itself seemed to pass by in a flash. The Verve looked assured, Ashcroft's eyes deep and dark and focused somewhere over the top of the hill. It was everything I liked about The Verve. It was passionate but not pompous. They sounded big but not overbearing. They were in a good groove, rather than being in a rut. One thing about The Verve: I never once saw them going through the motions. Just like T In The Park, they played this gig like it was their last.

To date we've broadcast this set three times on Radio 1 (twice is usually the maximum). And when I was asked to compile a show called *Steve Lamacq's Fantasy Festival*, it was the headline set.

24

SUMMER HERE KIDS

Phoenix Festival 1996: Neil Young is on stage. Neil Young has been on stage for what feels like three weeks. For the past two days he's been doing *Like A Hurricane.*

We can't go home till he's finished. I'm lying on the floor backstage by the BBC truck, pounding the ground with my fists. 'For the love of God, somebody stop him!'

T In The Park 1998: It seemed like a good idea at the time. The organizers of T In The Park, Scotland's first big two-day festival, asked if I'd like to DJ on the campsite on the Friday night as people arrived for the weekend. The idea was that it would give people something to do, instead of simply roaming the site bored or drunk, looking for their own ways of livening up the proceedings.

So this was OK. Between the T staff and Radio 1, they printed up some flyers and I duly arrived, expecting to see a hundred or so people sitting around on the grass, waiting to listen to some music. Instead, from the bottom of the field we were in, I could make out a large crowd pressed up against some barriers. And on the other side there was a tent that looked like it had been commandeered from a village garden party.

I'd invited a guy called Phelim along to give me a hand over the four hours we were supposed to fill. And together we walked up the hill and set up on the tiny stage. I think I said 'Hi' or something and we started seguing a few CDs. And within half an hour the crowd had swelled to around two thousand people. Two thousand increasingly drunk, mad-for-it people in a field at a festival. Where there was nothing else to do.

That's when the first beer can suddenly appeared out of nowhere and whistled past my ear, knocking over a pile of CDs at the back of the stage. Then came another. And another. This one half full. Then the can fight started in earnest. They weren't all heading at us, they were being lobbed back and forth between the crowd themselves.

'I'm not sure this is entirely good,' I turned around and said.

'Nonsense,' said one of the T In The Park bosses, 'they only do this if they like you.'

They must have liked Phelim even more than me, because two minutes later a three-quarters-full can of lager whizzed through the sky and hit him on the forehead. He had to go to the Red Cross tent, leaving me on my own, just as Jason Carter from Radio 1 spotted four ambulances making their way up around the edge of the crowd. By now the police were estimating there was a crowd of four thousand in front of us, and wanted to pull the plug (even though the ambulances were apparently just a precaution and no-one, apart from one sitting duck DJ, had been injured). We made an appeal for calm and played Fatboy Slim, and slowly the number of cans in the air stopped resembling a pattern of planes circling to land at Heathrow.

But the thing is, for all the fear of being hit (and believe me, that wasn't dancing up there, that was dodging and weaving), everyone did look like they were having a good time. Finally, after playing a few slightly restrained Britpop tunes, it was time to up the ante again and hope for the best. I cued up *Sabotage* by the Beastie Boys, hit the play button on the CD, and dived to the floor for cover. Literally. I hid on the floor behind the decks.

The whole field went apeshit.

Phoenix Festival 1997: It's the *Melody Maker* vs *Loaded* in the five-a-side football competition and we're holding them to a valiant 0–0 draw. *Loaded* magazine's team features several ex-pro stars including Gordon Strachan. In goal for the *Maker* is one Steve 'The Cat' Lamacq (can't remember who gave me the nickname, but I owe you!).

Loaded are getting increasingly bored with not scoring, while The Cat saves shots with knees, his elbow and, in one extreme case, manages to tip a shot over the bar with his ear. Honest. It hit me on the side of the head and went out of play. Strachan picks up the ball, beats two men, and BANG. As I fall over backwards, the shot cannons off my right foot and goes for a corner. We lost 2–0 in the end, I think, and got knocked out of the competition in the first round. Mind you, Strachan came over after the match and said, 'Well played, keeper. Couple of good saves there.' I was this far away from a trial with Coventry City!

Unfortunately, I'd just broken my wrist.

I didn't notice it at first. But I must have landed on it awkwardly while saving Strachan's piledriver. After two hours of wandering around the site watching bands, the nagging discomfort turned to full-scale agony. At the Red Cross tent a nurse gave me an ice pack to hold on it, and then wiggled my fingers around till my face went red. As I was waiting for the ambulance to take a group of casualties to hospital a chap in a suit came up. 'Steve Lamacq? I'm from the *Daily Telegraph*. I'm writing a piece about a day in the life of the Red Cross at Phoenix ... I was wondering if I could interview you?'

The hospital was miles away, somewhere in the direction of Warwick, but comfortingly it looked just like *Casualty* on TV. Only with fewer people.

A nurse who looked a little like Claire Goose handed me my X-rays and said, 'We checked, and you've broken two small bones in your wrist. If you take the X-rays down to the room at the end of the corridor someone will put you in plaster and give you a sling.'

Right. Erm, nurse? How long will it take, because I want to get back to the Phoenix to see The Charlatans.

Warning: British festivals can seriously damage your health! Think first. Most doctors don't go to Glastonbury.

I used to have just two rules in life. One: never go to gigs south of the river. Two: never go to outdoor festivals. Live your life by these easy guidelines and you can't go wrong.

Except then I moved to Brixton. So ignoring gigs at the Academy, five minutes' walk from the house, would have been a little churlish. And then the *NME* finally persuaded me to review a day at Reading. OK, I thought, but just this once. And now look what's happened (five festivals last year, and more this). A life in social disarray.

It wasn't meant to be like this. I had very strong reasons behind why I never went to festivals (I like gigs with roofs on and a tube station within walking distance. Call me old fashioned but that's the way I am). Festivals, it struck me, were cold and wet and miles from the tube and all you ever heard was the final strains of a band's set as it was whisked off by the wind and deposited in a ditch five miles away.

Fact: a good festival sound is like the pot of gold at the end of a rainbow (it's over there somewhere). Really, I could talk for hours on the subject.

Then the war of attrition began, and slowly I lost the battle with festivals (so yes, you can get an OK sound mix, and it doesn't always rain, and you can live without public transport for a couple of days if you really try. There, I've said it). But there's more to it than that. As a microcosm of the music scene, the summer festivals can tell you a lot about the pop landscape. They're some of the few chances you have to judge the comparative pulling power of bands and their ability to move an audience.

You have to take into account that some bands are just simply no good at festivals – they're like people who are ultra-bright for the majority of the year but can't do exams. And then there are the groups that have made them a speciality (James, Fun Lovin' Criminals, etc). Still, as a rough guide to who's on the way up and who's on the way down, the festival circuit is about as good as it gets for market research.

All those choices. Band A on the main stage, Band B in the *Evening Session* tent. It's an *al fresco* questionnaire. Not only that, but the changes in make-up of the summer festivals say much about developments in music over the last 10 years.

If anything points to the fact that fans have become less concerned about generic barriers, then it's the rock festivals introducing a variety of dance tents to their annual bill. I can go and see Breakbeat Era and The Charlatans in the same evening. Or the Prodigy and Ten Benson in the same day. Good.

And I know Glastonbury has been doing that for years, but Glastonbury is a law unto itself. It's the festival anomaly. It doesn't play to any of the rules and, as I'm always being reminded by people, it's not just about the music. It's about peach cider, the Green field, and by the end of the night your best friend turning into a pink elephant.

You could claim that the same degree of cross-culturization hasn't happened at the (relatively new) dance festivals. But look how many different styles of club music you can hear across 36 hours. Four hundred different dance genres and it's only three in the morning.

My final initiation into festival life happened in 1994, when I started compèring the main stage at Reading.

This means turning up with a box of records/CDs and playing music between bands. It also means standing to one side of the stage with a microphone and shouting up the arrival of some of the acts. This is the thing that causes me the greatest fear. My worst Reading nightmare is that I'll forget who I'm introducing. Or worse still, I'll introduce the wrong group. Death In Vegas will be standing backstage, ready to walk on, and I'll shout: 'Make some noise for Apollo 440.'

The nearest I've come to this was two years ago, when I forgot who was about to play next – but I'd already started talking. Fortunately my mouth kept going, as I frantically found a running order in my pocket. Even so, it was hard work: 'Time for more live music … please welcome to Reading Festival 1998 … a band who need no introduction … here on the main stage … make some noise for … Fountains Of Wayne.'

I've only really got into trouble once at Reading. Having consumed too much alcohol one Saturday night, I went for a lie-down in the Radio 1 truck. God knows how long I feel asleep for, but I was woken by Andy Rogers: 'Steve! Steve! You've got some guests here to interview.'

I had a vague recollection of arranging to interview someone.

BUGGER. In walked the Stone Roses. Fresh from a rather hostile press conference. They were here to introduce the new line-up, prior to headlining on the main stage (the now famous set where Ian Brown's singing left something to be desired). Luckily I found some notes I'd made the night before, and the interview happened, and they sloped away again. However, during the sleeping/interviewing interlude I'd missed two whole bands on stage. I've lived a very clean Reading life ever since.

Clean, though, isn't a word I'd use to describe Glastonbury. Not when it's raining. Radio 1 is big on Glasters, and we've done some ace shows there. But in 1997 and 1998 – the years of the mud – it was hard enough to get on site, let alone get on air.

The first year, the heavens had opened on Worthy Farm for most of the week leading up to the festival. Jo and I did a show there on the Thursday evening from an outside broadcast truck which was meant to set the scene for listeners at home, or *en route* to the event.

The scene we had to set was … damp.

'It's Thursday night, the *Session* live at Glastonbury,' I said, in the style of a frontline news veteran. 'And if you hear anyone saying that the conditions down here aren't really that bad … well, THEY ARE.' If the BBC ever need DJs to broadcast during an national emergency, then here are Jo's and my phone numbers.

'Bring wellingtons. And straw. Make sure you've got something waterproof …' I trailed off. If we hadn't played a record, the next line was going to be: 'Save us. Can anyone out there hear me …?'

The BBC's operation (including radio and TV coverage) is so big at Glastonbury that engineers rig up what's been dubbed 'The BBC Village' backstage (including an on-air studio, a truck for recording all the live music, a tent for TV, an editorial Portakabin and Jools Holland's caravan). By day two of 1997 it looked like the set from M*A*S*H. The incoming wounded included Live Music boss Chris Lycett who had broken an ankle after tripping over a badly covered pothole.

Of course, it couldn't be as bad the following year … could it? Nope. It was worse. In 1997 it was just muddy. In 1998 it poured down.

As part of our brief, producer Claire, myself and assistant Jo Tyler were sent out to the field where the Glasto organizers had erected a huge screen to show one of England's World Cup games. The field was rammed – and the rain sloshed down. Jo held the umbrella, Claire the DAT machine and I had to vox pop the crowd about England's chances and what sort of Glastonbury they were having.

Making our way through the drenched mass of humanity, I pointed to a likely suspect. 'He looks OK, let's try him.'

'Excuse me, it's Steve Lamacq from Radio 1,' I said as a drop of water formed on my nose. 'Who do you think's going to win …'

The guy just stared at me for a second. Then at the DAT machine. Then back at me.

Then he said, 'Steve? Are they really making you do this …?'

There are still some things about festivals that I don't understand. Like why is festival cider always that bright orange colour? Like radiation-affected Tizer. It never is anywhere else in the world.

And why do people who've managed to avail themselves of free passes spend 90 per cent of the day sitting in the Nest Of Vipers? The NOV is our nickname for the backstage bar area. Take Reading, for example. The Nest Of Vipers sits just to the back, and to one side of the main stage, so all you get is a muffled sound from the back of the PA. I'm being harsh in my generalizations here, because obviously I'm aware of the benefits of only standing behind five people in the queue for the toilets and the fact that there are chairs and tables and, occasionally, polite conversation. But don't feel for one second that you haven't lived till you've been backstage.

I spoke to one festival goer once who genuinely seemed to believe that the backstage toilets were fashioned out of marble and the champagne flowed like water, served by waiters with bow ties. It's not. It's not full of pop stars either (occasionally you might spot a bored American, who can't bear another minute on his tour bus, doing the rounds – The Offspring, Henry Rollins, etc. But Ice T took one look at the NOV at Reading a couple of years ago and fled to the sanctuary of the main arena.

Nevertheless, I'm still in favour of introducing a backstage timeshare scheme. This way everyone – the entire audience at the festival – could have 15 minutes to buy a drink and go to the loo. Seems much fairer.

So there's me and my mate Liam and we're on our way to the Reading Festival. We're stuck in a three-lane traffic jam on the way out of London (we're in the outside lane).

I open the passenger seat window for some air, and then someone says, 'Excuse me? Sorry. Hello?' I look round, and next to us there's a girl leaning out of an old Citroën (the sort that remind you of Inspector Clouseau films). Hello?

'Are you Steve Lamacq?'

'Erm, yeah.'

'Right. Thought you were … Can I give you a demo?'

Their lane of traffic moves forward and, looking pained, they inch forward about 10 feet. Then we catch them up. In the meantime, there's a lot of rummaging around in the glove compartment.

'We're just looking for it. You don't mind this, do you?'

'No, it's fine.'

Then the traffic dribbles forward again. First us, then them. Every time we get close, the cars in front start to move. It's like a *Pink Panther* car chase. In the end, she virtually heaves the cassette through the window. Thank you. Oh no. I realize she's still talking and looking across at us expectantly. She's thinking I'm going to put it straight into the stereo and give her an instant, blow-by-blow account of what I think. Just then we hit a roundabout, and Liam puts his foot down.

I've been given demos in all sorts of places now. The A40, gents' toilets at gigs, my old local Indian restaurant, and even one from the checkout girl at Tesco's in Brixton (sadly not very good. I was hoping she would be the new Kirsty MacColl). And I do try to listen to as many as possible, even though there never seem to be enough hours in the day to listen to music. Even so, it's rare that you find a tape that really bowls you over.

The first band I replied to after joining Radio 1 was 3 Colours Red. (I'd lost the biog that came with the tape, so I had no idea of who was in the band or anything about them. But it sounded fiery and hungry enough to warrant my finding out more.) And there have been a handful of others that I've fallen for over the last couple of years. Superfine from Sheffield, who sounded like Six By Seven-meets-Mogwai, the Kustom Built who I saw play live in Newcastle. And then there was a band called My Vitriol. Their singer gave me a CDR at a gig at the Garage in north London, and I found it the next morning in my jacket pocket and stuck it in the hi-fi. It was possibly one of the worst-recorded demos I've ever heard. It sounded like it had been recorded off the telly. The hiss was louder than the guitars. But if you turned the treble down, and strained your ears really hard, the songs were ace.

We managed to clean it up a little, and played a track on the show a couple of days later. After that we followed their career with growing interest (it transpired that at the time of the demo, the band wasn't even fully formed. There were only two of them and they'd never gigged. But a year later they released a single on Org Records, *Always Your Way*, which was a belter and made the Radio 1 playlist). The thing is that, given the state of my room, the CD might have been lost forever, or left for a couple of weeks in a pile of Waiting-To-Be-Played demos – but I have a vague notion that fate muscled in again here.

To me, the My Vitriol demo was incredibly important. It was evidence that not all bands in Britain were delivering tapes that sounded like third division Radioheads or Becks with no bottle. It's a cliché, I know, but just one demo like this is enough to fire your enthusiasm up again. It was like the first shoots of spring. It wasn't particularly commercial, and it didn't fit into any particular scene. But then again, at the end of the 90s, what did?

b side

'The most interesting work in any genre,' explains horror writer Clive Barker, 'is surely going to be on the perimeters, where definitions blur.'

I can't remember where I read this, but I wrote it down on a piece of paper and found it in a drawer the other day. It must have struck me when I saw it (as it does now) that it says everything you need to know about certain points in pop music. Although the centre, the mainstream, has the highest profile and generates the most sales, it is the stuff happening on the periphery that's probably more individual.

If the quote wasn't on a yellowing scrap of A4, indicating that it's a few years old, then Barker could have even been talking about the music scene at the end of the 90s.

I have come up with hundreds of theories to help explain what's happened in pop music over the years (and a hundred more to predict what will happen in the future). Some of them, as you might have noticed, are scattered throughout this book.

They're usually the product of one too many ciders at a gig, or a sudden mid-morning bout of insecurity about the future of rock'n'roll or dance or music in general. I suppose they do serve a purpose of sorts by putting bands and records and scenes into some kind of context. But if I really think about it, I don't want pop music to be a bunch of rules and theories. In fact, it's the total and utter lack of rules that makes it so interesting.

It's the completely arbitrary nature of success and failure that keeps music on its toes and gives it that level of unpredictability that makes it both fascinating and mind-bogglingly frustrating to watch. Imagine if there was a foolproof formula for making hit records or launching bands (and despite what people like Pete Waterman and Jonathan King might tell you, there isn't), then how dull would that be? No shocks, no upsets ... nothing that wasn't beyond our control. It's almost too awful to contemplate.

I know certain bands stand a better chance than others because of a whole list of reasons that aren't necessarily to do with their music or even their looks. Some bands come from fashionable towns, others have good managers or press firms or pluggers or mystery financial backers. But that still doesn't mean they're definitely 100 per cent sure of making it. And that's what's so great about the whole thing.

I've championed numerous bands who should, if we were working to the idea of a definitive winning formula, have gone straight to number one. In about four weeks. And when they haven't I've been mystified and miffed at the same time. But I love being proved wrong and then proved right and then proved wrong again. I love the way pop music is so erratic, and refuses to behave in character.

But I still do the theory thing (because I'm weak and hopeless and it's become a habit, and because one day one of them might work. And then I'll be jubilant and destroyed all at the same time).

My favourites are always about how music goes in cycles. About how you get peaks and troughs and watershed movements and you always get them in precise, recurring years.

I started with the Mid-Term theory. Every decade, somewhere in the middle, you'll find that pop goes through a massive facelift. It started with the arrival of *Rock Around The Clock* in 1955 and continued in the 60s and 70s (when between 1975 and 1977 glam and prog rock were all but swept away by the emergence of punk).

Of course this is baloney and, apart from the C86 movement, the 80s don't fit in at all (neither do the 90s for that matter), but it was worth a try. Then there was the Ten Year theory, which started with punk in 1976 and continued with the arrival of C86, the originally shy indie-pop scene which took its name from a compilation tape produced by *NME* ... But this train of thought ran off the rails in the 90s as well.

In fact, it's the bastard 90s that have done for virtually every rock blueprint I've ever dreamt up. Even the cunning Alternative Music Does Badly In The Charts During A Labour Government theory ran aground under Tony Blair (though you could argue that in the same way that The Beatles were never the same after meeting Harold Wilson, Oasis were never quite as popular or rock'n'roll after Noel visited Downing Street).

My favourite of them all, though, was the Double Digit theory. This was a refined version of the Ten Year gambit, again starting in 1955 with Bill Haley and the impact of rock'n'roll on the charts. Then you had 1966 with *Yellow Submarine* by The Beatles and *Good Vibrations* by the Beach Boys, followed by 1977 marking the media arrival of punk and the Sex Pistols. The next one is a little wobbly, but 1988 gave us sampling culture and *Pump Up The Volume* by MARRS, not to mention Chicago house, and the dawn of a new era around the Hacienda and the Happy Mondays.

And then in 1999 – nothing. Well, to be fair, not nothing. But not anything that can so far be identified as changing the course of pop music history. DAMN. The fact that I hadn't thought this one through at all – and that going by the double digits, the best year of the 90s would be followed by the most ground-breaking year of the noughties – is neither here nor there. Imagine if it had panned out this way, though. We'd have nothing to look forward to for another nine years.

So I'm glad in a way that none of these daft fancies are real. And I'm glad I found the sheet of paper with Barker's quote on.

• 25
EVOLUTION

Some people say that 1998 and 1999 were lean years for music, but the people who say that are usually the ones who had a financial stake in the game. From a commercial standpoint, it was 24 months of sales stress and marketing madness.

Post Britpop, the expectations for bands were huge (or, to put it another way, absolutely deranged). Three singles and if you're not in the Top 40, you're dropped; two failed attempts at the Radio 1 playlist, you're in trouble. What was all this about? Mail-outs, flyposters, double CD packs? And if none of them worked it was back to signing on. At least there's one comforting thing about the bosses in charge of the music industry – at least they're not running the country.

Clive Barker was right about the material being made on the perimeters. But what he wasn't to know, in the case of the music scene of the late 90s, was that the bands on the edge would be so different to the world within.

If Britpop had been the centre of many things in the mid 90s, then it had simply fallen out of the middle. Like a hole being punched in a Polo (except this time, the major labels weren't making a mint). Filling the gap left by the guitar bands and some of the more leftfield dance acts, the charts ran back to the people it had missed the most. Mother and the kids. Boy and girl bands for the young teens, Cliff Richard for the mums (and Ronan Keating and Robbie Williams to the lot of you).

But, heck, you know. Did we really care? Do the charts matter that much? If they do, then there were still the odd traces of mainstream alternative music to be found in the Top 40 (Travis and the Stereophonics going ballistic, Blur coming over all sentimental). But in a way, I think alternative and independent culture had become too worried about chart placings. And 1998 and 1999 gave bands and fans a chance to reflect.

Post Britpop, the lack of a centre – or an overriding scene – was both creatively exciting and commercially terrifying. Bands always get upset by musical tags because they believe that if they get lumped into a scene then they lose their precious individuality. More than that, they're not the centre of attention any more. But I'm with the press and most of my radio colleagues on this one: genres, scenes ... they make music easier to explain and to sell to the rest of the public. They flog more CDs. The groups involved will get their own turn in the spotlight, if they're good enough, but, in the meantime, what's wrong with being part of a movement which could change the course of pop history?

Only in 1998 and 1999, there wasn't a scene. And the lack of cohesion led to all kinds of oddities. It was like building a house without any plans (which sounds inventive, but who the hell's going to buy it?). There were Gomez, who didn't fit anywhere, Ooberman who were big tips for the top at one stage, and Gay Dad, who became famous for becoming famous.

With the *Evening Session* moving from 6.30 to its later time of 8 p.m., we didn't have to worry so much about delivering an endless stream of crossover hits, or Next Big Things (though we came through with some anyway. Coldplay, then unsigned, played live on the show in March 1999, and we featured *Aisha* by Death In Vegas months ahead of it becoming a hit). But there were scores of bands on the perimeters of the chart to make the hairs on the back of your neck stand up (a feeling once nicknamed by Frankie Stubbs from Leatherface as 'The Neck Mohican').

The original *Cedar Room* by Doves, hip-hop MCs The Arsonists, the return of Mercury Rev, anything by Le Tigre, The Vandals, Looper and My Vitriol. All neck mohicans. And farther out on the periphery, where our show blurs into John Peel's, there were Hefner and Mogwai, the Flaming Lips, Lolita Storm and all sorts of post-rock and drum'n'bass.

Romy from Lolita Storm had actually come up to me with their demo at a club off Tottenham Court Road, and told us that that her band blew everything else on the planet into oblivion. The demo was this magical piece of irate digital hardcore, and this is true: I took it into the office and played it to Peel, who stared at the stereo and then said: 'I'd have to say I'd be quite proud if one of my daughters was in a band like this.'

Over the past couple of years there's been more of a crossover between our show and Peelie's, even though I think there's still a perception from some quarters that we're the slightly evil, mainstream part of the duo. And I can see where these people are coming from. Or, at least, I've come to see it.

I was at the All Tomorrow's Parties weekender at Camber Sands recently, when a total stranger came up behind me and showered me with expletives before running away like a naughty schoolboy into the crowd. I mentioned this to a friend of mine from an independent label, who said, 'Well, some people don't think you're cool enough to be here because you play Travis on your show.' Oh my God!

Come back. Let me tell you about how I lugged some of Stereolab's gear to their second ever gig in Birmingham! I've got four New Bad Things LPs you know – and Stephen Pastel likes them.

I have to admit that for me as a kid, no-one came close to Peel, and although Mike Read played some good music he never seemed like the real deal. So, put that comparison into place now, and I understand the assumptions. But the critics don't see the person behind the presenter. They don't hear what I play at home or the arguments we have about music behind the scenes at the *Sesh*. But that's all part of the job.

Besides, there is only one John Peel and there will never be another one (and yes, I know people say I sound like him, but listening to Peel for hundreds of years is like moving to a different part of the country. Sooner or later you pick up the accent). And all this brings the DJ part of this story to some sort of conclusion. Because wanting to be Someone Like John Peel and actually wanting to *be* him are two totally different things. And, to be honest, I'm happy enough being myself.

Wouldn't mind his record collection though.

There's been something else happening on the peripheries of the chart during the last couple of years. The re-emergence of rock music. I'm loath to say rock made a comeback, because rock had never really been away. But what it sounded like – and maybe the purpose of it – had changed significantly in the past decade.

It's odd looking back now, but rock went through something of an identity crisis at the same time as Radio 1, and faced some of the same problems. After the arrival of Nirvana and grunge, there had been an uneasy period, where the old-skool and the nu-skool rockers existed together in a stand-off.

In the middle of rock's identity crisis, *Kerrang!* magazine – the bastion of rock writing since the glory days of British heavy metal – had to face the same sort of decisions as the Powers That Be at Radio 1. For Smashy and Nicey read Judas Priest and Saxon. To embrace the changing times, they had to start dragging rock properly into the 90s and appeal to the younger fans who scorned their elder brothers' Whitesnake collection.

Rather bravely, they went for it, erm, hell for leather. The mag not only broadened its definition of rock to include all sorts of guitar bands, but it started writing about the Prodigy, too. The Prodigy! In *Kerrang!*! You wouldn't bat an eyelid now, but the letters pages at the time were full of scorn from the denim and patch constituency. The Prodigy were a dance band, weren't they? What did they know?

Not all the bands were cleared out. After all, most of the emerging bands in this country, like Therapy? and The Wildhearts and Terror-vision, were still into their Motorhead and their Sabbath. But rock, in common, with most musical styles in the 90s, stopped being so elitist. Not only that, but it stopped being the subject of so much disdain from other musical genres (metal bands had always brought guffaws of laughter from the cool kids). The new rock wasn't so funny. It was larger than life and occasionally it bordered on pastiche, but that was OK. That was what rock was for. It was escapism and and being Over the Top. It was just the bad haircuts and the interminable drum solos we didn't like (and those 70s logos cast in dreadful metallic shapes).

You can probably tell – and I'll freely admit – that I'm piecing this together from a spectator's standpoint. There are rock writers who could put all this into a better context, but then I come from a strange background. I am one of only a handful of white, suburban boys who never had a metal phase.

I'm of the right age (just passed 30), I had the right amount of latent teenage angst and aggression (lots of it) and I liked loud music. But unlike most of the boys into music at my school, I didn't start buying Iron Maiden records when I was 13. Everyone else did.

I put this down to the time. Punk supplied everything my teen-anger strove for and the punks were new and wanted to change the world. I couldn't see the same attraction in Sammy Hagar. I have a few Motorhead singles and a UFO EP, but that's it. The metal kids grew out of their metal phase when they realized they stood a better chance of pulling girls if they had their hair cut and made an attempt to smarten themselves up a bit.

All that has changed now. The music, the fashion, the attitude, it's all more, for want of a better word, sussed. But the anger is still there. The point is, if I was 13 now, I WOULD have a rock phase. Except it might not even be a phase. It might just be that some of the bands around now would have the same life-changing effect that The Clash did on my teens. And even though I'm not a fan of all these bands, you can see the devotion in the eyes of the audience at gigs by Slipknot and Korn. The sort of devotion that comes with making a decision about your identity as an adolescent. The need to belong to something that other people – grown-ups mainly – just don't understand. Or better still, are a bit scared of.

In some cases rock music has become more articulate too. It has learnt to express its emotions better and, with bands like Rage Against the Machine, it has developed a new identity as a political commentator. Put Zak from Rage in power with Lemmy as Home Office Minister and you're sorted.

So Smashey and Nicey went, rock music went all cut-throat and cool on us and Radio 1 relaunched the *Rock Show*, presented by Mary Anne Hobbs.

Alan Freeman, who was both Mr Rock and the inspiration for S&N, must have wondered what on earth was going on.

Meanwhile, as all this was happening, there was a resurgence of another part of the rock family too – the American punk-pop side (which even as I type seems to be going through a baby boom. Excuse the kids metaphor, but I've just got in from watching American foursome the Get Up Kids in front of a packed house at the Highbury Garage). The punk underground appears to be as lively as it was when Green Day first toured here – playing the relatively tiny Boston Arms and sleeping on the front room floor of a nurse's house in Walthamstow. The bigger bands of the moment, such as Blink 182, might be having all the hits, but outside the charts there is a big and burgeoning following for US (and even European) skate and post-punk bands. Even bands who I've followed for years appear to be going through something of a rejuvenation (Britain's Snuff and American trio the Muffs).

It's another 'scene' that refuses to go away, and occasionally propels bands into the chart. It also reminds me of a letter journalist Mick Mercer sent me when I joined Radio 1.

'Dear Steve,' it said. 'Has Matthew Bannister put you in a glass cabinet in his office? "In case of Punk revival Break Glass".'

• 26
OI TO THE WORLD

Since starting to celebrate the 10th anniversary of the *Evening Session*, people have asked on a couple of occasions, 'How has the show changed over the years?' And the answer is, it hasn't really. That's the good thing. The music's changed. The bands and audience have changed. The staff have changed. But the *Sesh* effectively does now what it did in 1990. It plays new tunes from 50 different genres, some by bands you'll know. Some by people you might not. It fits somewhere between the more specialist, leftfield shows like John Peel's and Tim Westwood's on one side, and the daytime playlist on the other.

At least I think that's it. It's like an unwritten constitution. You know roughly what it stands for, but the exact wording and phrasing is open to different interpretation.

The next question is always, 'How do you pick the records?' Well, that's easy. Or to quote former producer Claire Pattenden, 'It's not rocket science, is it?'

To be honest, much of the music on the show virtually picks itself. I know even a varied programme like ours can't please everybody, but we try to spread the tracks around so everybody gets a look in.

Ever since I started on the show, I've always seen it as being as much the property of the listeners as it is the team's in the office. Without the listeners we can't do anything. Without any listeners we wouldn't even be here.

And this is probably the one practical time in my day-to-day life when having completely failed to grow up is actually a really good thing. The only worrying aspect is that there are probably people out there tuning in – younger than myself – who are more adult than I am. But for the most part, I and the hardcore fans who tune in all the time get on pretty well, I think, because we recognize certain characteristics about each other.

When we get happy or sad we listen to records. We're a little snobbish and we like hearing new bands first. We like a pretty broad range of music from hip-hop to pop to punk, and we recognize when the record industry is selling us a dud. Much of what we play is based on these things.

But at the same time, we try to present a radio show that isn't a closed shop. It shouldn't be a ghetto, or a gang that you can't join, just because you don't know the name of the drummer in Suede. At times we're accused of being *too* accessible – mainly when we play more established alternative acts (the likes of the Stereophonics or Travis). But everything's relative, isn't it? Supergrass might not be the cutting edge to some fans anymore, but there are still thousands of people who've probably never heard of them.

Besides, if the bigger bands keep coming back with good records we'll keep playing them. And it doesn't matter if daytime radio's playing them too. In fact, that's a result. It means someone we've championed from the word go has gone on to bigger and better things – and if there's an audience out there for Super Furry Animals, then maybe they'll like something else we're playing too. Something new.

So the *Session* is a mix of musics. Established and underground. But at the root of the musical policy is a burning desire to communicate our favourite records to as many people as possible. For as long as I can remember I've wanted to pervert the course of the chart, or even persuade people to get off their backsides and go see whatever new band I've fallen in love with at the time. And I think there's a part of our audience who quite often feel the same.

But all types of people tune into the *Session*. As well the schoolkids and students, there are people in cars, late-shift workers, clubbers getting ready to go out … and hopefully over the two hours there's something in the programme for all of them.

So when people ask if the programme is made up of all my own favourite records, the answer is usually no. Put it this way, if you invited me round your house, would you want me dictating what we listened to all night? I've been round to people's flats where they've droned on for hours about all their favourite music – and not let me get a word in edgeways. It's boring.

No, this show is for us. You, me, and anyone else who recognizes a brilliant record when they hear it. Whatever shape or form it comes in.

If that's the theory, then this is the practical bit. How do we actually get on air every night? What goes on during the day? Who does what? And why?

Well, I'm buggered if I know.

I suppose it starts here, where I'm sitting typing now. It's the room in my house where I keep all the records and CDs, and my computer and my stereo. Behind me there's a wall that's plastered with pictures and posters, and round the window in front of me is the Colchester United shrine (two replica shirts and an assortment of pictures, including a treasured Polaroid of me with former defender Peter Cawley in the bar at Fulham FC). I stumble down here at about eight in the morning and – apart from the time when we're actually on air – that's the best bit of the day.

If I'm lucky I've got two or three hours of listening to music before the phone starts going, and the real world outside starts forcing its way in. I have four piles of CDs by my desk when I'm starting to work out a running order. The first is the tracks we should definitely play a couple of times during the week, the second is stuff that I think should be in at least once. And in the third are singles or albums that I'd like to get in, if I can find the space. Two hours a night might seem like a long time, but we never manage to play everything we want.

Next to the third pile is the biggest, most towering stack of the lot: the new stuff. That's where the gold's hidden. Somewhere in that pile there is a record that will blow the audience's speakers, or make people stop and turn their radios up. It's in there. You just have to wade through the also-rans to find it.

Of course, when you do, then you feel like you've hit the jackpot. People are always saying that I'm really lucky getting to listen to music for a living, and they're right. But at the same time it's not like I'm sitting at home listening to all my favourite records. You should hear some of the tripe that people release, or pester you to play. After an hour of finding nothing, though, just when I've got my head in my hands, there'll be THE record of the morning.

The debut Chicks EP, eels' first album, the latest Boss Hog single, or the Arsonists' album. It comes out of nowhere. And you want to play it 10 times on the spin.

I fax a rough draft of the running order to the office at about 11 a.m. and the team do the rest. At the time of writing there are four other people working on the show. There are the two producers, Sam Steele and Jane Graham (Sam came from journalism via several stints in TV researching programmes like *The White Room*, while Jane was another writer who previously worked on the *Breezeblock* and as agent provocateur in the arts department of Radio 4). And there are the two assistants, Louise and Rob. Between them they have to make sense of the list I've sent them, and then add their own choices and take out the records where I've clearly lost the plot.

Plus there's all the other day-to-day running of the show to do. Booking sessions, organizing the nightly competition, coming up with bands for live gigs, talking to pluggers and arranging interviews. Really, I've got the easy bit.

I turn up around 4 p.m., open some post and try to tidy my desk a bit. It has been a battle over recent months as to who has the untidiest desk in our open plan office – me or Annie Nightingale. Annie's winning, but I can console myself with the fact that when the Health and Safety officers last came round to check the building, they said I was a fire hazard. Not only that, but one of them came back an hour later and took a picture of my desk to use as an example of What Not To Do In An Office. But look, sorry, it was the same at *NME* and it's the same at home – and people with tidy desks have got too much time on their hands.

After throwing a couple of press releases in the bin I'll try to get through some e-mails. The arrival of the internet over recent years has been both a triumph and a disaster for us. On the plus side, it means you can get a much quicker reaction from listeners to the tracks we're playing. On the minus side, I now have 3465 unanswered e-mails, and there are more arriving every minute.

If we've got a pre-recorded package to prepare for the show (sometimes bands can only fit you in at certain times in their schedules) then we'll be in the studio at 5 p.m. If not, I might wander round to The Ship to read the music press, or write some links, or meet a couple of friends.

But it's strange … throughout all this routine, you find yourself subconsciously building up to the programme. The whole day really is geared around going on air (in the same way that a band's day is geared around going on stage). And yes, I still get nervous. When we push the green button on the control panel, which means we now have control of Radio 1's output, I still feel my stomach jump.

Eight o'clock, we're on air. We turn the studio lights down and the speakers up. What could possibly go wrong?

Some nights I'm aware I'm broadcasting to thousands and thousands of people and that if I cock it up, I'll sound like a prize tosser. But mostly I get over that. Mostly it's just me and the team and a box of records, and it's not that important if you get word blindness or the giggles.

All the *Evening Session* is really about … are the tunes.

OUTRO

Of all my senses, the one that's survived and is still the most evocative is hearing. For some of my friends it's smell. They only have to catch a whiff of, say, mashed potato, and they're transported back to primary school. My own sense of smell is appalling, and my taste isn't much better ... but my hearing works.

Physically, I imagine it must be deteriorating (I've noticed I've had to turn my headphones up a touch over the last year to compensate). But otherwise it works brilliantly. I only have to play certain records and I'm whisked away in space and time. For instance:

Lovecats by The Cure. Early 80s. Benny's Disco, Harlow Student Night. Completely failed to get off with Elaine Westley.

Strawberry Fields by Candyflip. Back of car listening to pirate radio coming home from seeing the Senseless Things in Bath.

Born Slippy by Underworld. The *NME* tent at Reading Festival. I can hear the beat thumping through the canvas as Neil Pengelly and I bowl up backstage on his scooter.

Creep by Radiohead. My old flat in Thorley Park just outside Bishop's Stortford. The Saturday morning routine of listening through piles of advance cassettes is broken up by the guitar noise that goes *jerging, jerging* ... just before the chorus. And then I sit the *NME* down on Monday and make them listen to it ... over and over again.

Mansize Rooster by Supergrass. Sheffield town centre. Ben Wardle and I have been to see Supergrass supported by The Bluetones in Manchester and have gone on to see Sleeper in Sheffield. We spend two hours roaming record shops looking for a bloody red vinyl version of *Mansize Rooster*, before it starts pissing down and we have to shelter in a pub.

The list goes on and on. And some of them aren't very healthy memories either. There are records which make me want to cry because the images they conjure up are too painful or too sensitive. And I curse the fact that I can't play various records any more, because they've become synonymous with bits of my life that I'd rather forget.

Which, by the way, is something I never understood about 'Our Tune' (or, as it later became nicknamed, 'And The Baby Died ...'). Why did all these people want to hear records that made them feel bad? I mean, I'm up for a spot of catharsis as much as the next man, but the last thing I'd want is Simon Bates playing a record that made me thoroughly miserable.

Virtually every record I've ever bought, though, has got some baggage attached to it. And despite the downside, I love the way they arouse all those emotions you associate with moments of nostalgia. I like the fact that in times of need I can go to my record collection and select a tune for all occasions (victorious, angry, sad, new girlfriend, old girlfriend, Saturday morning, Sunday evening, Colchester win, Colchester lose). The only problem with them is, I've sussed what they do. I know how all these records will make me feel. There's no element of surprise.

That's why it's the music of tomorrow that will always have the upper hand. You just never know what's out there – or what it's going to sound like. And though I still need my comfort blanket CDs, I have to own up and say, yes, I'd take the ultimate gamble. I really would swap one of the albums I know for one that hasn't even been made yet.

It's a mad scheme, I know, and I'm not sure how to explain it, but try this. You know when a friend says they remember hearing X record for the first time? And they tell you how their jaw hit the floor and they virtually fainted with excitement. Well, that's it. It's not *remembering* the first time you heard a record, it's the actual first-time experience itself. That's the thing that gets me every time. That's why the pile of un-listened-to singles by my desk holds just as much fascination as the racks of dutifully filed albums behind it.

It's the only facet of my life where I can say I'm an experience junkie.

All this, I've realized, creates a problem. Because between the time I finish this book and the moment you read it, pop music will have changed again. Not only that, it'll have changed in a month or a week from now. Who knows what fantastic musical genres or bright young things will have arrived during the summer of 2000?

Just this morning I've had an ace demo from someone called Three Inch Pornstars, not to mention the debut King Adora single and a whole pile of 12-inches from Moving Shadow. But if you think I'm going to make any cast-iron predictions here, then you must be mad. We like to think we know what's going on, but have you seen our record for tipping new bands? Never snog a media pundit ... they have the kiss of death.

But it's not just music that's still evolving. It's technology too.

Already I can see live gigs streamed through my computer from the Bull & Gate (OK, I haven't tried it yet, but the possibility is there). And how much will that alter the course of A&R when venues across London or – better still – venues all over the UK have their own webcams? Scouts will be able to see 50 groups in a night instead of two or three. If you're a group from Scotland looking for a record deal in London, well, forget having to traipse down to the Smoke to play a lifeless showcase gig in front of five people in Camden. Do a show at home (remind me to register a&rshowcase.com before it's too late).

Of course there are failings with this. You don't get the atmosphere of the gig, or the heated exchange at the bar afterwards between the mouthy lead singer and the sceptical A&R scout. But it could seriously alter the way bands approach getting seen or signed.

The way we buy music, the way we listen to it, and the way we discover it ... it's all in theory about to change. Over the last few months the number of e-mails we receive at the *Evening Session* has started to soar – and they're not just from the UK either. They come from people listening on their computers all around the world (just a week ago we had one from the offices of Grand Royale, the Beastie Boys' label, where the staff were listening at work in the States). The implications of all this are huge. Too big to go into here.

And I haven't even mentioned the onset of digital radio either (CD quality radio with all sorts of bonus bolt-on extras).

I'd be a total fraud if I pretended to know where all this is taking us, but I know the technology relies on one thing. It needs music to help drive it. And it needs people who believe in the music to listen to it. So we need more bands, please, and more ideas, and more injustices, and more hype and more petty squabbling over the Next Big Thing.

After all, we've all got more second childhoods in us yet.

Index

OUT NOW
IN PRINT
ONLY **£3.99**

store.rpipress.cc

WELCOME TO
CONQUER THE
COMMAND LINE

S ometimes only words will do. Graphic user interfaces (GUIs) were a great advance, creating an easy route into computer use for many non-technical users. For complex tasks, though, the interface can become a limitation: blocking off choices, and leaving a circuitous route even for only moderately complicated jobs.

(Re-)Enter the command line: the blinking cursor that many thought had faded away in the 1990s. For getting instructions from user to computer – in a clear, quick, and unambiguous form – the command line is often the best way. It never disappeared on UNIX systems, and now, thanks to Raspbian on the Raspberry Pi, a new generation is discovering the power of the command line to simplify complex tasks, or instantly carry out simple ones.

If you're not comfortable when faced with the $ prompt, then don't panic! In this fully updated book, we'll quickly make you feel at home, and able to find your way around the terminal on the Pi, or any other GNU/Linux computer: getting things done, and unlocking the power of the command line.

FIND US ONLINE raspberrypi.org/magpi   **GET IN TOUCH** magpi@raspberrypi.org

PUBLISHING
Publishing Director: **Russell Barnes**
Director of Communications: **Liz Upton**
CEO: **Eben Upton**

DESIGN
Critical Media: **criticalmedia.co.uk**
Head of Design: **Lee Allen**
Designer: **Mike Kay**

EDITORIAL
Editor: **Phil King**
Writer: **Richard Smedley**
Contributors: **Lucy Hattersley,
Simon Long**

The MagPi ESSENTIALS

CONTENTS

[RICHARD SMEDLEY]

Since soldering
together his first
computer – a ZX81
kit – and gaining
an amateur
radio licence as
GW6PCB, Richard
has fallen in
and out of love
with technology.
Swapping the
ZX81 for a guitar,
and dropping ham
radio for organic
horticulture,
he eventually
returned to the
command line,
beginning with a
computer to run
his own business,
and progressing
to running all the
computers of
an international
sustainability
institution. Now
he writes about
Free Software and
teaches edible
landscaping.

[CHAPTER ONE]
DON'T PANIC

In the first chapter, we take a look around and discover that things aren't as strange as they might appear…

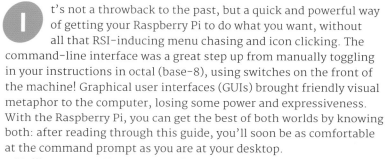

t's not a throwback to the past, but a quick and powerful way of getting your Raspberry Pi to do what you want, without all that RSI-inducing menu chasing and icon clicking. The command-line interface was a great step up from manually toggling in your instructions in octal (base-8), using switches on the front of the machine! Graphical user interfaces (GUIs) brought friendly visual metaphor to the computer, losing some power and expressiveness. With the Raspberry Pi, you can get the best of both worlds by knowing both: after reading through this guide, you'll soon be as comfortable at the command prompt as you are at your desktop.

Unlike some earlier versions of Raspbian, Stretch boots you straight to a GUI, although you can change this behaviour in the settings. The command-line environment is still there: hold down the **ALT+CTRL** keys and press **F1** (the first function key on the keyboard), and you'll arrive at a 'virtual console'. Press **ALT+F2** through to **F6** and you'll find five further consoles waiting for you to log in.

You can drop into these any time you like, but for now press **ALT+F7** and you'll be back in mouse and menu land. The command line is also available through a program called a terminal emulator (often referred to as a term or xterm). You'll also find people referring to the shell, or Bash. Don't worry about that for now; just click on the icon at the top of the screen that looks like a black television screen,

[READ THE MANUAL]

Help is included, with man(ual) pages, but they can be a little overwhelming. Use them to check out some extra options beyond the switches like -a we use here. To read the ls man page, type man ls.

The command line is only a click away: it is called Terminal and you can find it under Accessories in the menu

Commands are terse, but, once learned, they're a quick way of navigating and reading your files and folders

Fig 1 Switches modify behaviour in commands; ls -a shows (dot) files in your listing that are usually hidden from view

or go to Accessories>Terminal in the menu: the terminal now awaits your commands.

Look around

If you're used to looking at files and folders in a file manager, try to clear your mind of the icons and concentrate on the names. Type **ls** and press **RETURN** (see 'Press Return' box). On a fresh Raspbian Stretch with Recommended Software install, you'll just see a few directories, including **MagPi**. Type **ls MagPi** (see 'Lazy Completion' box) and you'll see a listing of what's in it.

Commands like **ls** are not cryptic (at least not intentionally) but they are terse, dating back to a time when the connection to the computer was over a 110 baud serial line, from an ASR 33 teletype terminal. If you think it's strange to be defined by 50-year-old technology, just remember that your QWERTY keyboard layout was reputedly designed both to stop mechanical typewriter keys jamming, and to enable salespeople to quickly type 'typewriter' using the top row!

File path

You can list files and folders anywhere in your system (or other connected systems) by providing the path as an argument to your

[PRESS RETURN]

To save repeating it in the text, we'll confirm here that each time you type in a command, you need to hit the **RETURN** or **ENTER** key at the end, to tell the Pi you've issued Bash with a command.

command. The path is the folder hierarchy: on a Windows computer, in a graphical file browser, it starts with 'My Computer'; on your Pi it starts at **/**, pronounced 'root' when used on its own as the root of your file system. Try entering **ls /** – again we get terseness, and names like 'bin', which is short for binary, and is the directory where many programs are kept (enter **ls /bin** to see the details). **ls /dev** shows hardware devices in the Pi. Try **ls /home** – see that 'pi'? That's you: you are logged in as user pi. If you've changed your login name, or if you have created extra users, they'll all be listed there too: every user gets their own home directory; yours is the **/home/pi** folder in which we found ourselves in earlier. Before, with **MagPi**, we used the relative path (the absolute path would be **/home/pi/MagPi**) because we're already home. If you need to check your location, type **pwd** (present working directory).

> # Commands are not cryptic (at least not intentionally), but they are terse

There's no place like ~

For any logged-in user, their home directory is abbreviated as ~ (the tilde character). Type **ls ~** and you'll see. There's apparently not much in your home directory yet, but Raspbian keeps a lot hidden from the casual glance: files and folders beginning with a dot, known as 'dot files', contain configuration information for your system and its programs. You don't need to see these files normally, but when you do, just ask **ls** to show you all files with a command switch. You can do this with either the full switch **--all**, or the abbreviation **-a** like so: **ls -a ~**. Traversing the pathways of the directory hierarchy can be easier from the command line than clicking up and down a directory tree, particularly with all the shortcuts given. Your **ls -a** showed you **.** and **..** as the first two directories; these shortcuts represent the current and the parent directory respectively. Try listing the parent directory – from **/home/pi**, entering **ls ../../** will show you two layers up. If you want to list the hidden files without the **.** and **..** appearing (after all, they're present in every directory, so you don't need to be told), then the switch to use is **-A**.

Before we move on to other commands, let's look briefly at chaining switches together: `ls -lh ~`

`-l` gives you more information about the files and folders, and `-h` changes the units from bytes to kB, MB, or GB as appropriate. We'll look at some of the extras the `-l` listing shows you in more detail later, particularly in chapters two and three.

Time for change

That's enough looking: let's start moving. `cd` is short for change directory, and moves you to anywhere you want in the file system: try `cd /var/log` and have a look (`ls`, remember). Files here are logs, or messages on the state of your system that are saved for analysis later. It's not something you'll often need to think about: Raspbian is a version of an operating system that also runs across data centres and supercomputers, where problem monitoring is very important. It is, however, useful to know, particularly if you have a problem and someone on a forum advises you to check your logs.

`cd ~` will take you where you expect it. Try it, then `pwd` to check. Now try `cd -` (that's a hyphen), the '-' is a shortcut for 'wherever I was before I came here'. Now we've looked around, we can move on to beginning to do things to our files.

Right Who needs icons when you can fit a listing of 78 files into a small window? Coloured fonts indicate file types

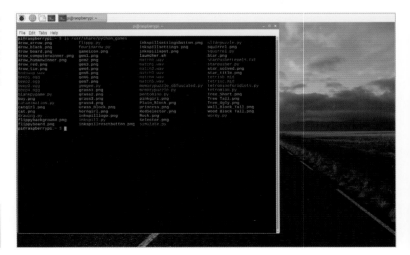

[CHAPTER TWO]
READ/WRITE TEXT

In this chapter, we get working on files

The command line offers tools to get text from different parts of a file, like skipping to the conclusion

Create and name files and directories with keystrokes, rather than mouse-clicks and keystrokes

N ow that we can navigate folders and list files, it's time to learn how to create, view, and alter both files and folders. Once more, it's not that the task is difficult, rather that the forms of the commands (particularly when editing) are unfamiliar, coming from an era before Common User Access (CUA) standards were created to ease switching between applications and operating systems.

Stick with it: with just the first two chapters of this book under your belt, you'll be able to do plenty of work at the command line, and start getting comfortable there.

Creating a directory

We're going to dive straight into working with files and folders by creating a new directory. Assuming you already have a terminal open (see 'Instant applications' box), and you're in your home directory (**pwd** to check, **cd ~** to get back there if necessary), type **mkdir tempfolder** and have a look with **ls**.

mkdir, as you've probably guessed, creates a new directory or folder. Let's use it to experiment with altering one of the included Python games. Don't worry: we're not going to be programming Python, just making a small change by way of illustration. **cd tempfolder** (use tab completion: **cd t** then hit the **TAB** key). In the following example, we'll be copying some files to this directory.

First, make sure Python Games is installed – if not, click the top-left Raspberry Pi icon on the desktop, select Preferences, then Recommended Software, tick the box next to Python Games in the list, and then click Apply to install it.

We'll copy over the files from the **python_games** directory:

```
cp /usr/share/python_games/fourinarow.py .
cp /usr/share/python_games/4row_* .
```

Wildcard

The **.** (dot) at the end of the commands refers to 'just here', which is where we want the files copied. Also, **4row_*** is read by the Pi as 'every file beginning **4row_**' – the ***** is known as a wildcard, and this one represents any number of characters (including none); there are other wildcards, including **?**, which means any single character.

Try **python fourinarow.py** and you'll see you can run the local copy of the game. To change the game, we need an editor – sidestepping the UNIX debate about which one is best, we'll use the Pi's built-in editor: nano. Unless you've previously used the Pico

> ## We're going to dive straight into working with files and folders by creating a new directory

editor, which accompanied the Pine email client on many university terminals in the 1980s and 1990s, it will seem a little odd (**Fig 1**, overleaf). That's because its conventions predate the **CTRL+C** for copy type standards found in most modern programs. Bear with us.

Editing and paging

nano fourinarow.py will open the game for editing; use the arrow keys to go down nine lines, and along to the **BOARDHEIGHT** value of **6**. Change it to **10** (both the **BACKSPACE** and **DELETE** keys will work in nano). The last two lines of the screen show some shortcuts, with

^ (the caret symbol) representing the **CTRL** key: **CTRL+O**, followed by **RETURN** will 'write out' (save) the file; then use **CTRL+X** to exit. Now, `python fourinarow.py` will open an oversize board, giving you more time to beat the computer, should you need it. However, there's now no room to drag the token over the top of the board: go back and change the **BOARDHEIGHT** value to **9**, with nano.

If you want to take a look through the **fourinarow.py** listing without entering the strange environment of nano, you can see the entire text of any file using `cat`: e.g., `cat fourinarow.py`. Unfortunately, a big file quickly scrolls off the screen; to look through a page at a time, you need a 'pager' program. `less fourinarow.py` will let you scroll up and down through the text with the **PAGE UP** and **PAGE DOWN** keys. Other keys will do the same job, but we'll leave you to discover these yourself. To exit `less`, hit **Q** (this also works from man and info pages, which use a pager to display text).

Cats, heads & tails

If editor wars are a UNIX tradition we can safely ignore, there's no getting away from another tradition: bad puns. `less` is an improvement over **more**, a simple pager; the respective man pages will show you the differences. One advantage the relatively primitive **more** has is that at the end of a file it exits automatically, saving you reaching for the **Q** button. Admittedly, this is not a huge advantage, and you can always use **cat**.

Fortunately, **cat** is not a feline-based pun, but simply short for 'concatenate': use it with more than one file and it concatenates them together. Used with no argument – type `cat` – it echoes back what you type after each **ENTER**. Hit **CTRL+C** to get out of this when you've finished typing in silly words to try it. And remember that **CTRL+C** shortcut: it closes most command-line programs, in the same way that **ALT+F4** closes most windowed programs.

Fig 1 The default editor, nano, has unusual command shortcuts, but they're worth learning, as you'll find nano installed on virtually all Linux boxes, such as your web host

```
pi@raspberrypi ~/tempfolder
File  Edit  Tabs  Help
pi@raspberr...  ×  pi@raspberr...  ×
  GNU nano 2.2.6          File: fourinarow.py

# Four-In-A-Row (a Connect Four clone)
# By Al Sweigart al@inventwithpython.com
# http://inventwithpython.com/pygame
# Released under a "Simplified BSD" license

import random, copy, sys, pygame
from pygame.locals import *

BOARDWIDTH = 7  # how many spaces wide the board is
BOARDHEIGHT = 8 # how many spaces tall the board is
assert BOARDWIDTH >= 4 and BOARDHEIGHT >= 4, 'Board must be at least 4x$

DIFFICULTY = 2 # how many moves to look ahead. (>2 is usually too much)

SPACESIZE = 50 # size of the tokens and individual board spaces in pixe$

FPS = 30 # frames per second to update the screen
WINDOWWIDTH = 640 # width of the program's window, in pixels
WINDOWHEIGHT = 480 # height in pixels
```

You can peek at the first or last few lines of a text file with **head** and **tail** commands. **head fourinarow.py** will show you the first ten lines of the file. **head -n 5 fourinarow.py** shows just five lines, as does **tail -n 5 fourinarow.py** with the last five lines. On the Pi, **head -5 fourinarow.py** will also work.

Fig 2 rm is a powerful removal tool: use with great care!

Remove with care

nano afile.txt will create a new file if **afile.txt** does not already exist: try it, and see if it works when you exit the file before writing and saving anything. We've done a lot already (at least, nano makes it feel like a lot), but it's never too early to learn how to clean up after ourselves. We'll remove the files we've created with **rm**. The remove tool should always be used with care: it has some built-in safeguards, but even these are easy to override (**Fig 2**). In particular, *never* let anyone persuade you to type **rm -rf /** – this will delete the entire contents of your Pi, all the programs, everything, with little to no chance of recovery.

Have a look at what files we have: if you're still in the **tempfolder** you made, then **ls** will show you the Four-in-a-Row files you copied here. Remove the program, then the .png files with careful use of the ***** wildcard.

```
rm fourinarow.py
rm 4row_*.png
```

cd .. to get back to **/home/pi** and **rm -r tempfolder** will remove the now empty folder. The **-r** (recursive) option is necessary for directories, and will also remove the contents if any remain.

In the next chapter, we'll delve into file permissions and updating your Pi's software from the command line.

[CHAPTER THREE]
PERMISSION TO INSTALL

We look at Raspbian's efficient system for installing
and updating software, among other things

nstalling software should be easy, but behind every piece of software is an evolving set of dependencies that also need installing and updating. Keeping them separate reduces unnecessary bloat and duplication, but adds the potential for bugs, missing files, and even totally unresolvable clashes.

Fortunately, Debian GNU/Linux cracked the problem back in the 1990s with the Debian Package Management system and the Advanced Package Tool (APT) – and Debian-based systems, like Ubuntu and the Pi's Raspbian, inherit all of the benefits. Here we'll show you the basics you need to know to install new software and keep your system up to date from the command line, and then look at the not entirely unrelated field of file ownership and permissions.

Using the **apt** command to update your system's list of installable software should be as simple as issuing the command like so: **apt-get update**. Try this logged in as user pi, though, and you'll just get error messages. The reason for this is that changing system software on a GNU/Linux (or any type of UNIX) system is a task restricted to those with administrative permissions: the godlike superuser, or admin, also known as root.

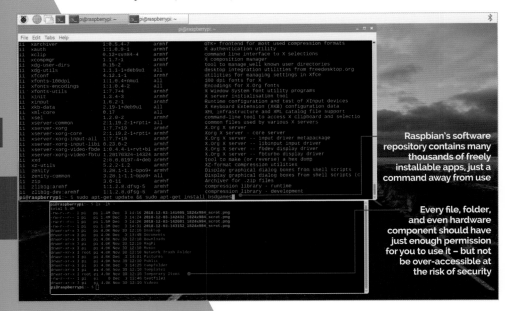

Raspbian's software repository contains many thousands of freely installable apps, just a command away from use

Every file, folder, and even hardware component should have just enough permission for you to use it – but not be over-accessible at the risk of security

Fig 1 Raspbian updates its listing of thousands of available apps, providing you give it admin permissions

Pseudo root, su do

We'll get onto permissions properly a bit later, but for now you'll be pleased to know that you can fake it, using the **sudo** command. **sudo** potentially offers a fine-grained choice of permissions for users and groups to access portions of the admin user's powers. However, on the Pi, Raspbian assumes, quite rightly, that the default user will be someone just wanting to get on with things, and **sudo** in front of a command will pretty much let you do anything. You have been warned!

The following two commands will update Raspbian's installed software (**Fig 1**):

```
sudo apt-get update
sudo apt-get upgrade
```

You can wait for one to finish, check everything is OK, then issue the other command, or you can save waiting and enter both together with:

```
sudo apt-get update && sudo apt-get upgrade
```

The **&&** is a Boolean (logical) AND, so if the first command doesn't run properly, the second one will not run at all. This is because for a logical AND to be true, both of its conditions must be true.

It's always worth running the **update** command before installing new software, too – minor updates are made even in stable distributions such as Raspbian, to address any issues. We've just run an update, so no need to repeat that for now. Sticking with a command-line theme, we're going to install an old suite of terminal games:

```
sudo apt-get install bsdgames
```

Searchable list

It is possible to find particular apps with apt-cache search: **apt-cache search games**. You can also examine individual packages with apt-cache show: **apt-cache show bsdgames**.

APT is actually a front end to the lower-level **dpkg**, which you can call to see what you have installed on the system: **dpkg -l**. Even on a fresh system, that's a large listing: we'll show you how to get useful information from such listings another time.

Downloaded packages hang around in **/var/cache/apt** and if you find yourself short on disk space, issuing **sudo apt-get clean** will clear out the archive, without affecting the installed software.

Now, remember the extra details that **ls -lh** showed us in chapter 1? Try **ls -lh /etc/apt**.

That **-rw-rw-r--** at the beginning of the listing for **sources.list** comprises file attributes, telling you who may use the file. Other entries in the listing have a **d** at the beginning, indicating they are directories. You'll also see hardware devices have a **c** here, for character device – **ls -l** on **/dev/input**, for example. On Linux, everything is a file, even your mouse! A dash (-) at the start tells us this is just a regular file; it's the remaining nine characters that cover permissions.

Every file has an owner and a group membership. Files in your home directory belong to you. If you're logged in as user pi and **ls ~ -l**, you'll see **pi pi** in each listing, telling you the owner and the group. Note that we put the switch at the end this time: that's a bad habit under certain circumstances, but we're just showing you what's possible. Owner and group aren't always the same, as **ls -l /dev** will show you.

File attributes

The file attributes, after the file type, are three groups of three characters (rwx) telling you which users may read, write or execute the file or directory for, respectively, the user who owns the file, the group

[FREE TO USE]

Software in the Raspbian repository is not just free to use, but freely modifiable and redistributable. Free software, like Raspbian's Debian base, is built on sharing: for education and for building community.

owner, and everyone else ('others'). Execute permissions are needed to run a file if it's a program – such as **launcher.sh** which runs the Python games in your **usr/share/python_games** folder, and thus it has the x – and for directories, so that you may **cd** into them.

cd into **usr/share/python_games** and then enter the command `sudo chmod a-x launcher.sh` – the **a** stands for all (user, group and others), use **u**, **g**, or **o** to just change one. Try opening Python Games from the main menu and it won't work. We could restore normal running with `sudo chmod a+x launcher.sh`, but instead we'll use: `sudo chmod 755 launcher.sh`.

Octal version

Those numbers are an octal representation of user, group, and others' permissions: in each case, read is represented by 4, write by 2, and execute by 1, all added together. So here we have 7s for read+write+execute for user, and 5 for read+execute for group and all other users. `ls -l` and you'll see we're back to -rwxr-xr-x.

You can use **chown** to change who owns a file and **chgrp** to change which group it belongs to. Make a new text file and `sudo chown root myfile.txt` – now try editing it and you'll find that while you can read the file, you can no longer write to it. You can also make a file that you can write to and run, but not read!

In the next chapter, we'll be doing useful things with the output of our commands; before moving on, though, why not try your hand at **robots** from the **bsdgames** package we installed?

The **id** command shows what group access you have, for permission to use and alter files and devices

```
pi@raspberrypi: ~
File  Edit  Tabs  Help
pi@raspberr...  ×   pi@raspberr...  ×
proxy:x:13:13:proxy:/bin:/bin/sh
www-data:x:33:33:www-data:/var/www:/bin/sh
backup:x:34:34:backup:/var/backups:/bin/sh
list:x:38:38:Mailing List Manager:/var/list:/bin/sh
irc:x:39:39:ircd:/var/run/ircd:/bin/sh
gnats:x:41:41:Gnats Bug-Reporting System (admin):/var/lib/gnats:/bin/sh
nobody:x:65534:65534:nobody:/nonexistent:/bin/sh
libuuid:x:100:101::/var/lib/libuuid:/bin/sh
pi:x:1000:1000:,,,:/home/pi:/bin/bash
sshd:x:101:65534::/var/run/sshd:/usr/sbin/nologin
ntp:x:102:104::/home/ntp:/bin/false
statd:x:103:65534::/var/lib/nfs:/bin/false
messagebus:x:104:106::/var/run/dbus:/bin/false
usbmux:x:105:46:usbmux daemon,,,:/home/usbmux:/bin/false
lightdm:x:106:109:Light Display Manager:/var/lib/lightdm:/bin/false
pi@raspberrypi ~ $
pi@raspberrypi ~ $ whoami
pi
pi@raspberrypi ~ $
pi@raspberrypi ~ $ id
uid=1000(pi) gid=1000(pi) groups=1000(pi),4(adm),20(dialout),24(cdrom),27(su
```

[CHAPTER FOUR]
MANIPULATING TEXT

Discover pipes and learn how to connect multiple simple
commands together for more powerful text processing

[ABSOLUTE PATH]

We're using ~/ mylisting4.txt with ~ short for /home/pi. If you cd to ~ then you can simply use the file name without the ~/

The UNIX family of operating systems, which includes other flavours of GNU/Linux and also Apple's macOS, deals with data from commands as streams of text. This means that commands can be chained together in countless useful ways. For now, though, we'll focus on giving you a firm foundation to building your own custom commands.

Getting our feet wet

When a command is called at the terminal, it is given three streams, known as standard input (stdin), standard output (stdout), and standard error (stderr). These streams are plain text, and treated by the Pi as special files. As we noted in chapter 3, 'everything is a file': this is what gives the Pi and other UNIX family systems the ability to put together simple commands and programs to build complex but reliable systems.

Normally, stdin is what you enter into the terminal, while stdout (command output) and stderr (any error messages) appear together. The reason the last two have a separate existence is that you may want to redirect one of them – error messages, for example – somewhere away from the regular output your commands produce. We'll look at separate error messages later, but first we need to know how to redirect and connect our output to other commands or files.

Connecting commands together are pipes, the '|' symbol found above the backslash on both GB and US keyboards (although the two keyboards for English speakers place the \ respectively to the left of Z, and at the far right of the home row). When you type a command such as `ls -l`, the output is sent by Raspbian to the stdout stream, which by default is shown in your terminal. Adding a pipe connects that output to the input (stdin stream) of the next command you type. So…

```
ls -l /usr/bin | wc -l
```

…will pass the long listing of the **/usr/bin** directory to the wordcount (`wc`) program which, called with the `-l` (line) option, will tell you how many lines of output `ls` has. In other words, it's a way of counting how many files and folders are in a particular directory.

Search with grep

One of the most useful commands to pass output to is **grep**, which searches for words (or 'regular expressions', which are powerful search patterns understood by a number of commands and languages), like so:

```
grep if /usr/share/python_games/catanimation.py
```

This displays every line in the **catanimation.py** file containing the character sequence 'if' (**Fig 1**, overleaf) – in other words not just the word 'if', but words like 'elif' (Python's **else if**), and words like 'gift' if they were present. You can use regular expressions to just find lines with 'if', or lines beginning with 'if', for example.

Piping search results and listings to **grep** is the way we find a needle in one of Pi's haystacks. Remember **dpkg** from the last chapter, to see what was installed? Try…

```
dpkg -l | grep -i game
```

…to remind yourself which games you've installed (or are already installed). The `-i` switch makes the search case insensitive, as the program may be a 'Game' or 'game' in the description column. A simple **dpkg -l | more** lets you see output a page at a time.

sort will, as the name suggests, sort a listing into order, with various tweaks available such as `-f` to bring upper and lower case together.

[REGEXP]

Regular expressions (regexp) are special characters used in text searches, such as [a-z] to match any letter (but not numbers), and ^ to match to the beginning of a line.

Fig 1 No matter how long the file, grep will dig out the lines you need. It's also handy for finding the results you want from a multi-page output

One way to collect unsorted data is to combine lists. **sort** will put the combined listing back in alphabetical order:

```
ls ~ /usr/share/python_games | sort -f
```

Suppose you copied one of the games to your home directory to modify: you know it's there, but you don't want to see the same name twice in the listings. **uniq** will omit the duplicated lines or, with the **-d** switch, show only those duplicates.

```
ls ~ /usr/share/python_games | sort  -f | uniq
```

File it away

Pipes are not the only form of redirection. **>** (the 'greater than' symbol) sends the output of a program into a text file, either creating that text file in the process, or writing over the contents of an existing one.

```
ls /usr/bin > ~/mylisting4.txt
```

Now look in **mylisting4.txt** and you'll see the output of **ls /usr/bin**. Note that each item is on a separate line (**Fig 2**). Your terminal displays multiple listings per line for space efficiency; however, for easy compatibility between commands, one listing per line is used. Most commands operate on lines of text; e.g., **grep** showed you in which lines it found 'if'. Note that some commands need a dash as a placeholder for the stdin stream being piped to them:

```
echo "zzzz is not a real program here" | cat mylisting4.txt -
```

Appending

If you want to add something to the end of a file without overwriting the contents, you need **>>**.

```
echo "& one more for luck!" >> ~/mylisting4.txt
```

echo simply displays whatever is in the quote marks to stdout; the **-e** switch lets you add in special characters, like **\n** for newline (see below). You can look at the last few lines of a file with **tail ~/mylisting4.txt**. **<** will link a program's input stream to the contents of a file or stream. Make an unsorted list to work on, and sort it:

```
echo -e "aardvark\nplatypus\njellyfish\naardvark" >
list1
sort < list1
```

You can also combine **<** and **>**:

```
head -n 2 < list1 > list2
```

...will read from **list1**, passing it to **head** to take the first two lines, then putting these in a file called **list2**. Add in a pipe:

```
sort < list1 | uniq > list3
```

Lastly, let's separate that stderr stream: it has file descriptor 2 (don't worry too much about this), and **2>** sends the error messages to any file you choose:

```
cat list1 list2 list3
list42 2>errors.txt
```

The screen will display the 'list' files you do have, and the 'No such file or directory' message(s) will end up in **errors.txt** – **2>>** will append the messages to the file without overwriting previous contents.

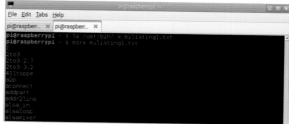

Fig 2 **With redirection, you can get all of the output from a command saved straight into a text file. Save your error messages to ask about them on the forums!**

[CHAPTER FIVE]
CUSTOMISE THE
COMMAND LINE

We make Raspbian a little more personal as we get it
to behave and look just the way we want it to

Share your Pi: make new user accounts and others can log in or switch users from a command-line session

The command-line environment is personal to each user. You can change your identity with or without a change of environment, depending upon what you need to do in another role

Take a look at that blinking cursor on your terminal, and at what's behind it: **pi@raspberrypi ~ $**

The $ is known as the 'dollar prompt', awaiting your command; before it you see the **~** (tilde), shorthand for 'home' – which is **/home/pi** in this case. Before that is [user name]@[computer name], in the form **pi@raspberrypi**. Not only is this informative (at least if you've forgotten who and where you are), but it's also something you can change and personalise.

New user

Let's start with that user name: pi. If more than one person in your family uses the Pi, you may want to keep the pi user for shared projects, but set up individual login accounts for family members, including yourself. Creating a new user in Raspbian is easy: **sudo adduser jo** will create a new user account named **jo**. You will be prompted for a password (pick a good one) and lots of irrelevant info (dating back to shared university computers of the 1970s) that you can safely ignore by just pressing **ENTER** at each prompt. Now we have a user account for jo, have a look at **/home/jo**. Does it look empty? Use **ls -A**. Jo has never logged into the computer, so you will see the absence of most of the contents of **/home/pi** for now, but there is a **.bashrc** and a couple of other config files.

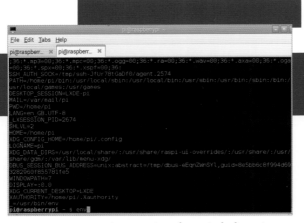

Not every user has a home directory and logs in: enter `cat /etc/passwd` and you'll see a lot of users listed that aren't people. This is because files and programs running on a UNIX-type system have to belong to a user (and a group – take a look at **/etc/group**), as we saw back in chapter 1 when we did `ls -l`. The user passwords are fortunately not listed in the **/etc/passwd** file in plain text, so if you want to change a password you'll need to use the `passwd` command: `sudo passwd jo` will change the password for user jo. If you're logged in as user pi, then simply calling `passwd` will prompt you to change pi's password.

Transformations in the virtual world are always easier than those in nature, and this is the case with switching from being 'pi' to 'jo': we use the change (or substitute) user command, `su`, like so: `su jo`. After typing this, you should see the prompt change to **jo@raspberry**; you can also confirm who you are logged in as with `whoami`.

Changing identity

`su - jo` (note the dash) is usually preferred, as you'll gain all of jo's specific environment settings, including placing you in **/home/jo.** Note that on many other Linux systems, `su` on its own will enable you to become the root or superuser, with absolute powers (permissions to run, edit, or delete anything). Raspbian (and some other popular GNU/Linux systems like Ubuntu) prefer **sudo** to run individual programs with root permissions. Root's godlike powers may be temporarily attained with `sudo -s` – try it (as user pi) and note how the prompt changes (enter **exit** to exit) – but it's generally a bad idea to run with more permissions than you need! For any user, you can customise elements of their command-line use most simply by editing **~/.bashrc**. Take a look through that configuration file now (as user jo): **more ~/.bashrc**. Note a number of variables in all capital letters, such as **HISTSIZE** and **PS1**. The last of these controls the prompt you see, currently **jo@raspberry ~ $**. To change it (for the duration of your current terminal session), try something like: **export PS1="tutorial@magpi > "**.

This is a temporary change: type **exit** and you've left the **su** value of **jo**, so you'll see **pi@raspberry ~ $** once more. If you **su** back to jo, the magpi prompt will still be gone. To make your change permanent, you need to put the **PS1** value you want into **~/.bashrc**. A search around the web will bring up many fancy options for better customising the Bash prompt.

The **~/.bashrc** file is read upon each login to a Bash session, or in other words, every time you log into a console or open a terminal. That's unless you change Raspbian's default shell away from Bash,

> # Transformations in the virtual world are always easier than those in nature

something you may have reason to do in the future – there are interesting alternatives available for extra features or for smaller memory footprint – but let's not worry about that for now. You can put all sorts of commands in there to personalise your environment: command aliases are great for regularly used combinations.

Alias

As user pi, see what's there with: **grep alias ~/.bashrc**. There are a few aliases already in there, particularly for the **ls** command. One entry is: **# alias ll='ls -l'**. This sounds quite useful, although the # indicates that it is 'commented out', which means that it will not be read by Bash. Open **.bashrc** in your text editor (double-click the file in File Manager after pressing **CTRL+H** to show hidden files) – the simple Text Editor will do for now as although we've touched on using nano for editing text from the command line, we aren't going to go into this

[BASIC ACCOUNT]

adduser creates a new user, then takes care of all of the extra details like making a home directory. If all you want is a user created with no extra frills, then the command you want is **useradd**.

[WHO AM I?]

From a virtual console (**CTRL+ ALT+F1** to **F6**), su and that's who you're logged in as. From an xterm, you can change to someone else, but start another app from the menu and you'll be back to your original login.

in detail until the next chapter. Removing the # will mean that now when you type **ll**, you'll get the action of running **ls -l**. Handy, but we could make it better. Change it to: **alias ll='ls -lAhF'** and you'll get an output in kB or MB, rather than bytes, along with trailing slashes on directory names and the omission of the ever present **.** and **..** (current and parent) directories. Changes take effect after you next start a Bash session, but then you can just run that alias as a command (**Fig 1**). To disable an alias for a session, use: **unalias ll**.

Key point

We'll end with the very first thing many users need to change: the keyboard map. The system-wide setting is found in **/etc/default/keyboard**, but often you need to change it just for individual users. If £ signs and letters without accents are not sufficient for them, log in as the user who wants a different keyboard, or add **sudo** and the correct path to the commands below. For example, for a Greek keyboard:

```
touch ~/.xsessionrc
echo "setxkbmap el" > ~/.xsessionrc
```

Replace **el** with **pt**, **us**, or whatever language you desire. Note that the config file we created – **.xsessionrc** – holds settings that are read when we log in to the GUI, so the keyboard setting will cover not just the terminal, but every app used in the session.

Fig 1 Those terse, two- or three-letter commands are not set in stone: make your own shortcuts to keep, or just for use over a specific session

[CHAPTER SIX]
CONNECTING
DISKS

For chapter six, we're tackling the
management of removable storage

Raspbian, while presenting a simple surface, also lets you dig deep for information when you need to change default behaviour. That's real user-friendliness!

Even simple utilities have multiple uses: df, by showing space available, reminds the user which disks are mounted and can be accessed by the Pi

(A) lthough Raspbian will, when booted as far as the GUI, automatically mount any disk-type device (USB flash key, camera, etc.) plugged into the USB port and offer to open it for you (**Fig 1**, overleaf), you may wish to get more direct control of the process. Or, as is more often the case, you may want to mount a disk when the Raspberry Pi is running a project that doesn't involve booting as far as the GUI, as it's not necessary for most sensor projects.

Connected or mounted?

Plugging a drive or flash memory device into your Pi (*connecting* it to your computer) is not the same as making it available for the Pi to interact with (*mounting* it) so that Raspbian knows what's on it and can read, write, and alter files there. It's an odd concept to accept: the computer knows there's a disk plugged in, but its contents remain invisible until the Pi is told to mount it. It's a bit like seeing a book on your shelf, but not being allowed to open or read it.

Disks and disk-like devices are mounted by Raspbian on a virtual file system, and you'll rarely need to worry about what goes on beneath that layer of abstraction, but to see some of it, type **mount**. The information displayed is of the form *device* on *mount point, file-system type, options*. You'll see lots of device 'none' for parts of the virtual

[IN DEPTH]

If you want to delve deeper into what goes on inside Raspbian and other GNU/Linux systems, try Brian Ward's excellent book, *How LinuxWorks* (**magpi.cc/ ZEhaBF**).

system that you don't need to worry about; the devices that concern us start with **/dev/** and have names like **/dev/mmcblk0p1** for partitions of the Pi's SD card, and **/dev/sda1** for plugged-in USB drives.

Plug in a USB drive (a flash drive should work fine, but some hard drives may require a separate power supply). Like most computer desktops, Raspbian automatically mounts the disks, so (unless you boot to a virtual console) you'll need to unmount it. **mount** will show an entry beginning something like **/dev/sda1 on /media/pi/ UNTITLED...** and you can unmount with `sudo umount /dev/sda1` (yes, that is umount without an 'n'). An error will result if the device is in use, so change directory and/or close apps using files from the device. Now we can mount it just the way we want.

[DISK & DISK SPACE]

The **df** command shows you space on mounted drives: just type df and you'll also get a list of connected drives. It's more readable than mount -l, though lacking file type info. It's also quicker to type!

Finding the disk

The **/dev/sda1** refers to the first, or only, partition (a section of the hard drive that is separated from other segments) on **/dev/sda**. The next device plugged in will be **/dev/sdb1**. You can see what's being assigned by running `tail -f /var/log/messages`, then plugging in the USB device. On other Linux systems, if **/var/log/**messages draws a blank,

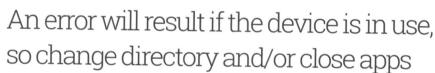

> An error will result if the device is in use, so change directory and/or close apps

try **/var/log/syslog**. Stop the tail with **CTRL+C**. Another way of seeing connected devices that aren't necessarily mounted is fdisk, a low-level tool used to divide disks up into partitions, before creating file systems on those disks (see the 'Format' box on page 35). Called with the list option, `sudo fdisk -l`, it performs no partitioning, but simply lists partitions on those disks connected to your Pi. It also gives file-system information, which you need in order to mount the disk. Lastly, you need a mount point (somewhere to place the device on the file-system hierarchy) with appropriate permissions. Create one with:

```
sudo mkdir /media/usb
sudo chmod 775 /media/usb
```

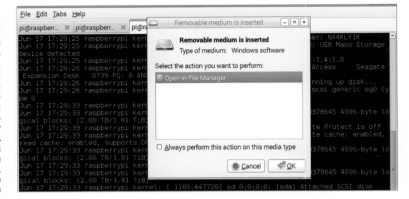

Fig 1 Raspbian wants to mount plugged-in disks, and take care of the details for you – note that the GUI tells you it's 'Windows software' – while the command line beneath has information for you to take control when you need the job done in a particular way, telling you it's an NTFS file system

Mount the disk with **sudo mount -t vfat /dev/sda1 /media/usb**, where vfat (or NTFS or ext2) is the file-system type.

File-system table

Raspbian knows which disks to mount at boot time by reading the file-system table (**/etc/fstab**), and we could put our **/dev/sda1** in there, but if we start up with two drives plugged in, the wrong one may be selected. Fortunately, disks (or rather, disk partitions) have unique labels known as UUIDs randomly allocated when the partition is created. Find them with **sudo blkid**, which also helpfully tells you the label, if any, that often contains the make and model of external drives, or look in **/dev/disk/by-uuid**.

For an NTFS-formatted drive, we called **sudo nano /etc/fstab** and added the following line to the end of the file:

```
/dev/disk/by-uuid/E4EE32B4EE327EBC /media/usb
ntfs defaults 0 0
```

This gives the device name (yours will be different, of course), mount point, file-system type, options, and two numeric fields: the first of these should be zero (it relates to the unused dump backup program), while the second is the order of check and repair at boot: 1 for the root file system, 2 for other permanently mounted disks for data, and 0 (no check) for all others. **man mount** will tell you about possible options.

Editing with nano

We touched briefly on nano in chapter 2. Looking in a little more depth, the first thing to be aware of is the dozen shortcuts listed across the bottom two lines of the terminal: each is the **CTRL** key (represented by the caret ^) held at the same time as a single letter key. For example, **^R** for ReadFile (*i.e. open*), **^O** for WriteOut (in other words, *save*), and **^X** for Exit. Remember those last two for

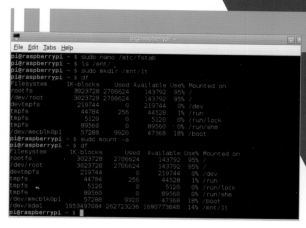

now, and you'll be able to manage nano. However, if you learn more of them, you will really race through your editing tasks.

While nano lacks the power features of Emacs and Vim, its two main command-line code editor rivals, it has useful features such as a powerful Justify (**^J**), which will reassemble a paragraph of line-break strewn text into an unbroken paragraph, or apply line breaks at a fixed character length. This is a legacy of its development for email composition. **^K** cuts the line of text the cursor is on, but it isn't just a delete function: each cut is added to a clipboard. **^U** will paste the entire clipboard at the cursor position: it's great for gathering together useful snippets from a longer text.

Hit **^O** to save fstab, and the shortcut listing changes, with many now beginning M instead of ^ – this is short for Meta, which means the **ALT** key on your keyboard (once upon a time, some computers had several modifier keys, such as Super and Hyper). One 'hidden' shortcut after **^O** is that at this point, **^T** now opens a file manager to search for the file/directory where you want to save.

After saving, exit nano; now `sudo mount -a` will mount the external drive at the desired mount point (**Fig 2**), regardless of what else is plugged in. If you have other new entries in **/etc/fstab**, then `sudo mount /media/usb1t` (or whatever entry you put in fstab) will mount just that chosen device if you don't want to mount any of the others.

Having got inside connected disks, the next chapter will see us accessing all of the Pi, but remotely, from anywhere on the planet with an internet connection.

Fig 2 Once we've put our removable disk in the file-system table (/etc/fstab), `mount -a` will read the config from there to mount your disks, saving you from having to remember the details

[FORMAT]

Copying a disk image negates the need to format the disk. Should you need to format a new partition, or convert a disk to ext4 format, read the manual: `man mkfs` and for individual file-system types such as `man mkfs.ext4`

[CHAPTER SEVEN]
PREDICTABLE
NETWORKING

In this chapter, we give the Raspberry Pi a permanent
network address of its own

Raspbian takes care of automatically connecting in most situations, but sometimes you need to override automatic configurations to ensure a consistent network setting for your Raspberry Pi project: Raspbian has the tools, and we'll show you the essentials you need to stay connected.

Plug an Ethernet cable from your ADSL router / modem to your Raspberry Pi (or connect via wireless LAN) and, automatically, Raspbian knows where it is on the network, and can talk to the outside world.

All of this is thanks to DHCP – Dynamic Host Configuration Protocol – which provides network configuration for every device connected into a network. Typically, this comes in the form of an IPv4 (Internet Protocol version 4) address, a pair of four numbers separated by a period. For example: 192.168.0.37

The first two sets of numbers, 192.168, mark the start of a private range. These are the numbers for all devices in your house, ranging from 192.168.0.0 to 192.168.255.255.

Check your Raspberry Pi's current connection with the `ifconfig` command. This should show, amongst others, a line like inet 192.168.0.37 (with your own numbers). This will be below the eth0

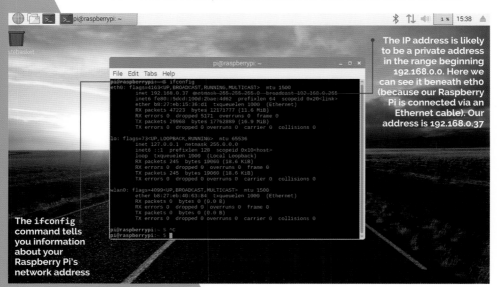

The `ifconfig` command tells you information about your Raspberry Pi's network address

The IP address is likely to be a private address in the range beginning 192.168.0.0. Here we can see it beneath eth0 (because our Raspberry Pi is connected via an Ethernet cable). Our address is 192.168.0.37

section if you are connected via Ethernet, or under the wlano section if you're connected wire wireless LAN.

A faster way to get your IP address is to enter **hostname -I** on the command line.

How to set up up your Raspberry Pi to have a static IP address

Usually when you connect a Raspberry Pi to a local area network (LAN), it is automatically assigned an IP address. Typically, this address will change each time you connect.

> # You might want your Pi to boot up with the same IP address each time

Sometimes, however, you might want your Pi to boot up with the same IP address each time. This can be useful if you are making a small self-contained network, or building a standalone project such as a robot. Here's how to do it.

Edit the file **/etc/dhcpcd.conf** as follows (**Fig 1**):

Type **sudo nano /etc/dhcpcd.conf** at the command prompt. Scroll to the bottom of the script, and add the following lines:

Fig 1 Edit the /etc/dhcpcd.conf file to determine which static IP address to use with a Raspberry Pi

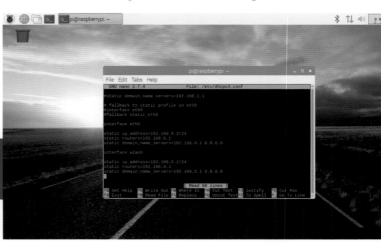

Fig 2 Use ping from another computer to detect if your Raspberry Pi is responding to network requests

```
interface eth0
static ip_address=192.168.0.2/24
static routers=192.168.0.1
static domain_name_servers=192.168.0.1 8.8.8.8

interface wlan0
static ip_address=192.168.0.2/24
static routers=192.168.0.1
static domain_name_servers=192.168.0.1 8.8.8.8
```

Save the file with **CTRL+O** and then exit nano with **CTRL+X**.

Your Raspberry Pi will now boot up with the IP address 192.168.0.2 every time; we didn't use 192.168.0.1 as this is reserved for the router. You can of course use any address you like, but in the configuration above, the range must be between 192.168.0.2 and 192.168.0.255.

Reboot with **sudo shutdown -r now**. Log in and type **hostname -I**. You should then see the IP address you set in the eth0 or wlan0 entry (192.168.0.2).

Normally you don't want your computer set to use a static IP address. You can change the network configuration back by editing **dhcpcd.conf** again using `sudo nano /etc/dhcpcd.conf`. Remove all the lines you added in the previous step, then save the file again.

Ping!

Ping is the most basic tool in the network testing armoury, but one which is often called upon. It sends an ICMP (Internet Control Message Protocol) ECHO_REQUEST to a device on the network. ICMP is built into every connected device and used for diagnostics and error messages: a ping will produce a reply from the pinged machine, which tells you it is on, and connected, and that the network is working between you and it. Information about packets lost, and time taken, also helps with fault diagnosis.

A successful `ping localhost` from the Raspberry Pi tells you not just that the local loopback interface is working, but that localhost resolves to 127.0.0.1, the local loopback address. Name resolution is the cause of many computing problems – see 'Domain Name Servers' box. Now ping the Pi from another machine on your local network: `ping 192.168.0.2` (**Fig 2**) – you'll need to use the static IPv4 address you set, rather than ours, of course. If you're doing this from a Windows machine, ping defaults to five attempts; from another UNIX machine (another Pi, a Mac, or Ubuntu or other GNU/Linux), it will carry on until you stop it with **CTRL+C,** unless you set a number of ECHO_REQUEST sends with **-c** like so:

```
ping -c 5 raspberrypi.org
```

IPv6

The four-digit IP address style we use (such as 192.168.0.2) is IPv4. A newer standard, IPv6, is becoming more common. These are longer 128-bit addresses represented in hexadecimal (for example, fd51:42f8:caae:d92e::1). Look at the example code in **dhcpcd.conf** for setting up a static address with IPv6.

Free / public DNS

As well as dynamic DNS providers, some of those listed at **FreeDNS.com** offer public DNS servers. For a wider listing of alternatives to Google's DNS servers, have a search on Google itself.

[DOMAIN NAME SERVERS]

We added 192.168.0.1 8.8.8.8 to our domain_name_servers line in /etc/dhcpcd.conf. This is for the Google public domain name server (DNS). The DNS maps public IP addresses like raspberrypi.org to IP addresses (in this case 93.93.128.230). You'll need to add a DNS reference to access websites in a browser.

[**CHAPTER** EIGHT]
STOPPING A
PROCESS

As close to perfect as Raspbian is, things can go wrong . In this chapter,
we learn that there's no need to turn the Raspberry Pi off and on again:
just kill the process!

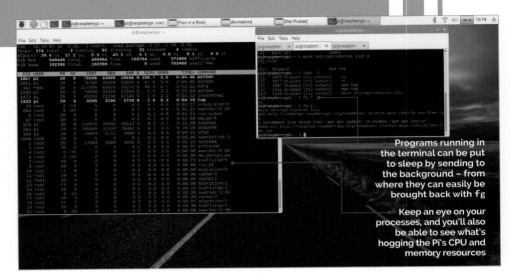

Programs running in the terminal can be put to sleep by sending to the background – from where they can easily be brought back with **fg**

Keep an eye on your processes, and you'll also be able to see what's hogging the Pi's CPU and memory resources

E ver lost the 'off switch' for a program? Sometimes a piece of software you're running seems to have no inclination to stop: either you cannot find how to quit, or the app has a problem, and won't respond to your **Q**, **CTRL+C**, or whatever command should close it down.

There's no need to panic, and certainly no need to reboot: just identify the process and quietly kill it. We'll show you how, and look at what else can be done with knowledge of processes.

Processes

Find the many processes running on your Pi with the **ps** command. As a minimum, on Raspbian, it's usually called with the **a** and **x** switches – which together give all processes, rather than just those belonging to a user, and attached to a tty – and with **u** to see processes by user; **w** adds wider output, and **ww** will wrap over the line end to display information without truncating.

Type **ps auxww** to see, then try with just **a** or other combinations. You will notice that these options work without the leading dash seen for other commands. Both the lack of dashes, and the particular letters, **a** and **x**, date back to the original UNIX ps of the early 1970s, maintained through various revisions by one of UNIX's two family branches, BSD, and baked into the first GNU/Linux ps. UNIX's other branch, System V, had extended and changed ps with new options and new abbreviations for command switches, so for **ps ax** you may see elsewhere **ps -e** (or **-ef** or **-ely** to show in long format).

The **ps aux** listing has various headers, including the USER which owns the process, and the PID, or Process IDentification number. This starts with 1 for init, the parent process of everything that happens in userspace after the Linux kernel starts up when you switch the Pi on.

Knowing the PID makes it easy to kill a process, should that be the easiest way of shutting it down. For example, to kill a program with a PID of 3012, simply enter **kill 3012**, and to quickly find the process in the first place, use **grep** on the ps list. For example, locating vi processes:

```
ps aux | grep -i  vi
```

The **-i** (ignore case) isn't usually necessary, but occasionally a program may break convention and contain upper-case letters in its file name. You can also use **killall** to kill by program name:
killall firefox

Piping commands
Naturally, you can pipe ps's output to select the PID and feed directly to the kill command:

```
kill $(ps aux | grep '[f]irefox' | awk '{print $2}')
```

We don't have space for an in-depth look at awk (we're using it here to print the second field of grep's output: the PID), but the **[f]** trick at the beginning of Firefox (or whatever named process you want to kill) prevents the grep process itself being listed in the results; in the vi example above, grep found the grep process itself as well as vi (and anything with the letter sequence vi in its name).

The output of ps also shows you useful information like percentage of memory and CPU time used, but it's more useful to see these changing in real time. For this, use **top**, which also shows total CPU and memory use in the header lines, the latter in the format that you can also find by issuing the command **free**. For an improved top:

[KEEP ON TOP]

When using a virtual console, it can be worth keeping htop running so that if there are any problems, you can CTRL+ALT-FN there for a quick look for any problems – even if the GUI freezes.

[QUICKER BOOT]

The start up
process of
Raspbian
Wheezy is
controlled by the
traditional SysV
init. Raspbian
Jessie, like other
GNU/Linux
distributions,
has moved to
the faster (but
monolithic)
SystemD – we
touch on some of
the differences in
chapter 11.

```
sudo apt-get install htop
```

htop is scrollable, both horizontally and vertically, and allows you to issue commands (such as **k** for kill) to highlighted processes. When you've finished, both top and htop are exited with **Q**, although in htop you may care to practise by highlighting the htop process and killing it from there (see **Fig 1**). htop also shows load over the separate cores of the processor if you have a Pi 2 or 3.

Background job

Placing an ampersand (&) after a command in the shell, places the program in the background – try with: **man top &** and you'll get an output like: **[1] 12768**.

The first number is a job number, assigned by the shell, and the second the PID we've been working with above. man top is now running in the background, and you can use the job control number to work with the process in the shell. Start some other processes in the background if you wish (by appending **&**), then bring the first – man top – to the foreground with **fg 1**. Now you should see man running again.

You can place a running shell program in the background by 'suspending' it with **CTRL+Z**. fg will always bring back the most recently suspended or backgrounded job, unless a job number is specified. Note that these job numbers apply only within the shell where the process started. Type **jobs** to see background processes; **jobs -l** adds in process IDs (PID) to the listing.

Fig 1 htop tells you what's running, what resources it's using, and lets you interact with the process, even killing htop from within htop

Signals

When we send a kill signal from htop, we are given a choice of signal to send. The most important are **SIGTERM**, **SIGINT**, and **SIGKILL**.

The first is also the signal **kill** will send from the command line if not called with a modifier: it tells a process to stop, and most programs will respond by catching the signal, and first saving any data they need to save and releasing system resources before quitting.

kill -2 sends SIGINT, which is equivalent to stopping a program from the terminal with **CTRL+C**: you could lose data. Most drastic is **kill -9** to send SIGKILL, telling the kernel to let the process go with no warning. Save this one for when nothing else works.

Mildest of all is the Hang Up (HUP) signal, called with **kill -1**, which many daemons are programmed to treat as a call to simply re-read their configuration files and carry on running. It's certainly the safest signal to send on a critical machine.

Fig 2 **Everything running has a process ID (PID) that can be used to control that program; find them all with ps aux**

Staying on

nohup will run a program which will continue after the terminal from which it is started has closed, ignoring the consequent SIGHUP (hangup) signal. As the process is detached from the terminal, error messages and output are sent to the file **nohup.out** in whichever directory you were in when you started the process. You can redirect it – as we did in chapter 4 – with **1>** for stdout and **2>** for stderr; **&>** is a special case for redirecting both stdout and stderr:

```
nohup myprog &>backgroundoutput.txt &
```

One use of nohup is to be able to set something in motion from a SSH session, which will continue after an interruption. For example, restarting the network connection to which you are connected:

```
sudo nohup sh -c "ifconfig wlan0 down && ifconfig
wlan0 up"
```

Note that the **nohup.out** log file created here will need sudo privileges to read – or reassign with:

```
sudo chown pi:pi nohup.out
```

[KEEP ON RUNNING]

nohup is useful for a program that will be running for some time in the background – perhaps a sensor project you are working on – until you feel happy enough to add it to Raspbian's startup processes.

[CHAPTER NINE]

REMOTE PI

Learn how to access the Raspberry Pi from remote PCs
and devices with Secure Shell (SSH)

t's great that the Raspberry Pi is so portable, but sometimes you may want to use it without taking it with you. Here, the Pi's default Raspbian OS is a real strength, as UNIX-like operating systems have been used this way for over 40 years.

Over time, as the internet has given the opportunity for malicious users to connect to computers, old standards like Telnet and rlogin have been replaced by Secure Shell (SSH), based on public-key cryptography. Once set up, secure connections are simple, and open to scripted, automatic connection for your projects. Note: you're advised to change your Pi's login password – with **passwd** – before using SSH.

If the SSH server is not enabled by default on your version of Raspbian, run **sudo raspi-config** and go to the advanced settings to enable SSH. Check the IP address assigned to the Pi with **ifconfig** (note the 'inet addr' for the eth0 or wlan0 interface). Now you can try connecting from another computer on your network.

Connecting with SSH

From a Mac or GNU/Linux computer, use **ssh** from a terminal to connect to the Pi. Assuming a default setup, and **ifconfig** revealing an IP address of 192.168.0.2, connect with **ssh pi@192.168.0.2** and enter your password. You can use the OpenSSH client on Windows 10 PCs; for earlier PCs, install an SSH client like PuTTY (**magpi.cc/uLytfk**), which also works with SCP, Telnet, and rlogin, and can connect to a serial port. Android users can try the ConnectBot client.

You can test on the Pi if SSH is running, and start the service from the command line – as you can any service (look in /etc/init.d/ and /etc/init/ if you're curious about other services)

The Raspbian install image shares its keys with everyone else who has a copy. Generate your own, and personal keys for the user account, for secure remote access

You should now be at the command-line interface of your Pi. If you got any sort of error, check from the Pi that SSH is really up and running by entering **ssh@localhost** on the Pi itself. If that works, SSH is up and running on the Pi, so take a closer look at network settings at both ends.

Hello, World

Now we can access the Pi on the local network, it's time to share with the world. Step one, for security reasons, change the **PermitRootLogin yes** entry in **/etc/ssh/sshd_config** to read: **PermitRootLogin no** using **sudo nano**. After making any changes to the SSH server's configuration, you must restart the service for them to take effect, or at least reload the configuration file: **sudo service ssh reload**. Note there's also a file in **/etc/ssh/** called **ssh_config**, which is for the SSH client; the **d** in **sshd_config** is short for 'daemon', the UNIX term for a service which runs constantly in the background.

You can also change port 22 to any unlikely number, but be sure to check it still works. You'll need to begin **ssh -p 12123** (or whichever port you have chosen) to tell your client you're not using the default port 22.

To reach your Pi from anywhere on the internet, you need an IP address, which will connect you to your board even though it's behind an ADSL router. Of course, if your Pi is in a data centre, with its own public IP address, you don't need any workaround.

There are numerous services such as **DuckDNS.org** providing free-of-charge dynamic DNS (DDNS), to point a constant IP address to the changing one allocated to you by your ISP. However, the largest of these, DynDNS, has ended its free service, which provides a useful reminder that you cannot assume that a free service will be around for ever.

There are several steps to configuring a DDNS setup, no matter which service and software client you choose. Some are detailed in the **raspberrypi.org** forums, and there's a good guide to ddclient at **samhobbs.co.uk**.

Otherwise, if your broadband router can handle both port forwarding and dynamic DNS, you can set it up to point to port 22 (or a chosen alternate port) on the Pi. You may even find your ISP offers static IP addresses.

Bye bye FTP

File Transfer Protocol (FTP) was not designed for security: data, and even passwords, are transmitted unencrypted. The Secure Copy

[INTERRUPTED SERVICE]

While you can restart most services with **sudo service ssh restart**, replacing **restart** with **reload** permits configuration changes to be registered with less disruption, which is key for some projects.

Program (SCP), which runs over SSH, is best for transferring files. The syntax of the command mimics the command-line cp program:

```
scp pi@192.168.0.2:/home/pi/testfile1 .
```

Here we're transferring a file from the Pi, across a local network, to the current location (the dot shortcut). Note that you can use wildcards for groups of similarly named files, and can recursively copy directories and their contents with the **-r** switch after **scp**.

A secure key

If you're trying this on something other than Raspbian, you may not have the SSH server installed. It's often found in a package called **openssh-server**. With Raspbian, you have a pair of keys (public and private) in **/etc/ssh/**. Unfortunately, they'll be the same as those held by everyone else with a copy of the Raspbian image that you downloaded. First, remove the existing keys:

```
sudo rm /etc/ssh/ssh_host_*
```

Alternatively, you can move them somewhere out of the way. Regenerate the system-wide keys with:

```
sudo dpkg-reconfigure openssh-server
```

For keys personal to you as a user, type **ssh-keygen -t rsa -C "comment"**, where **"comment"** is anything you want to identify the key with: name, email, or machine and project, for example. You'll be asked for a passphrase to secure the key – if you press **ENTER**, you'll get a key with no passphrase, which makes life easier when making scripted (automated) connections, but removes an extra layer of security. You can create keys from any computer with the SSH package, and move the public key to the Pi, but we'll work on the assumption that the Pi is the only handy UNIX-like computer, and we'll be generating the keys there.

If you accepted the defaults, your personal keys will now be in **~/.ssh** with the correct permissions. By default, sshd looks in **~/.ssh/authorized_keys** for public keys, so we need to copy the

[SAMBA STEPS]

Samba is *extremely* well documented, with separate man pages for everything from **smb.conf** to **smbpasswd**, and excellent online books at **samba.org** – look for smb.conf examples.

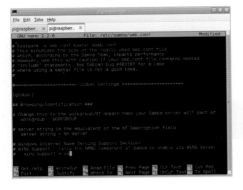

Fig 1 There's a lot of configuration in Samba, but simply adding your WORKGROUP name to the default settings should get you up and running

contents of **id_rsa.pub** to there. The following command will work even if you already have an **authorized_keys** with contents (make sure you use both **>>** symbols with no gap between them):

```
cd ~/.ssh && cat id_rsa.pub >>
authorized_keys
```

Using SCP, copy the private key to **~/.ssh** on your laptop, or wherever you will access the Pi from, removing it from the Pi if it's to act as the server. Once you confirm SSH works without passwords, you can edit **/etc/ssh/sshd_config** to include **PasswordAuthentication no**. If you are sticking with passwords, replace 'raspberry' with something stronger.

Shared drive

You may be using a service like Dropbox to share files between machines. There is no need to do this on a local network, as the Samba networking protocol on the Pi lets Windows PCs access it as a shared drive (**Fig 1**, page 48). Samba is already installed in recent versions of Raspbian, or you can install it using:

```
sudo apt-get install samba samba-common-bin
```

Edit **/etc/samba/smb.conf** with a WORKGROUP value (for Windows XP and earlier; try **workgroup = WORKGROUP**) and/or HOME (For Windows 7 and above). Ensure that Samba knows **pi** is a network user:

```
sudo smbpasswd -a pi
```

Then restart with:

```
sudo service samba restart
```

[LOST KEYS?]

The private key half of your key pair should be kept secure – but safe, too. Keep a backup of the private key on a memory card in a safe place.

The Pi should now show up in Windows Explorer under Network. You can fine-tune **smb.conf** for what's shared (including printers), and permissions.

[CHAPTER TEN]
DOWNLOADING
& INSTALLING

We look at downloading and unpacking software,
and show you how to create new Raspbian SD cards

curl can be used in place of wget for simply downloading files, but its strengths lie elsewhere, in its extensive features – these take in everything from proxy support and user authentication, to FTP upload and cookies

The tar command packs or unpacks an archive of files and directories; it also handles uncompressing the download first

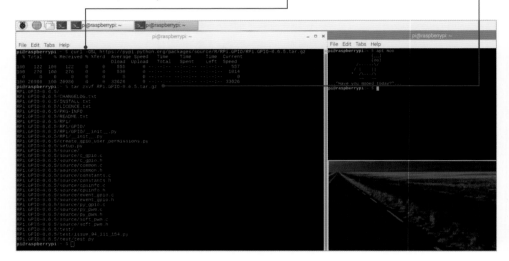

Running an **apt** command (see chapter 3) allows access to a huge collection of software – several thousands of packages in the main Raspbian repository – but sometimes we need to add software from outside the main repository.

If we are lucky, we find that someone has packaged up the software in the .deb format used by Raspbian, or even created a whole repository to take care of the dependencies. We'll look briefly both at adding repositories, and dealing with other kinds of downloads, trying the venerable vi editor along the way.

Information about repositories is kept in the **/etc/apt/sources.list** file, which on a new install just contains the Raspbian repository. Rather than editing this file to add other repositories, you are advised to add them in a .list file to the **/etc/apt/sources.list.d** directory. To add a new repository, use **sudo nano** to create a .list file there and inside it, add a source in the following format:

```
deb http://apt.pi-top.com/raspbian/ jessie main
```

Here, **jessie** is a Debian (and Raspbian) release name: all Debian releases have been named after characters in the *Toy Story* series of films since 1996 (former Debian project leader Bruce Perens was involved in the early development of Debian while working at Pixar). Stretch followed Jessie in June 2017.

Most software is in the **main** repository, which can be freely copied or mirrored anywhere. Other components, like **non-free**, allow repositories to contain software you may not be free to pass on, keeping it separate from Raspbian's FOSS repository.

wget & curl

Having added our repository source in a file in **sources.list.d**, we need to get the key for it and use **apt-key** to install it. Packages authenticated using keys added by **apt-key** will be considered trusted.

```
wget -O - -q http://apt.pi-top.com/apt.pi-top.com.
gpg.key | sudo apt-key add -
```

Wget downloads from the URL given. The **-O** switch directs the download to stdout, from where it is piped to apt-key (the trailing dash there tells apt-key to read its input from the stdin stream, which is where it receives the output from wget). After any change to the **sources.list.d** directory, you should run:

```
sudo apt-get update
```

This updates Raspbian's knowledge of what's available to install from pi-top's packages – for a full list, enter:

```
grep ^Package /var/lib/apt/lists/apt.pi-top.com_
raspbian_dists_jessie_main_binary-armhf_Packages
```

To install one, for example, **sudo apt-get install 3d-slash**.

Wget is a simple but robust download tool, with a powerful recursive feature that helps fetch entire websites, but it does have mild security risks, so be careful using it to fetch scripts. An alternative is curl, a file transfer tool that works with many protocols and can be used for simple

[VI IMPROVED]

If you really want to get to grips with vim, you'll need to **sudo apt-get install vim** – the vim.tiny package already in Raspbian is very limited.

downloads. It dumps to stdout by default; to save as a file with the same name as the resource in the URL, use the **-O** switch. For instance:

```
curl -OSL https://pypi.python.org/packages/source/R/
RPi.GPIO/RPi.GPIO-0.6.5.tar.gz
```

Here, the **-S** switch will show any errors, while the **-L** switch will enable curl to reattempt to fetch the requested file if the server reports that it has a different location.

Unzip

The Python GPIO library downloaded above is compressed with gzip, which losslessly reduces the size of files, and can be decompressed with **gunzip**. The contents here are files rolled into a tar archive (instead of **.tar.gz**, you'll sometimes find similar archives ending **.tgz**), and the **tar** command can do the decompression and untarring in one:

```
tar zxvf RPi.GPIO-0.6.5.tar.gz
```

[EASTER EGG]

Read man **apt**, and you may see: "This APT has Super Cow Powers." If it's there, try typing **apt-get moo** to see what happens.

Note that the dash is not needed for single letter options in tar. The first switch, **z**, calls gzip to decompress the archive, then **x** extracts the contents. **v** is verbose, informing you of the process as it happens, and **f** tells tar to work with the named file(s), rather than stdin. Miss out the **z** and tar should automatically detect the necessary compression operation.

The result in this case is a folder containing, among other things, a setup script to run the installation (read the **INSTALL.txt** file first):

```
cd RPi.GPIO-0.6.5
sudo python setup.py install
```

While gzip is more efficient than zip (and even more efficient options like bzip2 are available), sometimes you'll get a plain old zip file, in which case **unzip** is the command you want.

```
unzip 2018-11-13-raspbian-stretch-lite.zip
```

Disk image

Having downloaded and unzipped an image for Raspbian, you cannot copy it across to a second microSD card (connected to the Pi via a USB card reader) with regular **cp**, which would simply put a copy of it as a file on the card. We need something to replace the SD card's file system with the file system and contents that exist inside the Raspbian disk image, byte-for-byte, and for this we can use a handy little built-in utility called dd.

dd converts and copies files – any files, even special devices like **/dev/zero** or **/dev/random** (you can make a file full of zeroes or random noise) – precisely copying blocks of bytes. To copy our Raspbian image,

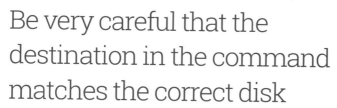

> Be very careful that the destination in the command matches the correct disk

we will need to unmount the secondary microSD card we've plugged in via a USB card reader. Use **sudo fdisk -l** both before and after plugging in the card (you can also use **df** to see what's mounted) to see attached devices. If, say, a /dev/sdb appears, with the size equal to the SD card, then unmount with **umount /dev/sdb1**. Now copy the disk image with:

```
sudo dd if=~/Downloads/2018-11-13-raspbian-stretch-
lite.img of=/dev/sdb bs=1M
```

Development of Raspbian's ancestor UNIX started in 1969, so we've covered a few utilities with a long heritage in this book, but that **if=** in place of the usual dashes for command-line options indicates a lineage stretching back to the early 1960s, and IBM's Data Definition (DD) statement from the OS/360 Job Control Language (JCL).

Be very careful that the destination matches the correct disk, or you will lose the contents of another storage device! The **bs=1M** is a block size default; **4M** would be another safe option. Now put the card in another Pi and go and have fun!

[CHAPTER ELEVEN]
START AND STOP AT
YOUR COMMAND

We take a look at scripts to manage the way Raspbian
starts and shuts down

ver the last few years, every major GNU/Linux distribution – Raspbian included – has changed the way that it starts up. This means that much of the older literature on bookshelves and websites, dealing with where to put files in **rc.local** to get them to automatically run at startup, is no longer correct – unless you've yet to upgrade from Raspbian Wheezy.

One thing remains the same: although the first process the kernel starts is not **/sbin/init**, but **/lib/systemd/systemd** (still with a PID of 1), it is still the parent process of everything that happens in user space once the Linux kernel has finished initialising devices and drivers, and mounted the file system.

init gets everything else started, and usually ends with the prompt inviting you to log in to your Pi. Recent versions of Raspbian hide most of the messages that this startup process generates, but you can see them by typing **dmesg**. They're also stored in **/var/log/kern.log**.

Startup – **init** – is the start of user space; this is the place where you can put your own programs to affect how the Raspberry Pi runs, without having to modify the code of your Linux kernel! Traditionally, GNU/Linux distributions implemented a version of the UNIX System V init, which had a well-defined startup process with run levels that would indicate whether the system was at startup, 'single user mode' (rescue mode – a handy way to get back in when you've lost your password, or a security headache), console mode, the GUI, or heading for shutdown.

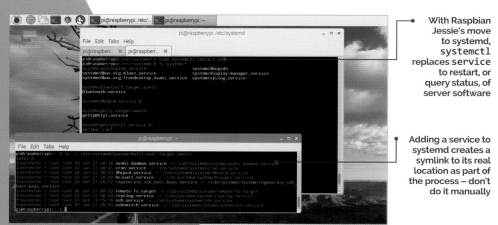

With Raspbian Jessie's move to systemd, `systemctl` replaces `service` to restart, or query status, of server software

Adding a service to systemd creates a symlink to its real location as part of the process – don't do it manually

dmesg gives you the startup messages from the kernel – nuggets of useful info buried in plenty of legacy boot information

Along the way, files in **/etc** with names beginning **rc0** through **rc6** get called – running startup scripts in **/etc/init.d** – and **/etc/rcS.d** which contains files always called at startup, regardless of run level.

Those **/etc/init.d** scripts can be called directly to start or stop your databases, web servers, or anything else that needs intervention. Many support further commands such as **status**, to check a service is running properly, and **reload** – the latter useful if you want a service to take a look at fresh config settings without doing a full restart.

```
sudo /etc/init.d/couchbase-server status
```

Although the regular and predictable scripted startup of Sys-V init makes it easy to place your own programs in the startup process – particularly useful on an unattended Pi – the performance of a purely sequential startup process is poor, even when booting from a solid state disk. Enter systemd...

Systemd

Systemd (like Upstart – see 'Refuseniks' box on p62) can start services in parallel, and can defer service starts until they are needed. Rather than many scripts for individual components, a target is set, and systemd resolves the dependencies until it reaches that target, avoiding any fixed startup sequence along the way.

Files are found under **/etc/systemd/system** and there's a lot to learn, but as Raspbian now starts up far more quickly, at least we've created extra time for all that learning. The one thing to remember for any user is that systemd and its service manager are controlled with the `systemctl` command.

```
sudo systemctl restart ssh
```

…will restart the SSH server – something you'll need to do if you change the port it listens on, for example. For compatibility, as well as **/etc/init.d** scripts to start and stop services, the system of service commands that worked on older versions of Raspbian, such as

```
sudo service apache2 reload
```

…still works (here we ask a running Apache2 Web server to reread its configuration files).

Under **/etc/systemd/system/multi-user.target.wants** you will find files like **cron.service** which, when examined closely with `ls -l`, you'll see are links to files of the same name in **/lib/systemd/system** (other GNU/Linux distributions may place the files under **/usr/lib**).

Don't worry if what's inside these files looks confusing; there's a logic to them with their conditional dependencies, but you can safely forget about them until you need to get some software working automatically on every system restart for your Pi project. Even then, we'll show you another way with crontab – otherwise you'll need to be aware of the following, as those links aren't created manually:

```
sudo systemctl enable postgresql.service
```

…will create the link, and means PostgreSQL will be enabled upon startup. To control the service before the next restart:

```
sudo systemctl daemon-reload
```

…will make systemd aware of the changes.

[WHO / WHERE]

Although run levels are no longer particularly meaningful under systemd, you can still check which run level you are in with **who -r**

Linked In

Systemd makes links between files automatically, but there will be times you'll want a file to appear to be in a local directory when it is elsewhere, with a handy little command we have not so far had a chance to show you: **ln**.

ln makes a link which allows a file to effectively exist in two places at once. In the following example:

```
sudo ln -s /usr/share/doc/python-numpy/THANKS.txt
numpy-THANKS.txt
```

…a file will appear in your current working directory. But **ls -l** and you'll see that it's a special type of file, a link pointing to the actual file. Edit **numpy-THANKS.txt** and you'll find that **THANKS.txt** in the linked directory will be edited.

Soft, or 'symbolic' links, are created with the **-s** switch – you don't even need the file to which you're linking to actually exist, which makes it handy if you're linking across a network, or to a removable drive.

Backwards compatibility with init.d scripts – and even run levels – is maintained by systemd

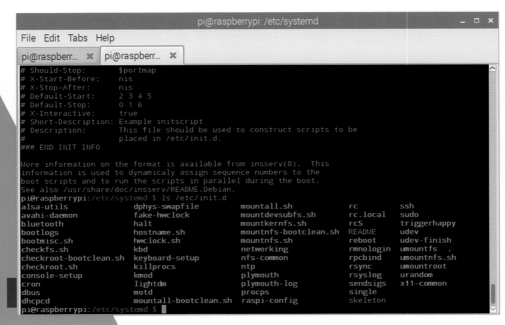

It's called a symbolic link because it works by linking to the name of the target file, rather than to the file data itself. Create a hard link:

```
sudo ln /etc/bluetooth/main.conf mybluetooth.conf
```

...and you have two names (and locations) for the same file – sounds like the same thing? Not exactly: if you delete the original file in the first example, you can replace it with a new file of the same name, but different contents, and the symbolic link will point to the new file. Remove the original file in the hard link case, and the link still points to the data.

Location, location

The startup scripts – whether init.d or systemd – are generally for daemons, processes you want running all of the time, like web servers and databases. There are plenty of programs which do housekeeping that need to be run periodically – hourly, daily, weekly. For this purpose, the cron software utility is ideal for scheduling the running of such programs and tasks. Cron searches its configuration directories and runs through the scripts it finds there – have a look at the different folders in **/etc** with names beginning with 'cron'.

The easiest way to get to know where things like this are on your system is to search with **locate** – which is not installed by default on Raspbian. Enter **sudo apt-get install mlocate**, followed by **sudo updatedb**, then **locate cron** – which will find you every file or directory with cron as its name or as part of its name.

The **locate** tool maintains a database of every file on the system, which itself is updated daily by cron. If you've made a lot of changes, or want to find out where some software you've just installed has put its config file, get locate to update its database with **sudo updatedb**.

The built-in alternative is **find**, a powerful utility which enables you to search particular directories – or the whole file system – by name or name fragment, size of file, how long ago they were modified, or whether they're bigger than another file – enough to deserve a whole chapter of its own. Because it searches the file system, rather than a cached listing, it takes longer than a locate, but it is always up to date, and has search options not found in locate (see the 'RegExp' box). To replicate our **locate cron** command with the **find** tool:

[REGEXP]

The **find** tool can search by regular expressions, as well as (part) name. They're a whole book topic in themselves, but well worth investigating once you've got command-line basics under your belt, as regexps can be used with many commands.

```
find / -name '*cron*'
```

If you were looking for cron or crontab, but not anacron, you could search for 'cron*' instead. There will be more output than you want, so pipe it through a pager, or perhaps a grep. Back to using cron – the easiest way is via crontab, which maintains a table where each row specifies a command, and how often it is to run.

You edit the crontab file not directly, but with **crontab -e**, which calls up the default editor to do it. To take an example from Michael Stutz's *Linux Cookbook* (No Starch Press), add an entry in the form:

```
45 05 * * 1-5 calendar | mail -s 'Your calendar'
me@myemailaddress.com
```

… which grabs the output from the venerable UNIX calendar program and emails it to you every morning. The first five crontab fields cover minute, hour, day of month, month, day of the week, and can all be replaced with a single special value, like **@daily** or **@hourly**. While **man crontab** tells you a little about crontab, **man 5 crontab** is far more useful as it covers the layout of the file, with examples. Run **man man** for more on the numbered sections available with **man** commands.

Note that traditional UNIX command-line mail is not installed by default on the Pi, so if you wanted to follow the example, you would need to install a simple mailer – we recommend ssmtp, and the Raspberry Pi forums contain plenty of tips on command-line mail, as it can be used in all sorts of projects.

A fresh startup

Using the value **@reboot**, we can easily run our own scripts on startup, without messing about with system startup scripts. There are times when a full systemd startup script will be more appropriate, but for quickly getting something tested, put the script into crontab.

There are two things that may catch you out. Firstly, you might be running scripts out of a directory that you have in your $PATH, which defines where Bash looks for commands. As $PATH is only set once you log in and your personalised **.bashrc** file is read, scripts running from

```
                               pi@raspberrypi: ~                        _  □  ×
File  Edit  Tabs  Help

 pi@raspberr...  ✕    pi@raspberr...  ✕
pi@raspberrypi:~ $ ls /etc/cron*
/etc/crontab

/etc/cron.d:

/etc/cron.daily:
apt   aptitude   bsdmainutils   dpkg   logrotate   man-db   ntp   passwd

/etc/cron.hourly:
fake-hwclock

/etc/cron.monthly:

/etc/cron.weekly:
man-db
pi@raspberrypi:~ $ ls /etc/cron.daily
apt   aptitude   bsdmainutils   dpkg   logrotate   man-db   mlocate   ntp   passwd
pi@raspberrypi:~ $ █
```

crontab which are run immediately upon startup will not be aware of your $PATH setting. So, you will need to express all commands by their full paths, such as **/home/pi/bin/test.sh** – as well as making sure that the permissions are sufficient.

Secondly, systemd's parallel service starts also mean that some services, such as the network, as well as environment variables, may not be ready when your **@reboot** commands are called. If you have problems, try giving a short pause first. It's ten seconds in this example crontab entry, but you could use the smallest time that consistently works on testing:

```
@reboot sleep 10; /usr/bin/python3 /home/pi/Documents/
Python_Projects/hello_gpio.py
```

One of the scripts that you'll see called by cron, is to run anacron, designed to periodically run tasks on machines that were not always switched on – so it is very useful on laptops, too – with tasks specified, in anacrontab, to run after so many days have passed since they last ran. You can also use the automation of crontab or anacron to run your own backup scripts, so we'll discuss backup options in the next chapter.

Installing mlocate adds a script to /etc/cron.daily to update its database of files and folders every day

[CHAPTER TWELVE]

SAVE IT NOW!

Learn how to protect your data with backups and disk wipes

Perhaps you've got backups running automatically on your main computer, or perhaps you just back up what's important now and then – it's OK, we're not here to judge. But we will say that anything you don't have backed up, you don't have. Computers break. Hard disks and SSDs break. Accidents happen. The unexpected is somewhat inevitable.

IT professionals prepare as if they could lose everything at any moment, at least the best do. That might sound a tall order for a small single-board computer you bought at a disposable price to use in a hobby project, but your data is the most important thing on it, and good backups are a useful discipline to take elsewhere. Fortunately, the command line can actually make this easier; we'll show you some of your best options for (relatively) painless backups.

Simplest of all is to copy the data and move it elsewhere. It's labour-intensive, compared to automatic solutions, but for only-very-occasional backups it's certainly better than nothing, so we will not ignore this option.

Whether you're copying to disk, or moving the backup to another machine, it's best to make it as small as practically possible. The zip compression format may not compress as much as some specialist UNIX choices, but it does mean that other users should be able to open the file(s) with their standard compression software. You could go with LZMA or bzip2 compression (from tar, **-J** or **-j**, respectively) – both more widely installed than they used to be – for better compression to

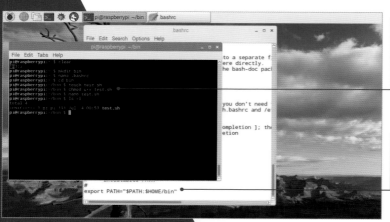

By putting commands in a .sh file and making it executable, you create your own scripts

Making a ~/bin folder and adding it to the PATH directive in ~/.bashrc means you'll be able to run your scripts by name

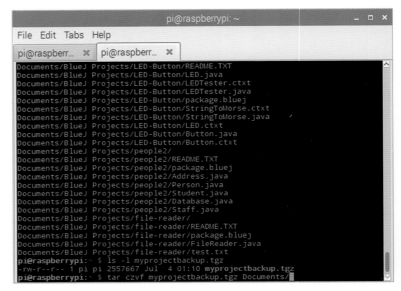

A single command wraps up all of the files and subfolders, then compresses the tar archive with gzip

a smaller file size, but although alternatives to gzip save a little more space, they can take far longer to perform the compression.

Taking a directory of files that needs collecting together, then compressing it, can be done with a single tar command:

```
tar czvf mybackup.tgz myfolder
```

The **c** switch tells tar to create the archive, diving into all subfolders found; **f**, use the named file (here, **mybackup.tgz**), is necessary to direct the output away from the terminal, or – historically – a tape device. Yes, tape, for tar is short for 'tape archive', as telling a sign of its longevity as its frequent use without a dash in front of the command-line options. **v**, as with many commands, asks for more verbose output, so the program tells you what it is doing and what (if anything) has gone wrong.

Lastly, **z** invokes gzip compression – saving the extra step of creating a .tar archive, then running it through gzip. To unpack the archive, substitute **x** for extract in place of **c** – you can omit the **z**, as tar will recognise the compression type and automagically deal with it:

```
tar xvf mybackup.tgz
```

A safe home

Often, using tar to back up **/home/pi** – with **cd /home**, then **tar** on the **pi** folder – will be all you need, but if you have data across directories, from **/etc** to **/var/www**, it's simplest to back up the entire microSD card. We looked at copying a new Raspbian image onto a card in chapter 10; backing up your disk is almost a mirror image of that process, which you can do on the Pi, with a USB card reader – with one important caveat.

You'll be creating a file as big as the entire SD card – usually 8GB or more – onto a Pi with a lot less space to spare. The solution is to compress the image file as it is created, which, for a Pi with a modest amount of data on it, will result in an image of around 2.5GB. Look back at chapter 10 for how to be sure which device the USB card reader is – for a card plugged in as **/dev/sdb**, and unmounted, do:

```
dd bs=4M if=/dev/sdb | gzip > back-raspbian.img.gz
```

Open another Terminal tab and monitor your disappearing disk space with **df** – if you don't think that it will fit, stop the dd operation with the usual **CTRL+C**, then **rm** the image file that you have partially created, and go and perform the backup on a computer with more disk space – or with a backup drive mounted, which you copy the archive to directly. Turning the backup into a usable microSD for the Pi means piping the other way, from gzip to dd:

```
gzip -cd back-raspbian.img.gz | dd bs=4M of=/dev/sdb
```

For disk operations like dd, you'll need root permissions: you can prefix **dd** with **sudo**, but for saving the file outside of **/home/pi** you may also need **sudo** – which means typing it in front of **gzip** as well.

This is only mildly inconvenient on the Pi, where **sudo** does not demand your password – but on a multi-user computer, or any setup with greater security, you need a reliable way of becoming the root user for every operation: running **sudo -s** will give you a shell with root permissions, but remember to **exit** afterwards. Alternatively, a chain of commands can be run with full admin permissions like so:

```
sudo bash -c "gzip -cd back-raspbian.img.gz | dd bs=4M
of=/dev/sdb"
```

[TAPE ARCHIVE]

tar dates from the days when computers backed up to big tape reels, those essential props of 1960s and 1970s sci-fi films. The lack of file structure on tapes means that tar can save all of the file system info such as ownership and timestamps.

Remote copy

It's good to be able to make backups as required, using removable drives, but to move towards systematic backups you will need to copy across the network. We mentioned SCP in chapter 9. To copy your backup file to another machine, one that allows SSH login (so is running a SSH server), pass your login name with the command:

```
scp -p back-raspbian.img.gz pi@192.168.0.207:/home/pi/bak/
```

You will then be prompted for the user password. Change the **pi@** to whatever your user name is on the remote machine, not the Pi you're copying from. The **-p** preserves information such as when the files were last accessed. Note that **-P** (capital p) can be used to specify a particular port number.

We showed you how to set up a Pi with a fixed IP address in chapter 7; that Pi, with a plugged in USB disk drive, could be an inexpensive backup machine, as well as media server or whatever else your home or office needs.

Because you're sending these commands through the Bash shell, you get all the usual Bash advantages, from tab completion (just type **bac**, or however much of the file name is unique in your present working directory) to wildcards. If you have disparate archives

SCP makes command-line copying to remote machines as easy as moving files around on your Pi

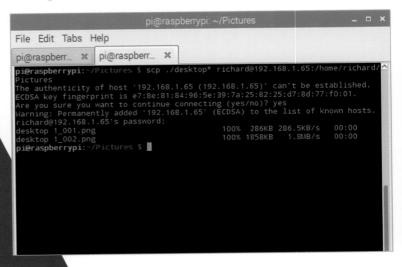

in the same directory – such as **www-backup-20181225.gz** and **data-backup-20181226.gz** – then copy them all with:

```
scp -p ./*backup*gz pi@192.168.0.207:/home/pi/bak/
```

So far so good, but there are possibilities to automate your backup process later in the chapter, so the interactive element – having to give a password – would be better avoided. As long as you can maintain security in some other way, of course.

Key to logins

Back in chapter 9 when we set up our SSH server, we generated keys with **ssh-keygen** – these keys can be used to provide passwordless login. You can copy them across to other machines manually, as we did earlier, but a handy shortcut is to use the command **ssh-copy-id**.

```
ssh-copy-id pi@192.168.0.207
```

If you have more than one key pair, use **-i** to specify which .pub file you're copying. **-p** allows you to specify an alternate port number – always a good thing in an internet-connected server, but not so necessary on a local network. Now we're all set for remote backups – but if you do them regularly, you'll waste a lot of disk space duplicating unchanging data.

rsync lets you copy data in much the same way as **scp**, but uses a delta-transfer algorithm, to only transfer the difference between the copies of the source file on your disk, and the remote, saved version. This both saves bandwidth used, and avoid cluttering up your backup disk with multiple near-identical versions of a file. It's also handy if you're paying a cloud provider for storage and data transfer.

If your version of Raspbian doesn't have rsync, it's just an **apt-get** away. Typically, rsync uses SSH for transport, but you can set up a server running an rsync daemon, and directly contact the **rsync://** URL over TCP (defaults to port 873). In this case, set an RSYNC_PASSWORD environment variable or use the **--password-file** switch.

While rsync is not a built-in Bash command, we are highlighting it here as part of the array of command-line utility choices that users face when considering whether or not to simply employ

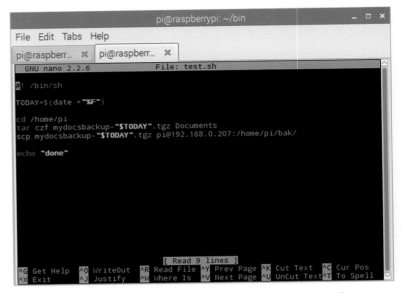

```
pi@raspberrypi: ~/bin                    _ □ ✕

File  Edit  Tabs  Help

 pi@raspberr...  ✕    pi@raspberr...  ✕
  GNU nano 2.2.6              File: test.sh

#! /bin/sh

TODAY=$(date +"%F")

cd /home/pi
tar czf mydocsbackup-"$TODAY".tgz Documents
scp mydocsbackup-"$TODAY".tgz pi@192.168.0.207:/home/pi/bak/

echo "done"

                    [ Read 9 lines ]
^G Get Help  ^O WriteOut  ^R Read File  ^Y Prev Page  ^K Cut Text  ^C Cur Pos
^X Exit      ^J Justify   ^W Where Is   ^V Next Page  ^U UnCut Text^T To Spell
```

A datestamp in our script means that we are not producing a backup with the same name each day we run it

built-in commands or to try something more complex instead.
In addition, there is the possibility of using version control
systems, such as git, for both backing up, and tracking changes on,
important files.

Script-it-yourself!

But let's row back to simpler commands. We have seen from early
on how powerful Bash can be by chaining together a few commands;
another way of putting commands together is to bundle them into a
script – a short program simply comprising a small number of Bash
commands, and known as a shell script. Take a look at this code – try
typing it in to your favourite text editor, adjusting it for the IP address
of your networked backup server, and backup folder location (or
change the **scp** line to a **cp** to a plugged-in backup drive), and saving it
as **test.sh**.

```
#! /bin/sh
cd /home/pi
tar czf mydocsbackup.tgz Documents
scp mydocsbackup.tgz pi@192.168.0.207:/home/pi/bak/
```

Then make the script executable with:

```
chmod u+x test.sh
```

...and run it with **./test.sh** – any problems, then check the names, network address, and did you perform the **ssh-copy-id** step?

Now we have a script that saves a folder, and copies it remotely, do you notice any potential problems? Each time you run it, it will overwrite the previous **mydocsbackup.tgz**, both locally and remotely. We need a way to put a timestamp on the backup name:

```
#! /bin/sh

TODAY=$(date +"%F")

cd /home/pi
tar czf mydocsbackup-"$TODAY".tgz Documents
scp mydocsbackup-"$TODAY".tgz pi@192.168.0.207:/home/pi/bak/
```

What we have done is set a variable – **TODAY** – to the current date, in YYYY-MM-DD format, which we can now access with **$TODAY** (remember, we permanently set variables for the shell named this way, when changing the prompt in chapter 5). You can run **date +%F** in the terminal – **date --help** will show you the many other format options. Now you can automate it by putting the script somewhere like **/usr/bin** (and with a better name than **test.sh**), and running it regularly with cron, as we covered in chapter 11.

Shell scripts tend to grow; there is always room for improvement. Here, you may want to back up more than one directory, for example, or use **echo** to let users know what the script is doing at each stage. You could even make it interactive, letting users choose which directories to back up.

There are plenty of shell scripting tutorials online, and great books (see *The MagPi* book reviews) to take it further, but Raspbian itself holds many great shell scripts, from which you can learn by example. To see how a script can be organised to still be maintainable with over a thousand lines of code, have a look at **/usr/bin/raspi-config**.

However grand or modest your scripting ambitions, don't be afraid to try things out: build up gradually, and test your code each time, so

[PASSWORD FREE]

Using your key to log in is a convenience you quickly get used to – beyond **scp** to your backup server, try it on any machine under your control that you have to log in to.

that you know where to look for any errors that you introduce. Help is at hand from the Raspberry Pi forums, and pasting your code into **shellcheck.net** will give you valuable feedback – for example, advising you the **cd** line of our backup script should be:

```
cd /home/pi || exit
```

...in case the **cd** step fails – this is generally a good idea, although not so important in this particular case. Now that we have a choice of backup options, one task remains: securely getting rid of data from disks. This is a concern for anyone handling other people's data, or just protecting their own privacy and security.

Through the shredder

Back in the 1960s, if you wished to cover your tracks, *Mission Impossible* told us it was done by the show opening's taped mission assignment finishing, "This message will self destruct in ten seconds...", and boom went the tape player.

In these digital days, protecting privacy or security means understanding how a disk drive actually stores data, so that you don't dispose of old disks under the mistaken impression that you've securely erased data, when you haven't.

Disk space is collected into blocks, sized typically at 4096kB, that are indexed by the file system with inodes so that the disk controller knows where to send the read head to retrieve information. SSDs and flash drives don't have read heads, but still organise the data in a similar fashion. Most disk operations occur at the inode level – so moving a file between directories on the same disk partition is simply done by relabelling an inode. **rm** does not delete the data stored, just the reference to its blocks on the inode.

Plug in a disk drive after someone has done **rm -rf** on it and it will look empty, but use a low-level utility and you'll have access to all of the jigsaw puzzle pieces needed to put the data back together again. So far, so *NCIS*, but can this be significant to the average Pi user? Given the range of projects out there, and the multifaceted data that they collect, to stay on the right side of new and future data protection laws it will be useful to know how to securely remove data from your disks.

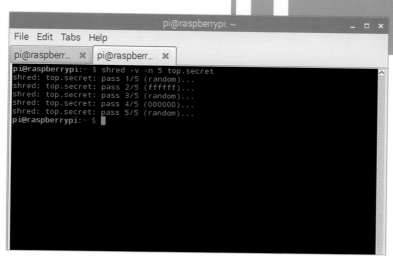

Shred will securely overwrite (then optionaly erase) files of sensitive data – or entire disk drives

Caution

Before we start erasing disks, think of the carpentry maxim, 'measure twice, cut once'. It's easy to mistakenly erase the wrong disk or partition if you're not paying attention. Given enough opportunities, most of us do it, and it's often the lesson that teaches us to make proper backups! Running through other operations on the disk (**mount**, **df**, **ls**, **umount**), before erasing, works as a sanity check that you're addressing the correct partition.

Now to those blocks. You can overwrite every bit of information, either with all 1 digits, or with totally random data, using **dd**. Even then, with magnetic disks, it's theoretically possible to recover the data, and multiple overwrites will be necessary – but before you worry about writing a script to do that, let us introduce **shred**, a utility that does just that, overwriting with as many passes as you select as a command switch (or defaulting to three):

```
shred -vf -n 5 /dev/sdb
```

Adding a **-z** switch will overwrite the random data shred has used with zeroes, leaving a new-looking disk. **-u** will delete the file after the secure overwrite. Shred can also safely overwrite and/or remove individual files.

[WHERE AM I?]

If you follow our tip on SSH keys everywhere, and end up hopping from machine to machine, remember to customise your Bash prompt so that you are always sure on which machine you're about to erase a file.

[CHAPTER THIRTEEN]

EASY COMPILATION

Here we look at how to install software
and build it from the source code

Just paste the URI ending .git after `git clone` at the Terminal and you'll have the very latest source code

Install alien and you'll be able to swap packages between Raspbian, Fedora, and other systems' packages

t's so easy to install most software on Raspbian – provided it's mature enough to have been packaged as a .deb archive. Often, however, there's some great code available you'd love to try, but it asks you to compile it – sometimes after first cloning it from GitHub.

While not so straightforward as running an **apt-get install** command, there's little to fear in stepping through the decades-old ritual of compiling software – and when errors do occur, it's often quite easy to get back on track. We'll also look at scripted installs and Python packages, but first let's find out what to do if a package is in the wrong format.

Raspbian isn't the only distribution of GNU/Linux based upon Debian – **distrowatch.com** lists more than a hundred – and the ones you're most likely to have heard of include Linux Mint and Ubuntu. Ubuntu – the name derived from an Nguni Bantu term meaning 'humanity towards others' – is so popular that many projects, including ones not in the Debian and Raspbian repositories, maintain .deb packages for each version released.

Ubuntu also introduced the idea of Personal Package Archives (PPA) to the Debian family – special software repositories for uploading source packages to be built and published as an APT repository by Ubuntu's Launchpad software like the official Ubuntu repository, but for unofficial software from outside. You won't tend to find these with Pi software, but if you've been inspired to try one of Raspbian's relatives on your main PC, you'll find plenty of instructions on them in the Ubuntu community documentation.

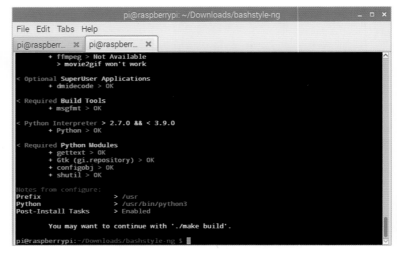

When you run **apt-get**, or you **apt-cache search** to look for a package, APT quizzes its local record of what packages are available to it. The record of where it gets these packages from – the address of the repositories – is kept in the file **/etc/apt/sources.list** and at files in **/etc/apt/sources.list.d/** to which you can also add repositories by hand should a project you are interested in maintain one.

You can also edit **sources.list** (not advised) – editing all mentions of wheezy to jessie was an (unsupported) way of upgrading without overwriting your SD card when Raspbian updated. Meanwhile, plain old .deb files can be downloaded, and then installed with the command:

```
sudo dpkg -i example.deb
```

And any missing dependencies resolved with an:

```
apt-get install -f
```

There is another popular family of GNU/Linux distributions, based upon Red Hat, and including Fedora and CentOS. Fedora is available as an alternative to Raspbian (on the Pi 2 or 3), should you wish to try it out. What we're concerned with here is situations where you may need to install packages for one distribution, onto a system of the other type. Your friend here is Raspbian's alien package, which will convert software between .debs and packages in .rpm (Red Hat Package Management) format.

```
alien some-package.rpm
```

...will convert from .rpm to .deb. You're more likely – on the Pi at least, where RPM-only packages are rarer – to need to convert the other way:

```
alien -r mysoftware.deb
```

Friendly triad

Before package managers, it was normal to compile your own software, obtaining source code – usually written in the C or C++ languages – and running it through the GCC compiler, before linking libraries, and installing to the correct place on your disk drive.

Many of the headaches involved in the process are long gone as **configure** and **make** scripts do all of the hard work, checking dependencies are installed, then running the correct compiler flags for the project and the platform, and even installing the man page in the correct place.

Although most of the software you'll want to run will be available as a .deb to install with **apt** or **dpkg**, or come with a shell script which deals with installation (see below), plenty of projects, particularly those you'll find on GitHub or FreshCode, need unpacking then compiling.

After unpacking the archive with:

```
tar xvf latest-software.tgz
```

...**cd** into the directory created, and look for a file called **README** or **README.md**, or perhaps one called **INSTALL**. It will usually tell you to run a trio of commands that will become familiar – but read the instructions as there are variations, and some software even bypasses make with its own local version which you'll need to run as **./make**. The norm is:

```
./configure
make
sudo make install
```

[TRACK YOUR INSTALLS]

Installing software from outside of Raspbian's repository means it must be looked after separately: updates, bug-fixes, security patches, and disaster recovery if something happens to your Pi. Keep track of what you install.

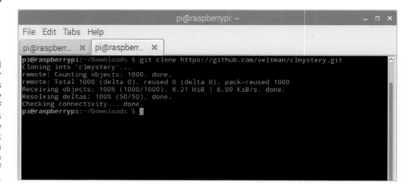

Git was developed by Linux creator Linus Torvalds to handle the complexities of multi-million lines of kernel code – yet makes it simple to maintain version control on the simplest of software.

However, on the Pi, `./configure` on its own may well result in programs (and particularly libraries) being built so they install in a not-quite-standard location – **/usr/local/lib** instead of **/usr/lib**. This can cause problems if these directories aren't on the library search path. In particular, if building a new version of a library that is already on the system, you will often end up with two versions of the library on the system – and the system will continue to use the old one. So, instead of plain `./configure`, we advise using the following to avoid issues:

```
./configure --prefix=/usr --libdir=/usr/lib/arm-linux-
gnueabihf
```

Dependencies

Commercial software (open-source or proprietary) often comes as a large binary file containing all of the dependencies, statically linked into the application. With most non-commercial software projects, however, it is more common to just get a list of which version of which library will be needed to compile and run the software. Luckily, for a standard Debian package, there's a simple command that will install all the dependencies required to build it:

```
sudo apt-get build-dep <package name>
```

However, occasionally you'll need to compile and install something else first. Often the reason for compiling is to get the very latest version of the software from the developers, for new features, compatibility, or bug fixes. In the last few years, GitHub has become the default place to host free software projects; other repositories are available, but we'll just look at fetching software from GitHub, to quickly show you what you need to know.

Your first encounter with GitHub's existence may be seeing a banner on a project page inviting you to 'fork me on GitHub', or an invitation to 'clone' the software. Yes, we're in the world of a project big enough to sustain its own jargon. A fork is simply your own development copy to work on, after which you can offer the changes back to the project, or publish them (on GitHub or elsewhere) for others to try or build upon.

You don't even need to be able to code – many people are now using GitHub for collaborative development of documentation, including scientific research, and even fiction. But to simply download something, we don't need to worry about other Git methods – just 'clone' the application's source to your Pi with the following command:

```
git clone https://github.com/veltman/clmystery.git
```

…which will make a local directory containing all of the source files. **cd** into the subdirectory just created. Then follow the configure/make instructions as above.

Nil desperandum

Sometimes, somewhere along the compilation, something goes wrong, and the script terminates with a complaint of some missing package. On a good day, you'll **apt-cache search** for the name of the missing dependency and there it will be, easy to install on Raspbian.

On a slightly-less-good day, you're going to have to dig around a bit to find the software, or the latest version that's being called for. Maybe having to go to GitHub or **SourceForge.net**. This is OK if the developer has a setup not too far removed from your own; the extra install steps may go smoothly. Otherwise, don't despair: help is available.

Most projects have one or more ways of reporting a problem and seeking help: a mailing list or Google Group; a wiki on the project SourceForge page; an email address for the lead developer; or even a Twitter account. Try to state your problem with plenty of detail, and

[IT'S A MYSTERY]

The clmystery in the GitHub example is The Command Line Mystery – a text game which teaches you command line use. Entertaining and very useful.

The MagPi
ESSENTIALS

[GOING FOR UBUNTU]

Ubuntu, can be installed on the Pi (2 or 3), as well as your PC, Mac or laptop,

remain polite and patient, and usually you'll find helpful people. Remember, although people want to be helpful, you are asking them to give up time to answer you – if you're frustrated with the installation process, and we've all been there, don't let that stop you being respectful of anyone going out of their way to help you.

If you don't have time for chasing up answers, but remain interested in a project, another option is to wait for the project's next release. By this time the dependencies may have become more widely available, even making their way into the Raspbian repositories, or the problem may simply no longer arise.

A scripted install

You'll sometimes be asked to grab an installation script and run it directly – as is the case with the excellent EduBlocks, a half-way house between Scratch and Python which is helping young coders get over the large step between the two languages. The EduBlocks install wants you to run:

```
curl -sSL get.edublocks.org | bash
```

...which takes the shell script at **get.edublocks.org** (you can look at it there in your browser) and pipes it through to a Bash process to run. The **-s** switch tells curl not to show a progress meter or error messages; **-S** overrides this to show an error message if it fails; while **-L** tells it to follow to wherever the site redirects to for the script.

If you don't like running software without knowing what it is doing to your Pi, or simply wish to take a look inside the script and see what the installation does, instead, download and save as **edu-install.sh** or just **install.sh** if that won't overwrite anything of the same name in your current working directory:

```
curl -o install.sh -L get.edublocks.org
```

...and you'll see the script downloads and unpacks a tarball with more than one script inside, first running the one that installs dependencies.

You can run the downloaded script – which you can do with **sh edu-install.sh**. If you don't read the script before running it, you're

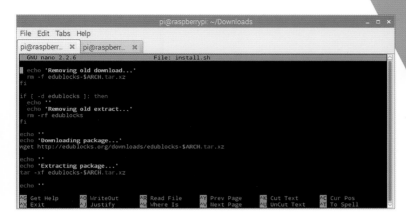

EduBlocks is a good example of a project that makes your life easy by putting every stage of the installation into a shell script, and giving you just one command to run the installation

placing a lot of trust not just in the developer(s) who wrote it, but every step of its journey before it reached your machine.

Python, please

Over the years of installing software from various sources, you learn to recognise signs of whether or not it's likely to be a painless installation – and one cause for hope is something written in Python. Although both good and bad software can be written in any language, Python software and Python libraries just seem to be well-packaged and reliable.

Although Debian-based GNU/Linux distributions like Raspbian come with the excellent APT and dpkg (Debian Package Manager), many popular programming languages have evolved their own ecosystems of packing tools and repositories – there are several for the Emacs text editor alone! Two that you are most likely to come across are JavaScript's npm and Python's pip. After using apt, the command format will be familiar, and:

```
sudo pip3 install numpy
```

…won't be a stretch to remember if the installation instructions tell you to install Python libraries such as NumPy. Happy installing, and above all, don't worry – it's quite hard to mess up the Raspbian installation, but if you do, at least those backups you made earlier will get tested out.

[CHAPTER FOURTEEN]
COMMANDING THE INTERNET

Yes, it is possible to get online from the command line. Here's how…

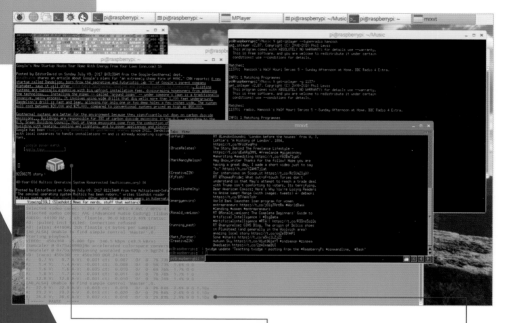

Text-mode browsing keeps the pics (but not the animated ads), thanks to w3m-img

Keep up with Twitter in the terminal, or send tweets from shell scripts

Now that you're getting comfortable at the command line, and perhaps finding it faster for some tasks, you may want to increase the amount of time you spend there, trying to improve your productivity on everyday tasks. Here we survey internet software – a diverse field, covering clients for protocols (IRC, Jabber), specific services (Twitter, BBC iPlayer), and tasks (search), as well as general web browsers, mail clients, and even surprising uses of the venerable Telnet client.

Don't get carried away: command-line alternatives vary from essentials you'll see often used in scripts and Pi projects, to less satisfactory alternatives you'd only use when there is no GUI available – so don't plan to switch all of your Facebook and Instagram use to the terminal. We concentrate here on internet interactions which will be useful for your Pi project, but sometimes you may be using the command line on the Pi and just need to look something up on the web, so welcome back to the Internet of Text.

If you've ever had to fall back on the Pi as a desktop machine, you'll know that capable as it is – particularly the four-core Pi 3 – you don't want to have too many browser tabs open at once. Some websites are so dependent upon JavaScript, though, that for all the memory that they hog on the Pi, you can only access them via Chrome (or Firefox). For others, try the retro world of the command-line web browser.

In the early 1990s, most people who had internet access browsed with a command-line browser called Lynx. After a quarter of a century, it's still in use! If not being able to see any pics makes the web pointless for you, consider the advantages. No tracking, no distractions from reading the text, and quicker page loads. Screen reader users and the mobility impaired can benefit from the simpler keyboard navigation, and as pages can be dumped to stdout, you can pipe it through other command-line applications:

```
lynx -dump https://duckduckgo.com/?q=gpio+bash | tail -n 30
```

Lynx isn't the only choice in command-line browsing – Raspbian also offers links2 and w3m; the latter is even usable from within the Emacs text editor. Install xterm (an alternative to Raspbian's default Terminal application) and w3m-img, and you can even view images when browsing from the terminal.

Commanding the web

Telnet – short for teletype network – is the protocol developed at the end of the 1960s to provide two-way text communication between computers. It dates from an era without security concerns, and was long ago replaced by SSH as a means of connecting directly to other machines over open networks, but the Telnet client remains useful for interactively querying services such as mail or web for testing, by connecting to the appropriate port on the server, then issuing commands in the service's protocol:

```
telnet example.com 80
GET / HTTP/1.1
HOST: example.com
```

…which (after pressing **ENTER** again) should dump a webpage onto

[MOBILE]

Responsive web design should mean that w3m works with more modern sites. While we wait for reality to catch up with the ideal, use mobile websites: w3m https://m. facebook.com

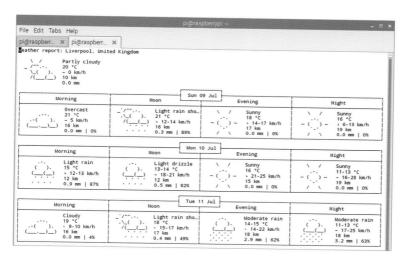

Command-line browsing is all about the information – mostly text, but not entirely

the terminal. It's a basic but useful diagnostic tool, but also gets used in some fun applications that we'll take a look at later in this chapter.

Surfraw

As we have seen earlier, with wget and curl, functions such as downloading can be removed from the web browser. Another case where specialist commands seem most appropriate is searching. Looking things up from the command line can be done directly with a nifty little program called surfraw, which uses helpers called elvi to tackle different search tasks – see them all with:

```
surfraw -elvi
```

As a good citizen of the command-line world, surfraw pays due regard to your time and your tendons, and can be called simply with **sr**.

```
sr google -results=2 raspberry pi clojure gpio
sr translate peloton
sr gutenberg dickens
sr wikipedia permaculture
sr bbcnews tim peake
sr rhyme orange
```

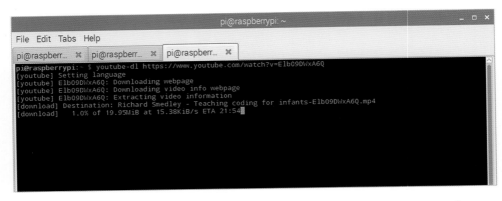

The results are displayed in your browser, which you can set in **/etc/xdg/surfraw/conf**:

No spare memory to open a YouTube link? Download the video to watch later

```
def       SURFRAW_text_browser  /usr/bin/lynx
defyn     SURFRAW_graphical            no
```

The Beeb

YouTube videos also won't work from a text mode browser, but it's easy enough to grab them with youtube-dl.

```
sudo apt-get install youtube-dl
youtube-dl https://www.youtube.com/watch?v=Elb09DWxA6Q
```

Each downloaded video is saved as an MP4 file which, thanks to MPlayer's ability to output video through a choice of libraries, can even be rendered in ASCII through the terminal, using the **-vo caca** option. It can also be output via an SSH session, although forwarding the sound is an exercise we leave the reader to research. ASCII rendering is far from high-resolution, but if you run **mplayer** from one of the virtual consoles (which we visited back in chapter 1), it will default to a framebuffer output, for regular-quality video overlaying the command line.

You can also access BBC content from the command line. Although television programmes are only available from IP addresses located in the UK, radio shows – from Radio 3 concerts to classic comedy and drama on Radio 4 Extra – can be downloaded for a few days after they have been broadcast, by the get-iplayer script; this saves them in the AAC format for listening to later. To keep within reasonable fair use terms – or at least be equivalent to the BBC's own iPlayer service – the programmes should be deleted after 30 days.

At the time of writing, the programme search function no longer seems to work properly. So instead, you'll need to use the iPlayer website to find the PID (Programme Identifier) of the desired show and then use it to 'record' (i.e. download) it. For example:

```
get_iplayer --pid=b0b95311
```

You can also use a comma-separated list of PIDs to download more than one show at a time.

```
get_iplayer --pid=b0b95311,b0b94zn8,b0b950c9
```

Calling with **--stream** sends the output to stdout, for redirecting via a pipe to an audio player (for radio shows). The **--stdout** switch does this in addition to recording.

Communication

We mentioned command-line mail – scripted directly – in the calendar example in chapter 11. ssmtp makes a fine choice for the **mail** command, to use in scripts that email you when your Pi does something. Nowadays, getting the Pi to post to a microblog is a far more popular choice – at least if the microblog is Twitter, although other choices are available.

There are instructions all over the web for using Python modules to tweet when your Pi detects various events on the GPIO pins. If Python suits your project, then go ahead, but for the simplest setups all that's needed is the easily scriptable twidge:

```
sudo apt-get install twidge
twidge setup
```

Setup is easy: twidge will give you a URL to visit, where you can authorise twidge to access your Twitter account; it passes you an authorisation code to use, after which twidge is ready to go. **twidge lscommands** will list the available commands. To post from the command line (or a script), try something like:

```
twidge update "Testing twidge - tweeting from the
#RaspberryPi #commandline."
```

The **update** command will also read from stdin. The helpful manual on the project's GitHub page will get you started. For an interactive (and very colourful) Twitter client on the command line, install Rainbowstream, which you can do with pip:

```
sudo pip3 install rainbowstream
```

More than just gimmicks

Command-line apps are also available for older means of internet communication, from IRC to Jabber, and Mutt is a powerful enough email client to keep people (who otherwise don't spend much time in the terminal) using it. Serious work gets done in a shell, but coders keep churning out command-line apps that are just for fun, too.

MapSCII is a Braille and ASCII map renderer for your console, using OpenStreetMap data, written by Michael Straßburger (**magpi.cc/znMzWa**). To connect from a remote computer:

```
telnet mapscii.me
```

ASCII Star Wars appeared at the end of the last century, and is still available at **asciimation.co.nz**. Ironically, you'll need a modern graphical browser to view it.

Some sites are designed to look good in text-mode browsers. A favourite is **wttr.in**, the weather website. Enter your location, and open in any of the text-mode browsers that we've mentioned; for example:

```
w3m wttr.in/Liverpool
```

THE *Official*
RASPBERRY PI
PROJECTS BOOK

VOLUME 4

200 PAGES OF
IDEAS & INSPIRATION

DIY Games
Console

Build
a Robot

Make a
Magic Mirror

Set up
a Spy Cam

55 PROJECTS
& GUIDES

FROM THE MAKERS OF *MagPi* THE OFFICIAL RASPBERRY PI MAGAZINE

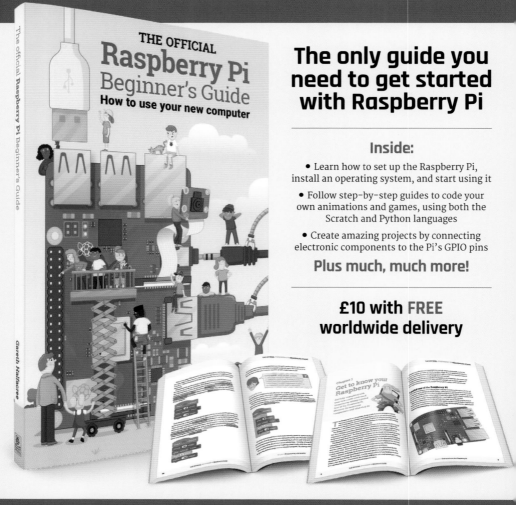

{code club}

Book of Scratch

Volume 1

Simple coding for total beginners

The first **Code Club book** has arrived!

- Learn to code using Scratch, the block-based language

- Follow step-by-step guides to create games and animations

- Includes 24 exclusive Code Club stickers!

- Use the magic glasses to reveal secret hints

- The special spiral binding allows the book to lay flat

Available at: magpi.cc/CCbook1

Raspberry Pi PRESS